The book is a refreshing illumination of not just ethics in social work practice, but social work practice itself. The use of paradoxes is a very apt way to characterise the daily choices which face practitioners. It is also a moving read, appropriate for not just students but experienced and senior practitioners alike.

Jan Fook, Leeds Trinity University, UK

The reality that social workers inevitably and unwittingly cause harm leads to confusion and distress. Merlinda Weinberg's book dynamically explains this and other obstacles to clear thinking in ethical conflicts. This book brings innovative thinking and suggestions for systemic and individual remedies – a game-changer for discussions of ethics in all settings. It is enlightening and a brilliant aid to teaching, supervision and direct practice.

Barrie Levy, University of California, Los Angeles, USA

This book is an exciting and much needed development in the field of ethics. For practitioners, academics and students seeking an alternative, more politicised and critical understanding of ethical practice, this research-based text offers sophisticated, yet highly accessible, analytical tools to navigate the contradictions inherent in the social work role with the aim of reducing ethical trespass.

Christine Morley, University of the Sunshine Coast, Australia

The author has deftly and lucidly engaged the vast complexity of ethical deliberation with all its inherent paradoxes, dilemmas, and trespasses, by weaving germane and critical theory with vivid, detailed and compelling lived social work examples. This book is about socially just ethical deliberations, taking the reader well past the ethical decision-making tradition, into the gritty and contextually nuanced world where social workers and clients, while unequal in their socially and professionally authorized power, are nonetheless both embedded and entangled – a truly impressive feat.

Marshall Fine, Wilfrid Laurier University, Canada

PARADOXES IN SOCIAL WORK PRACTICE

In the helping professions, codes of ethics and decision-making models have been the primary vehicles for determining what constitutes ethical practice. These strategies are insufficient since they assume that shared meanings exist and that the contradictory universal principles of codes can be reconciled. Also, these tools do not emphasize the significance of context for ethical practice.

This book takes a new critical theoretical approach, which involves exploring how social workers construct what is 'ethical' in their work, especially when they are positioned at the intersection of multiple paradoxes, including that of two opposing responsibilities in society: namely, to care for others but also to prevent others from harm. The book is built on narratives from actual front-line workers and therefore is more applicable and grounded for practitioners and students, offering many suggestions for sound practice. It illustrates that an understanding of ethics differs from worker to worker and is heavily influenced by context, workers' values, and what they take up as the primary discourses that frame their perceptions of the profession. While recognizing the oppressive potential of social work, the book is rooted in a perspective that ethical practice can contribute to a more socially just society.

Merlinda Weinberg is Associate Professor in the School of Social Work at Dalhousie University in Canada. Prior to this she worked for 25 years as a front-line social worker, manager, consultant and practitioner in private practice.

Contemporary Social Work Studies

Series Editors:
Lucy Jordan, The University of Hong Kong, China and
Patrick O'Leary, Griffith University, Australia

Series Advisory Board:
Lena Dominelli, University of Durham, UK
Jan Fook, South West London Academic Network, UK
Peter Ford, University of Southampton, UK
Lorraine Gutiérrez University of Michigan, USA
Lucy Jordan, The University of Hong Kong, China
Walter Lorenz, Free University of Bozen-Bolzano, Italy
Patrick O'Leary, Griffith University, Australia
Gillian Ruch, University of Southampton, UK
Sue White, University of Birmingham, UK

Contemporary Social Work Studies is a series disseminating high quality new research and scholarship in the discipline and profession of social work. The series promotes critical engagement with contemporary issues relevant across the social work community and captures the diversity of interests currently evident at national, international and local levels.

CSWS is located in the School of Social Sciences (Social Work Studies Division) at the University of Southampton, UK and is a development from the successful series of books published by Routledge in association with CEDR (the Centre for Evaluative and Developmental Research) from 1991.

Other titles in this series:

For information about other titles in this series, visit www.routledge.com

Paradoxes in Social Work Practice
Mitigating Ethical Trespass

MERLINDA WEINBERG
Dalhousie University, Canada

Routledge
Taylor & Francis Group

LONDON AND NEW YORK

First published 2016
by Routledge
2 Park Square, Milton Park, Abingdon, Oxon OX14 4RN

and by Routledge
711 Third Avenue, New York, NY 10017

Routledge is an imprint of the Taylor & Francis Group, an informa business

© 2016 Merlinda Weinberg

British Library Cataloguing in Publication Data
A catalogue record for this book is available from the British Library

Library of Congress Cataloging in Publication Data
Weinberg, Merlinda.
   Paradoxes in social work practice : mitigating ethical trespass /
by Merlinda Weinberg.
      pages cm. – (Contemporary social work studies)
   Includes bibliographical references and index.
   ISBN 978-1-4724-3109-7 (hardback) – ISBN 978-1-4724-3110-3
(ebook) – ISBN 978-1-4724-3111-0 (epub)   1. Social service–Moral and
ethical aspects.   I. Title.
   HV41.W367 2016
   174'.936132–dc23
   2015034831

ISBN 9781472431097 (hbk)
ISBN 9781315599373 (ebk)

Typeset in Times New Roman
by Apex CoVantage, LLC

Contents

Acknowledgments

Like the African maxim, "it takes whole village to raise a child," the same could be said about the creation of a book. There has been an entire village of souls who supported, nurtured, and sustained me through this process. Unending gratitude to:

The participants of this study. Without them, this work would have been an empty shell. Their generosity of time and openness of spirit cannot be measured.

The members of the committee for my dissertation at OISE/ University of Toronto, from which this book arose: Roger Simon, ע"ה, my supervisor, for his ability to teach me to think deeply and to respect my own capabilities. It was a great privilege to work with him. Kari Dehli and Amy Rossiter, accomplished educators who demanded academic rigor.

My parents, Sara and Murray, ע"ה, the start of it all. My sisters, Judi and Wendy, and my friends too numerous to name, who have cared for me in countless ways through thick and thin – and I've had my share of thin.

Many scholars (who are also thought/full friends) read drafts, critiqued ideas, and offered academic expertise. The folks at the School of Social Work at Dalhousie University for providing a collegial and supportive educational community for all my academic pursuits. Tracy Monaghan and Cindy Knapton for quality research and editorial assistance. The reviewers who provided constructive suggestions. A special thank you to Jan Fook who believed this book should come to light and pushed me to ensure that it did. And Barrie Levy for breathtaking wisdom and the creation of a safe emotional space.

With love to Micah and Alyza, my children, and their partners, Jess and Micah P. They are the stars in my firmament. Ultimately this book is not only for my readers but for them as well – To encourage a life devoted to social justice, learned exploration, and ethical behaviour.

Foreword

We live in times when it is becoming increasingly difficult to stipulate with any certainty, what is ethical. Yet paradoxically, we also live in times when more and more different groups are attempting to assert, with some force and corresponding certainty, their own ethical and moral code on those around them. It is no small wonder then that social workers are caught in what might feel like a tornado of conflicting pressures, trying to navigate often wildly divergent viewpoints and interests in order to facilitate a helpful outcome for the most vulnerable parties they are supposed to be supporting.

Merlinda Weinberg's work paints a vivid picture of this experience. In this climate it is not only timely, but thought-provoking enough to allow professional social workers to begin to navigate this pathway. There has been much work done on social work ethics, since of course we social workers take pride in recognizing that we are a profession which has a strong value base, and that our work is made the more challenging because of this. There is also beginning to be much more work done on the intricacies of social work practice. Merlinda manages to bring these two strands together beautifully. She not only manage to illustrate the ethical side of professional social work practice, she also manages to illuminate, in masterful style, the complexities of the "choices" involved. In this way she gives us an accurate and in-depth appreciation of the constant deliberation facing individual social workers.

As a piece of empirical work, Merlinda's study also demonstrates a model piece of social work research. It is well-conceived and solidly theorized, and utilizes methods which are highly appropriate to her subject matter. The use of stories enables her to delve in a complex way, into the heart of what is important to workers. This is all neatly integrated with an appreciation for the social and structural context in which workers are operating. What this means for me is that the work she has presented is applicable across many different contexts. I know that this is quite a tall order in social work, which is a profession strongly influenced by context and history. Much of our research does not even attempt to be able to speak across national contexts or even fields of study. Ye the way Merlinda has designed, theorized and conducted this study enables us to reach a depth of understanding which can influence the way we think about what we do in many different situations.

I found the concluding chapter, with its inclusion on several frameworks for better understanding of ethical practice, particularly helpful. The notions of "discursive fields" and "ethical trespass" in particular, are helpful in taking us forward to think in different ways about what we do, so that we are not trying to work in ways which are not relevant. For instance, the idea of working in "limited" ways which we assume are "limitless" is particularly poignant in an environment which often charges the social worker with assumed responsibility (or power) and who then attracts attendant blame when the expected societal outcome is not reached. This study reminds us of our fallibility when trying to assume that we can even understand the "Other" fully. It is awareness of this fallibility which keeps us constantly open to, and inquiring about, the world and people around us. This work, I do believe, makes an insightful and original contribution to social work practice right in the here and now.

I want to end this forward on a more personal note. I first met Merlinda just a few short years ago, when I went to work in Canada. We worked reasonably closely for a couple of years, and I was always impressed by her absolute passion for her work, and particular dedication to her research. I don't think she will mind me saying that she is a relative latecomer to academia, and I do think she is doing a wonderful job of "making up for lost time". She ensures that everything she does in her academic work is considered and thoughtful. She has a clear sense of what she feels is important, and is carving out a clear path to make this contribution in terms of ethical practice is social work. I am personally delighted that she has been able to publish this work so that the profession as a whole has access to it.

Jan Fook
Gomersal, Yorkshire
December 2015

Chapter 1

Introduction

Introduction – The Paradoxes and Complexity of Ethics in Practice

Paradox 1 – Care and Discipline

There is a fundamental structural paradox at the heart of all practice for social workers. As agents of the state, they are at the intersection of responsibilities to both care and to discipline. In public agencies and community settings, help takes many forms: amelioration, control, adaptation, reform and structural transformation (Gil, 1998). Some of these dimensions advance an agenda to meet the ascribed goals for clients, while other goals in social work support and maintain broader societal mandates (for example, ensuring the protection of those most vulnerable in society) that can perpetuate the marginalization of service users. As a result, social workers are caught between an ethic that informs social work as a vehicle of *social justice* dedicated to "the welfare and self-realization of human beings" (Canadian Association of Social Workers, 2005, p.3), and a bureaucratic regime where practitioners are responsible for social regulation and the ongoing *discipline* of others.

Social justice has been defined in a variety of ways (Gasker and Fischer, 2014), but for the purposes of this book, I am concerned about the redistribution of resources to foster a more equitable society. By discipline, I am referring both to "acts of punishment and correction and to fields of knowledge that diagnose deviance from the norm and intervene to remove it" (Chambon, Irving, and Epstein, 1999, p.271). However, not only does discipline work in repressive or autocratic ways, but also through the creation of new knowledges, focusing desires and energies in specific directions, and establishing what is taken as normative and adopted by individuals themselves (Sawicki, 1991). For example, given information about the health risks for cigarette smoking, a service user, in order to be a 'good mother' may decide she needs to quit this habit since it impedes the health of her foetus.

Discipline and regulation are central functions for helping professionals, as will be illustrated throughout this book. Therefore, this monograph explores how, if at all, it is possible to practice in an ethical fashion given the contradictions in the helping profession of social work.

What is more, there are other fundamental paradoxes in the nature of the helping relationship itself, which prevent the elimination of disciplinary and regulatory functions, while complicating the possibility of ethical, emancipatory practice. These paradoxes take the form of contradictory qualities, forces, tendencies, positionings or discursive frameworks that are well-established and assert the opposite of each other and are inherent in the work of practitioners. The additional paradoxes that will be examined in this book are:

Paradox 2 – More than one 'Client' in a Case

A structural anomaly exists for practitioners. The case[1] for social workers often involves more than one individual with differing and, at times, conflicting needs, for example, mother and child. Helping one may hinder the other. This conflict is exacerbated by organizations that may work with individuals in group settings, such as residences or classrooms. When there are a multiplicity of clients there is the possible amplification of conflicting wishes in which any outcome will potentially impact positively on some and not on others. And when the state is involved in contractual arrangements for services, might it be considered a client too? If this is the case, then the conflicts between the needs of society as a whole and that of individuals become even more complex.

Paradox 3 – Non-judgementalism vs. Need to Make Judgements

In the helping relationship itself, the principle of being non-judgemental is an underlying goal for workers and a dominant discourse in the profession. Being non-judgemental is viewed as particularly important in order to engage clients in the early stages of the relationship. Despite the intention of being non-judgemental, workers are mandated to engage in dividing practices (Foucault, 1982), or techniques of power, that create categories and classifications that distinguish one individual from another and create hierarchies which involve judgement and the objectification of individuals. In the process, people are constructed as: well or ill; fit or unfit; healthy or pathological; and deserving or undeserving. Determining eligibility for emergency food or assessing a mother's adequacy to parent, as illustrations, are ongoing enactments of judgements required of helping professionals in order to fulfill their responsibilities to the society-at-large. Furthermore, social workers have the mandate to develop knowledge as to what constitutes normal behaviour and then to evaluate whether individuals are meeting that standard. For example, assessing who is mentally ill or who requires admittance to a residential facility are tasks our society has authorized social workers to fulfill which ultimately contribute to normalization, "establishing the normal as a standard for judgment and against which to distinguish the pathological" (Chambon et al., 1999, p.276). Consequently, there is an inherent paradox between the requirement of judgement and non-judgementalism for practitioners.

---

1   While I find the term 'case' objectifying of clients, I have used it in order to suggest a more comprehensive concept that involves other people in a client's life, as well as institutional affiliations that can be broader than one agency.

Paradox 4 – The Setting of Norms vs. Encouraging 'Free Choice' and Client Empowerment

Practitioners contribute to moral regulation, processes that encourage individuals to accept certain practices, conditions and discourses as normative, taken-for-granted, or obvious, when in fact these are culturally and historically specific premises (Rousmaniere, Dehli, and deConinck-Smith, 1997). At the same time, workers value the principles of self-determination and self-empowerment for service users; believing that individuals should be making their own decisions, within limits concerning the rights of others. Nonetheless, professionals 'help' others towards 'self-actualization' by ascertaining what is normal, providing routes that foster self-discipline and regulation while attaching desire to individuals to be 'normal.' Individuals adopt these premises as their own, adhering "to explicit and implicit rules of conduct and norms of conscience" and believing themselves to be solely responsible for their own behaviour, as autonomous beings with choice to act morally or not (Rousmaniere et al., 1997, p.3). Epstein (1999, p.9) states,

> This is certainly what social workers try to do, with the caveat – more observed in the breach – that the persons being transformed should want this, should consent to it, and should do it of their own free will. This is the principle of self-determination.

In this riddle of self-determination and moral regulation is a paradox: by the utilization of power, the helper 'gives' power to those helped to make 'free' choices and decisions for themselves.

Paradox 5 – Self-disclosure as Necessary and Risky for Clients

Another contradictory aspect of the helping relationship flows from the notion that the 'good' client is one who self-discloses. Yet, the more a client reveals, the more likelihood she[2] will divulge information that puts her at risk for being disciplined by a helping professional. At the same time, the client who does not reveal can acquire the psychological label of 'resistant,' leading to the risk of disciplinary practices as well. Workers are aware of this puzzle, particularly with mandated clients who are especially at risk when they reveal information that could, for example, result in further jail time or losing a child. This restriction impedes the formation of relationships. Further, it places workers in the position of being disciplinary agents whose primary function becomes surveillance of the client, rather than support for the personal transformation of a client.

---

2   I will utilize the feminine form of pronouns as both a corrective to the dominant practice, which privileges men, but also because both the workers and most of the clients in my study were women.

Paradox 6 – Equality vs. Equity

One additional paradox is the unresolvable puzzle for workers of providing consistency to avoid favouritism versus offering dissimilar forms of help. This paradox is especially prevalent in group settings where the necessity of responding to the unique needs of individual clients who are different clashes with the needs for uniformity and impartiality. The perception of fairness in treatment of individuals is crucial to harmonious shared living situations. But there are times when special needs or circumstances require decisions that may seem to privilege one individual over another. This is the conundrum of equality versus equity; namely, treating everyone the same versus recognizing the need to respond to special circumstances or additional barriers for a particular individual. For example, dinner in a group home is served at 6 PM. But a Muslim client, celebrating Ramadan, cannot eat before sunset, which happens at 8 PM. A worker might give her permission to go into the kitchen and make herself a meal when generally clients do not have that privilege in that group home. Residents might resent the 'special treatment' she has received and not understand why, when given some situation in their own life, they were not granted the same exception.

A Question

Workers are aware of the dilemmas and tensions that arise from these conundrums, making their practice difficult, complex, and fraught with angst both for their clients and themselves. However, the inevitability of engaging in moral regulation runs concurrent to the potential for participating in social change. While social workers may collude in disciplinary practices, they may subvert and resist as well. This book explores the contradictions that arise, what forms they take in specific instances, how workers situate themselves within the contradictions, and how they resolve or live with the ambivalences and complexities that these paradoxes engender. Ultimately, the question is: what constitutes ethical practice given these core paradoxes?

The Traditional View of Ethics

In modern society, the study of ethics has traditionally been from a liberal-humanist perspective, which emphasizes principles to provide a basis for rational decision-making. Walker (1998, p.7) has referred to this approach to ethics as a "theoretical-juridical model." This is a system of compact "law-like propositions that 'explain' the moral behavior of a well-formed moral agent" (p.7–8).

The primary tool for a theoretical-juridical approach is a code of ethics. A code of ethics is "usually a written document produced by a professional association, occupational regulatory body or other professional body with the stated aim of guiding the practitioners who are members, protecting service users and safeguarding the reputation of the profession" (Banks, 2004, p.108). Codes are seen as universally applicable and objective, with solutions rule-bound and prescriptive. An ideal is laid out as a series of abstract principles. It is assumed that by applying the code, with clear rules for implementation, in combination with good decision-making and a method for tracking harms (Barsky, 2010; Congress, 2000; Guttmann, 2006; Robison and Reeser, 2000), a worker can move towards the avoidance of ethical breaches.

In the profession of social work, there is more than one code to which a practitioner can refer. For example, in Canada, there is a provincial code (Ontario College of Social Workers and Social Service Workers, 2008), a federal code (Canadian Association of Social Workers, 2005), and an international statement of principles (International Federation of Social Workers, 2012). While only one might be used for regulatory purposes (in the case of Canada, the provincial code), the others would offer guidance around values and principles for social workers.

Other countries identify different principles, or have alternate emphases from those in Canada. For example, the Aotearoa New Zealand Association of Social Workers puts prominence on responsibilities to their Indigenous people and greater concern about diversity and its implications in ethics (2013). In some countries, in addition to the dominant perspective laid out by the body responsible for qualification or licensure, particular groups have devised their own codes as critiques of those prevailing orientations. For instance, in the United States, the National Association of Black Social Workers has designed its own code of ethics that stresses very different principles than those in the conventional USA code (nd).

There are several features of a theoretical-juridical model, according to Walker (1998, p.8–9). First, it rests on the assumption that moral beliefs can be understood and verified by the use of intellectual activity and logical enquiry. (*Morality* refers here to distinctions between good and bad, right and wrong). Secondly, it assumes that the activities of ethical deliberation are the responsibility of individuals for whom these systems of principles will provide the necessary guidance to make ethical decisions. Thirdly, the view allows for an impersonal approach that is outside of time, context, culture, history or the material circumstances of those involved in the decisions.

Several theories of ethics fall under the umbrella of a theoretical-juridical approach. The two major ones are *deontology* and *utilitarianism*. The concept of deontology, crafted by Immanuel Kant, starts from the premise that one can articulate universal principles that can serve as the foundation for ethical thought and deliberation. These principles spell out individual obligations (from the word Greek for 'duty') (Hugman, 2005b) and are good in themselves, regardless of outcomes (Nash, 2002). So for example, killing would be viewed as wrong regardless of the circumstances. Utilitarianism, developed by J.S. Mill and Jeremy Bentham, assumes that moral decision-making will include ascertaining the benefit of the decisions made (Hugman, 2005b). Consequently, one major basis for decision-making would be to discern whether a choice resulted in the greatest good for the greatest number or resulted in the least harm. An offshoot of utilitarianism is consequentialism, which focuses on the consequences of one's actions (Gray and Webb, 2010).

A Critique of the Traditional Approach to Ethics and the Approach in this Book

Underlying the utilization of codes are some central assumptions (Weinberg and Campbell, 2014). Two of these are that there are universal values that apply to all peoples, often referred to as *universalism* (Hugman, 2010), and that there are shared meanings that are both possible and desirable to discern and utilize (Weinberg and Campbell, 2014). However, a counter-argument, referred to as *relativism*, is that values are specific to cultures and context, and no universal principles will be adequate to determine ethical practice. This debate in part has emerged from the criticisms that the supposed universal values are actually values that represent the perspective of Euro-Western countries, particularly those who are dominant in those countries (Hugman, 2010), and can lead to colonial domination and oppression of people elsewhere.

Another assumption is that conflicting principles can be reconciled. But some ethical principles are contradictory, preventing workers from using them as the sole means to resolve dilemmas (Weinberg and Campbell, 2014). An example would be that of self-determination for clients versus the need to act in the best interest of those who are most vulnerable (Weinberg and Campbell, 2014). And some principles are based on *incommensurate* values, meaning they cannot be compared (the old apples versus oranges issue). An illustration would be the dilemma of having to choose between an individual's duty and that person's well-being; such as an adult daughter whose elderly father can no longer live independently and would like to live with her, but she is so overwhelmed with pressures in her own life, that she is not sure she could manage this change (Hugman, 2007).

Furthermore, what workers take up as the knowledge of moral principles does not determine what they will actually *do* in response to these principles (Kendall and Hugman, 2013).

Moreover, a theoretical-juridical approach underscores an Enlightenment notion of the centrality of the practitioner as an autonomous individual, and of the utilization of rational cognitive processes, while de-emphasizing or ignoring the local, historical or contingent factors, including the structural inequities in which practitioners operate (at least in the codes that are dominant in North America) (Rossiter, Prilleltensky and Walsh-Bowers, 2000; Weinberg, 2010). Given the emphasis in codes on thinking and neutrality, they generally do not engender a "deep sense of personal involvement" (Oliver, 2013, p.208). Given the traditional emphases in organizational settings and in professional associations on principle-based approaches as the standards for ethical practice, these very approaches that are designed to support ethical deliberation may contribute to the distress that workers experience in their day-to-day practice, since they omit the relational and affective components that underpin workers' practice (Oliver, 2013).

Orlie (1997, p.195) explains that "code-oriented moralities tend to normalize principle because rather than continually questioning proper conduct, they express a desire to find the true ground of our being." She is suggesting that an emphasis on the codes ends up articulating norms and reifying what is taken as moral. This narrows the range of what workers should be addressing in ethics to an examination of principles (Kendall and Hugman, 2013). According to Orlie, what would be preferable is a system that encourages constant self-reflection about behaviour, recognizing that it is impossible to determine a universal and definitive 'good.' She adds that only through specific actions do those principles gain meaning and value (p. 195). Consequently, codes as the vehicle for ethics, are insufficient and may lead to more rigid and doctrinaire stances in making sense of what is moral, when what is required is the flexibility that would come from understanding the relevance of context and the history of practice.

Instead of a traditional approach to ethics, in this book, a critical approach that employs both structural and post-structural theorizing has been taken. Scientific objectivity and the empirical tradition, major tenets of Enlightenment thinking and of a theoretical-juridical approach, are viewed as problematic and therefore have led to a series of 'post' (after Enlightenment) theories such as post-structuralism, post-modernism and post-colonialism. Post-structural theorists assert that we all come to our understandings from standpoints that must be taken into account and reflected upon, and that one cannot obtain objectivity. Also, positivist explanations that arise from empiricism are viewed as one set of interpretations amongst many (Irving, 1999). Structural thinking centres on *structures* (the broader social and cultural in which an individual operates) and *agency* – an individual's ability to influence those structures or "the capacity for intentional acts" (Zembylas, 2003a, p.224). But *post-structuralism* bridges this sociological binary, which I will explain below. It examines "how institutional practices generate social identities, which in turn trigger new knowledge and practices" (Chambon, 1999, p.56). Post-structuralism puts the spotlight on local processes and examines language as the tool for meaning-making in those processes; thus being an appropriate approach for social work (Healy, 2005).

I have relied heavily on Michel Foucault, a French philosopher whose work is representative of post-structural thinking. His writings span a period from the middle to the late twentieth century. Earlier work focused on social practices and discourses in institutions (e.g. Foucault, 1977), but his later work shifted to practices of the self with an emphasis on ethics (e.g.Foucault, 1990). What individuals took to be ethical issues, what sources of authority they utilized to understand these as ethical, the work performed on the self to be ethical and the overarching type of person one wished to be (Nietsche and Haase, 2012) were all aspects he addressed. He was particularly interested in what he referred to as "technologies of the self" (Foucault, 1988), those practices through which an individual constitutes his/ herself, including notions of ethical behaviour. These practices arise from patterns that occur within that person's society, their culture and/or their social groups. Foucault's approach placed the emphasis on the individual agent as the source of morality (rather than on universal principles), and on the processes of self-reflection and critique (Hugman, 2003). Ethics is the "kind of relationship you ought to have with yourself," and how one constitutes oneself as a moral agent, according to Foucault (1984, p.352). Consequently, the definition of *ethics* that I rely on in this book is "a disposition of continual questioning and adjusting of thought and action in relation to notions of human good and how to be and act in relation to others" (Christie, 2005, p.39).

Foucault's body of work also applies to an exploration of the technologies used by individuals, such as social workers, on others – most particularly, one's clients. Foucault's theorizing brings together the micro-politics of the individual with macro concerns of the state or society generally (Dean, 1994), providing analytical tools to connect the effects of power at micro levels that make structural domination possible (Sawicki, 1991). I am using *micro* in two different senses of the word. By micro level in social work practice, I am referring to intervention with individuals, groups or families. But I am also intending that we understand micro technologies as Foucault's conception that power operates on an individual, on-the-ground level. An example would be the use of a particular recording tool that workers in Child Welfare need to use in their practice that constrains and demarcates what can be said and even thought about a particular client, since some aspects may not even emerge in an individual's thinking by the parameters that the form sets up.

Foucault's writing is particularly useful for examining ethics in practice and for ascertaining the links between individuals' practice and the historical time, place and institutions that influence what social workers take to be ethical. Other postmodernists have addressed unconscious processes and their connections to identity, and I will use some of their writing to explore linkages between identity and possible early biographical influences that may operate unconsciously for individuals.

One of the important shifts in post-structural theorizing was Foucault's emphasis on the productive aspects of power, rather than simply the repressive components. Power, according to Foucault, is productive in two ways (Chambon, 1999): it has positive effects but also, it contributes to producing identities, such as that of the 'client.' His work explores how the knowledges and practices of social institutions and social science, such as social work, contribute to governing with minimal coercion in democratic states. And when coercion is employed, he examines the processes by which those mechanisms are justified. Those mechanisms are disciplinary in that they work through the establishment of norms that individuals then desire to take in as their identity. His approach allows for a critique of the supposed benevolence of a profession such as social work, a disturbing prospect, but one that can be socially transformative (Chambon, 1999). Because social work is at the nexus of contradictory responsibilities of care and discipline, his theories provide a means of examining those paradoxical spaces in the profession, the theme of this book. This is especially the case regarding his view that practices often combine contradictory elements that can be both liberating and oppressive. It also explains, "how the effects of discipline can be veiled" (Chambon, 1999, p.690).

Foucault shifted notions of government to a broad range of diffuse tactics through which behaviour is regulated and controlled. He referred to this as "governmentality." The welfare and management of the population was the primary outcome of governmentality, with the family as an essential instrument to achieve the aims (Foucault, 1991, p.100). This concept allows for an analysis of the relationship between the state and everyday practices because it concerns both the conduct of government and the government of individuals' conduct (Dean and Hindess, 1998). It highlights the mechanisms and discourses by which people both are governed and govern themselves, and incorporates the dimensions of what is to be governed, and how, why and what is hoped to be produced by government (Dean, 1994). For this monograph, governmentality is especially useful as a concept to understand the construction and regulation of what is viewed as 'moral' behaviour by legitimating certain behaviours while marginalizing others (Valverde, 1994). Throughout the book, the abstractions of governmentality will be made concrete through illustrations in terms of both the constitutions of an ethical problem and the identities conferred on individuals through these constructions. Many theoreticians have taken up Foucault's ideas of governmentality and these will be utilized throughout this monograph.

Critiques of Post-structuralism for Ethics

One significant negative evaluation of Foucault's work is that by emphasizing the broad historical, political and social factors that contribute to the constitution of identity, there seems to be little room for personal agency. Sawicki (1991, p.99) questioned, "If much of history is beyond control, then what sense does it make to resist at all?" In an applied profession such as social work, with its goal of anti-oppressive practice and social transformation, this critique is very problematic. Part of the solution is to expose the processes by which these macro effects become commonsensical and taken-for-granted notions, a project that Foucault's theorizing supports. Furthermore, his conception of the fluidity of the self actually supports emancipatory action since a fixed self would have no means to resist. (I will elaborate on those concepts of self below). By connecting the cultural and institutional contexts of the operation of power with micro technologies, we are able to see how oppression functions.

The other major critique of Foucault and a post-structural approach to ethics, more generally, is the concern about moral relativity. I believe that all knowledge is situated. By situated, I mean, occurs in a context, and is shaped by time, place, as well as individuals' experience and the exercise of power. Therefore, all knowledge is only partial and consequently there is no possibility of discerning universal truths (Christie, 2005). Given the rejection of grand narratives and universal principles, the question becomes: if everything is relative, contextual and personal, then is everything equally valid from an ethical perspective? Are there not some common values that should underpin ethics in social work?

One response is to adopt an approach of *ethical pluralism*, which makes a distinction between primary values that "express broadly common human goals" (Hugman, 2007, p.25) and those secondary values that operationalize the primary values. Primary values are ones that can be pursued in and of themselves, such as social justice (Hugman, 2010). Secondary values are those that vary based on context and cultures, such as filial loyalty.

Another response to this dilemma, has been the emergence of two overlapping camps of postmodernists in the social sciences (Rosenau, 1992). Skeptical postmodernists contend that one cannot ascertain the preeminence of any particular values as the foundations for practice. Alternatively, although affirmative postmodernists recognize that while knowledge is shifting and constructed, and consequently can be inaccurate or wrong (Kendall and Hugman, 2013), they "do not … shy away from affirming an ethic, making normative choices, and striving to build issue-specific political coalitions" (Rosenau, 1992, p.16). I am in the affirmative faction, arguing, like Rosenau (1992, p.114) that "a plurality of legitimate value systems does not necessarily imply ethical relativism." What is required is to determine which values should prevail and what should constitute ethical behaviour. Then an understanding of ethical pluralism is useful as a means to move forward.

One can use critical theories, such as feminism and anti-racist theory, to determine which values should underpin social work. Those are the theoretical approaches utilized in this monograph. Hugman (2003, p. 1035) speaks about "critical postmodernism" which attempts to integrate understandings about diversity and the fluidity of meaning with an ethical lens that goes beyond the individual, incorporating the importance of context and history. Feminism is not only a constellation of theories but also a politics. While it began as a struggle over the unequal power relationships between men and women, it has expanded into a commitment to end all forms of oppression: between whites and people of colour, rich and poor, and within other social categories of marginality. It centres on an obligation to transform society to correct these imbalances through the development of knowledge and activism. Weedon (1987, p.179) makes the connection between post-structural and feminist theory. She states, "by questioning all essences and relativizing truth claims, postmodern feminisms create a space for political perspectives and interests that have hitherto been marginalized." Through it, alternate visions of how one could operate as a social worker are created.

Since the social work profession was founded on the 'goodness' of white middle-class women to manage social ills of more unfortunate others (Jeffery, 2005), it is necessary to examine how white supremacy is produced and maintained (Razack and Jeffery, 2002). Liberal theories either deny the importance of social difference or simply tolerate it, rather than seeing it as an essential component to be interrogated for ethical practice (Razack and Jeffery, 2002). Consequently, anti-racist theory is a useful adjunct since it critiques whiteness not just as identities but as social relations (Razack and Jeffery, 2002, p.265) and prevents an eclipsing of race found in cultural competence models of difference (Abrams, 2009). Social workers must start from a perspective of racism as the norm and reject a stance of 'colour-blindness' that is inherent in liberal humanist discourses (Razack and Jeffery, 2002, p.260). While the emphasis is on race, anti-racist theory includes an examination of the interlocking nature of oppressions, making it particularly useful for this book. Furthermore, one of its tenets is to bring in the voices of those marginalized, a necessary step in social work practice.

To bolster the emphasis on a struggle for social justice and collective action to alter society, there are times when I also apply the literature on structural theory, because a structural approach is concerned with issues at a macro level of practice and the fundamental transformation to a more ethical, socially equitable society. By macro, I am referring to that level of social work practice that is concerned with large-scale interventions that impact organizations, communities, systems of care, and includes attention to policy arenas.

Structural theory begins with "an assumption that inadequate social arrangements are predominantly responsible for the plight of many clients" (Middleman and Goldberg, as cited in Mullaly, 2007, p. 211) so there must be an emphasis on reforming the social structures in which social workers operate. Structural theory focuses on oppression in institutional and organizational arrangements rather than examining narrative or discourses, as post-structural theory does. This theoretical approach had its origins in North America (Lundy, 2004; Moreau, 1989) as an expression of socialist ideology about class struggles (Weinberg, 2008). An underlying supposition, in structural theory, is that society is comprised of groups with opposing interests and values. These groups compete for limited resources and those in dominant positions create social institutions to maintain their hegemony (Mullaly, 2007). This results in social inequality and the maintenance of structures that support the powerful at the expense of others. The aims of structural theory are political in attempts to articulate norms and provide vehicles of action towards a better society. Consequently, for a pursuit of ethics, structural theory is a helpful adjunct; both since post-structural theory has been criticized for its apolitical, relativistic approach to what constitutes 'the good,' and as an alternate means to examine broader social structures.

Accordingly, for this monograph, primarily a feminist anti-racist post-structural perspective has been employed, except in Chapters 4 and 5 where macro change is the emphasis so structural theory has also been utilized.

Theoretical Tools of Post-structural Theory

Discourse

Discourse is a central theoretical vehicle in post-structuralism. In this monograph, I examined discourse as providing an organizing frame or rationale for workers to make sense of the helping relationship. Discourses are "language practices through which we understand 'reality' and act upon it" (Healy, 2005, p.199). These varying "structures of knowledge and systematic ways of carving out reality" (Chambon et al., 1999, p.272) compete to give meaning to a particular concept or concepts that influence the possibility of how social institutions, processes, and relationships are organized. These organizing frames bring some kind of regularity, coherence, and sense to an understanding of the world, determining the rules for applying those concepts. By their formation, things are accomplished, regulated, enabled, and ordered, as well as constrained, delimited, and limited. Discourse is diffuse, pervasive and abstract. People both constitute discourse and are constituted by discourse. I envision discursive production as a swirling cloud of language and action that takes form as themes, ideas, and behaviours that bombard individuals on all sides. A person breathes in the elements of this mix, is affected by its vapours, and adds her own breath of language, creating a unique gaseous mist, which circulates through the atmosphere and becomes part of discourse 'out there.'

But this rendering is incomplete because it does not address the privilege accorded some discourses over others. All environments are not the same in terms of the availability of those gaseous mixtures. Some people live in more rarified atmospheres. Others live in more polluted environments. In the same way, all discourses are not as readily available or are privileged (accepted as the primary discourses). What constitutes privileged discourses varies from context to context and changes over time.

Since this is all very abstract, let us look at three discourses that circulate to understand young single mothers, the subjects of this book.

Contemporary Discourses on Young Single Mothers

What are the dominant discourses that frame how young single mothers are viewed in Euro-Western society? In the present, three competing explanatory discourses have emerged: the liberal discourse, the reactionary discourse and the revisionist discourse.

The Liberal Discourse

In the liberal discourse, these young women are seen as the products of unfortunate situations, either from within inadequate families of origin (usually white), such as 'broken homes' and/or inadequate cultural groups (usually non-white), making mistakes that have heartbreaking consequences. The literature of this liberal discourse (e.g. Dryfoos, 1990; McWhirter, McWhirter, McWhirter and McWhirter, 1998), while often recognizing the socioeconomic and structural disadvantages of poor young single mothers, has emphasized the intrapsychic difficulties, namely internal conflicts which are part of a system of unconscious processes (Bonac, 1996), rather than the environmental factors. Kelly (1996, p.428–9) describes this trope:

> The two most prominent psychological explanations of teen motherhood both infantilize these mothers and cast suspicion on their families. The first says that

these young women, many of whom are said to come from broken families themselves, have babies because of an unfulfilled need for somebody to love them ... The second psychological explanation holds that the young women have been abused (sexually or otherwise), and motherhood may help them escape a bad family situation ... . These two psychological explanations are not, of course, mutually exclusive.

Historically, interventions by social workers have focused on 'prevention' and on an amelioration of the perceived deleterious effects of being a young single mother (Rains, Davies, and McKinnon, 1998; Rains, Davies, and McKinnon, 2004). Often the 'problem' is located within the individual young woman. In those instances, the solutions are psychologically centred on therapeutic interventions and surveillance. These young women are seen as "in need of protection – from themselves, from their families, from their male partners" (Kelly, 1996, p.430). The discourse simultaneously destigmatizes pre-marital adolescent sexual activity while indirectly stigmatizing a young mother's pregnancy and decision to keep her child (Kelly, 1996; Rains, Davies, and McKinnon, 1998; Rains, Davies, and McKinnon, 2004).

The Reactionary Discourse
A second more reactionary discourse circulates as well. In this discourse, young single mothers are framed as irresponsible wanton young women or 'children having children' (Cornaccia, 1995; Fields, 2005; Pearce, 1993) at 'high risk' (MacVarish, 2010; Mitchell, Crawshaw, Bunton, and Green, 2001) for not being 'good enough' mothers (Silva, 1996). Despite the oft-times mention of environmental factors as the cause, the discourses conflate these causes with the mothers themselves (Breheny and Stephens, 2010). The consequences run the gamut from biological (Breheny and Stephens, 2010; Garn, Pesick and Petzold, 1986), to educational and economic (Breheny and Stephens, 2010; Butler, 1992; Klerman, 1986; Maynard, 1997; Wilson and Huntington, 2006), to social and emotional consequences (Maynard, 1997; Phipps-Yonas, 1980), for both themselves and their offspring. As politics have shifted in a more conservative climate, concern about the erosion of 'family values,' as personified by these young single mothers, has gained strength. A fiscally tight economic environment has resulted in putting more emphasis on accountability and private responsibility, rather than placing the onus on the community or broader society to support its most vulnerable citizens. Young single unmarried mothers have been an easy target for scapegoating, given their isolation and vulnerability. For instance, one construction of single teenage[3] mothers is as welfare mothers, who bleed the system economically because of laziness or lack of motivation (Wilson and Huntington, 2006). They represent the downfall of the

---

3 While 'teen' and 'teenager' represent an age group, and 'adolescence,' a stage of life, for the purposes of this book I have used these terms synonymously. My interest is in young single mothers, whatever their actual age or presumed developmental stage.

nuclear family and the rejection of men as primary breadwinners. Kelly (1996) has referred to this trope as the "wrong family" because "[a]n unwed teen mother who relies on any government program and does not give her child up for adoption is, in this construct, the epitome of the wrong family" (p.434). The individuals who articulate this discourse seek to "repatriate newly problematized needs to their former domestic or official economic enclaves" (Fraser, 1989, p.157); for example, by excluding teenage mothers from public places or returning responsibility for their behaviour to their families of origin. The Ontario government, a province in Canada, with policies of teenage mothers being required to live with their parents in order to receive benefits, is an example of the implementation of this discourse.

The Revisionist or Oppositional Discourse

Furstenberg (1991, p.127) has identified a third competing discourse, which he refers to as expressed by the "revisionists" or which Kelly (1996, p. 434) labels the "oppositional movement." The revisionists suggest that the issue of single teenage parenting has, in part, been "socially constructed to suit the political agenda of certain moral entrepreneurs" (Furstenberg, 1991, p.128), that the negative effects of early childbearing have been exaggerated, and that for some disadvantaged youth, mothering may be an adaptive strategy to poverty and/or racism (e.g. Stevens, 1996). In this discourse, the underlying differences in social background, family instability and academic problems are emphasized, leading this group of young women to be viewed by the oppositional movement as the more discouraged group of the disadvantaged (Luker, 1996). Kelly has termed this discourse as the "wrong-society" frame because it focuses on the "context of unequal power relations and advocates the transformation of social conditions" (1996, p.437).

In the following chapters, there will be many illustrations of how utilizing these different discourses shaped what workers took to be the 'truth' both about the young women they worked with, as well as their responsibilities as practitioners, and led to the construction of ethical issues that arose for a particular worker.

Discursive Fields and Ethical Dilemmas

While I understood discourses as the primary 'gases' which the workers would breathe in terms of young single mothers, I was interested in which of these gases were inhaled; i.e. how these discourses were taken up by the individual workers in the study to 'explain' their actions in relation to ethics. The discourses extended beyond those relating to the clients to encompass a wide range of related concerns such as what constitutes social work, the professional responsibilities of social workers, and ethical practice. Workers adopt certain discourses from the infinite array that are available as the framework by which they make sense of a situation, including the ethical challenges. Much has been written about codes of ethics, but much less has examined how the concepts, beliefs and assumptions, namely the organizing logic, both pre-determine what is perceived of as an ethical dilemma and shape what is manifest as the helping relationship by a practitioner. These constitute a worker's discursive field.

Discursive fields "consist of competing ways of giving meaning to the world and of organizing social institutions and processes" (Weedon, 1987, p.34). Every form of help has presumptions about the nature of the problem, the possible forms of practice, the positions of helper and the client/s, the nature of the helping relationship and the goals of helping. Different discursive fields provide alternate interpretations for understanding what 'help' is, exposing divergent underlying assumptions.

For example, a worker might perceive an ethical dilemma in fostering autonomy in clients if she subscribed to the 'reactionary discourse' and viewed a young single mother as 'an irresponsible child,' therefore seeing her duty to act *in loco parentis*. However, she might also subscribe to the articulated precept of fostering autonomy (a basic tenet of social work). Because of the two competing discourses taken up in her discursive field, she would find herself in an ethical dilemma between acting as a surrogate parent versus supporting the young mom's autonomy to make her own decisions. Therefore, the discursive field workers use to make sense of specific cases, at a particular moment in time, will be the grounds on which the notion of dilemma will be constituted and resolved. By *ethical dilemma*, I am referring to a situation in which a choice must be made between either two equally undesirable alternatives or an action performed in which there will be both positive and negative consequences.

I will enquire: How do social workers, caught within the actualities of practice and their understanding of principles of practice, respond to the paradoxes and dilemmas that arise? What do practitioners see as the dilemmas in their work? On what grounds do they constitute these as dilemmas? How do they resolve and/or live with these? What was not considered? What are those underlying assumptions for the workers? What are the discrepancies and contradictions that arise from their discursive fields?

I wish to examine how workers use their justificatory discourses, beliefs and assumptions to interpret and apply their understanding of proscriptive codes and principles within the context of a helping relationship. In short, my premise is that ethics in the social services cannot be understood outside of a study of discursive fields.

Subjectivity and Subject Positions

The constitution and resolution of dilemmas contribute to the creation and understanding of workers' own subjectivity, as well as that of their clients. Conversely, how subjectivity is fashioned impacts on what is constructed as a dilemma. Subjectivity is a post-structural term that rejects the liberal humanist notion of a unified and fixed self. Instead the individual is seen as a site of ongoing conflict, "precarious, contradictory and in process, constantly being reconstituted in discourse each time we think or speak" (Weedon, 1987, p.32), leading to the differing subject positions or "ways of being an individual" (Weedon, 1987, p.3). We both create and are created through discourse.

However, I subscribe to a belief that people do exercise agency within the limitations of context, history, and the pull of discourse. The subject positions that workers adopt for themselves and their clients, through their case interpretations and consequent decisions, as well as those positions the clients construct of themselves and their workers, lead to certain implications regarding what can take place and what cannot occur in the helping relationship. I will be highlighting the processes that allow workers to construct themselves and their clients in particular ways.

In the example just given, the subject position available to the worker by seeing her client as a reckless young woman making poor decisions (the subject position constructed by the worker for the client) led to the subject position of the worker as a substitute parent, having to operate in a paternalistic and 'protective' manner to safeguard a baby and to shield the young woman from herself. I will show that how the social workers constitute the problematic of an ethical dilemma relates to which discourses they privilege (or favour) from a discursive field regarding the nature of 'clients,' 'social work practice,' and 'help,' and consequently, constitute what subject positions are available for themselves and the service user.

Ethical Dilemmas/Preferred and Actualized Selves/Moral Distress

If one accepts the post-structuralist notion that identity is a shifting construction made up of an infinite number of subject positions, or ways of being an individual, which are impacted by history, context, relationships, and discourse, then there is no fixed and coherent self. However, given the emphasis of Enlightenment thinking that has dominated Euro-Western society in the modern era, most of us still believe that we do have a unified and stable self (Weinberg, 2007). Individuals also have an internalized ideal of the self (Benjamin, 1995). Subject positions that are a more comfortable psychological fit with notions of that idealized and coherent self are 'preferred.' In this monograph I have referred to these as the *'preferred self.'* However, the subject positions enacted at a particular point in time may not be in harmony with that preferred self, so there can be a discrepancy between the preferred self and one which I refer to as the *'actualized self.'* These theoretical concepts of 'preferred' and 'actualized' selves provide a way of examining the differences between how actors wish to view themselves ethically and what subject positions they may take up at a given moment in time.

At times, the structures social workers encounter contribute to actualized positions that are not consistent with their preferred selves. I want to introduce the term 'moral distress' at this point. This term is useful to include in the collection of theoretical resources in social work. Moral distress arises when "one knows the right thing to do, but institutional constraints make it nearly impossible to pursue the right course of action" (Jameton, 1984, p.6). It is distinguished from the notion of ethical dilemmas. Ethical dilemmas occur when two or more courses of action "are in conflict (and will potentially have both positive and negative consequences) but where each action can be defended as viable and appropriate" (Weinberg, 2009, p.144). Ethical dilemma assumes two equally viable options. However, moral distress identifies a preferred moral action, which the actor views as right but is blocked by factors outside of the self.

In more recent literature, the difficulty of separating internal constraints, such as fear of losing one's job, and external constraints has led to a change in the definition of moral distress. Now it is understood to be the product of an interaction between both internal and external factors (Oliver, 2013). It is a practical term to have in one's lexicon because it addresses contextual and political issues, and brings back the importance of affective components in the work for practitioners (Weinberg, 2009). When it arises, the discrepancy between preferred and actualized self emerges.

Moral distress is not a post-structural concept since the agency of a worker is viewed as compromised by unassailable structures. The problem with this idea is that we are not separate from structures; rather through one's actions, individuals create the structures that exist (Kondrat, 2002). Nonetheless, it is a term that has some prominence in the medical field in particular and adds a conceptual tool that practitioners find helpful when struggling with the complexities in ethical decision-making.

Ethical Trespass

Even when practitioners adopt subject positions that are preferred, harms may occur. A fundamental contributing component to ethical dilemmas are the primary paradoxes in practice. One of these relates to having more than one individual in a particular case, requiring meeting discrepant and contradictory needs. Melissa Orlie (1997, p.5) elaborates on a concept from Hannah Arendt (1958) that I believe is very useful in looking at practice in the helping fields. Orlie refers to ethical trespass as "the harmful effects ... that inevitably follow not from our intentions and malevolence but from our participation in social processes and identities." What she means is that social workers (as one group of citizens) are involved in harming others. This is not because of evil inclinations but because of the ways that social workers contribute to what is taken as healthy or normal. Those social processes and decisions may be inaccurate, unhelpful, or hurtful for particular individuals.

Orlie (1997) suggests that trespass is inherent in the world because there are a multiplicity of social actors all with conflicting wants and interests. Her contention is that in any decisions regarding those conflicts, some choices are opened, while others are closed. She maintains that harm, potentially invisible or unknown, follows inevitably from those decisions. Some ways of being in the world are supported while others are inhibited. The limits of any action cannot be transcended nor can all effects be predicted. Like the proverbial ripples from a stone thrown in a pond, one can never completely anticipate the consequences of an action, which go on and on. For instance, when a social worker supports an adult daughter that her elderly father should be in assisted living due to dementia, while he asserts he is capable of staying in his own home, this evaluation not only has effects on these individuals (and may be 'wrong') but may also result in some other person being denied a bed. Additionally, the decision reinforces social norms of 'health,' as well as the maintenance of the worker's power and authority.

How does trespass happen? Social norms develop through popular consensus and breed a level of thoughtlessness, according to Orlie (1997). In liberal democratic states, without a higher authority such as religion or totalitarianism, the potential for conflict and instability are great. Therefore, conformity to public reason and self-government are essential to avoid anarchy. Orlie asserts, "Our conformity to governing truths sustains social orderliness and thus solidifies the dubious foundations of modern governance" (p.32). Orlie argues that in modern states, citizens promise to give up individual power in order to constitute a government.

Professionals are key actors in the development of social norms. They participate in the definition of the public good and the processes of normalization. They are not 'neutral' players without vested interests. In fact, critical theoreticians have queried the beneficence of the helping professions as a whole. Power relations determine what is taken as truth, and critical postmodernists have begun to question their own metanarratives, "recognizing their dangers- the attractiveness of dogma, the temptations of certainty, the urge to control others 'in their own interests'" (Leonard, 1994, p.19). How as a society we ought to live is ultimately a moral and political question (Hugman and Smith, 1995). Critical social work maintains that professional disciplines control and regulate populations, reproducing social hierarchies and in the process preserving their own power and privilege.

The production of what is taken to be 'ethics' is not separate from this process. Orlie (1997) perceives that all of us trespass, including and most especially, "the 'responsible,' well-behaved, predictable subjects of social order who reinforce and extend its patterns of rule" (p.23). Helping professionals are those responsible subjects who through normalization, moral regulation, and dividing practices, support, amplify, and create the ruling social order. Therefore, all activities performed by social workers are vehicles for power, and inevitably trespass.

Orlie (1997, p.11) asks, "How can we conduct ourselves ethically when we are conditioned by history and by the governing power we carry as much as others are influenced or harmed by our effects?" This is a key concern addressed here. In this book I inquire if and how practitioners can edge towards a nonviolative relationship to others. I use the term 'edge' intentionally because, like Orlie, I do not believe total elimination of trespass is possible.

An Ethical Relationship

In this book, I am concerned about the potential of practitioners to create an ethical relation with a client, that is, "a nonviolative relationship to the Other ... that assumes responsibility to guard the Other against the appropriation that would deny her difference and singularity" (Cornell, 1992, p.62). The use of the term 'Other' is used in the social sciences to recognize that the construction of the self occurs, in part, through a differentiation of the self from others. It constructs a binary between the self and other human beings, with the Other in some manner objectified. Implicit in binaries is that one part of the pair is perceived as dominant (or preferred) over the other part. Even when one half of the binary is not articulated, its position in relation to the other side of the binary is implied. For instance, men are viewed as dominant over women; whites over people of colour. In the social work relationship, despite at times the best of intentions by professionals, in part, due their knowledge as experts and through the implementation of the policies and procedures in their organizations, professionals have advantages (Hardy, 2012) in the binary of worker and client, and may be involved in the Othering of their clients.

To return to Cornell's (1992) definition- she is suggesting that in order to create an ethical relationship requires first of all, doing no harm. What is meant by "guarding against appropriation" for social workers is eschewing power over, or taking custody of, or in some way possessing the 'Other.' But this is a tall order given the disciplinary nature of the profession. Additionally, we can never fully know any other human being. Cornell is saying that, to be ethical, the uniqueness of the other individual must be honoured and treating clients like objects must be avoided. While in theory that principle is supported by social workers, in practice, given institutional requirements, it is often difficult to implement. Cornell's definition of an ethical relation is central to the view taken in this book.

The orientation in this book, in addition to focusing on the dyadic relationships of workers and clients, also widens the ethical field beyond micro considerations. The individualized focus in codes of ethics scapegoats both clients and workers for profoundly complex systemic injustices. Emphasis on the worker-client relationship keeps from view the larger societal issues, such as class bias or the inadequacy of resources, which must be confronted to render a more just social order. An important consideration in ethics concerns the structural constraints that contribute to the limitations and framing of social workers' understanding of their practice. Social workers are not independent of institutional codes, material resources, or legal and policy imperatives. Tremendous demands and constraints are exerted on professionals by the state and broader institutional network within which workers operate. As I have identified, in fact, some might argue that the state itself should be considered a client, particularly when services are being contracted. This makes the pressures on workers all the more significant. Front-line workers' positions in organizational settings, legislative requirements, funding expectations, the restrictions of resources, all form and limit the directions in which workers can practice their craft. At the same time, it must always be remembered that helping professionals are not just passive players in the system. They are also agents who contribute to the social construction of Euro-Western society, by reinforcing some ways of being in the world while discouraging or denying others. This book also addresses the ways in which practitioners contribute to what is taken as the structures in society, including notions of race, class and age.

This book examines the constitution of the helping relationship within the context of workers' placements in institutional regimes. I ask: How are practitioners located within the institutional arrangements? What do the workers understand as the constraints, enablers and paradoxes in the work? Given those constraints and paradoxes, how do they try to be helpful? How does that affect what they understand to be help and what they practice? What do they not take into account? Why not?

Additionally, in Euro-Western society, the history of the development of the profession of social work, the process and outcomes of professionalization, particularly in the work with individual clients, have shaped and constrained what can and does occur between worker and client (Weinberg, 2010). At times, these pressures result in contradictory principles that must be resolved in the applied work in the field. This book will make a contribution to the debate about whether the profession as a whole is redeemable or whether, as some would suggest (e.g. Margolin, 1997), the whole enterprise of social work is flawed and potentially corrupt.

The Research Study

The Population for the Study – Social Workers and Young Single Mothers

I first became interested in the area of ethics when I worked as a social worker in two settings: as the clinical director in one social service agency and a consultant in another, both of whose primary work was with young single mothers. The inherent paradoxical structural dimension that complicated the work of helping in these agencies was questioning who was the client – the mother, the baby or both? Whose needs and protection were workers responsible for ultimately, and when conflicts arose, how did practitioners resolve the tensions when the resolution might have contradictory effects? I frequently was consulted about the 'treatment' of these young women and was troubled and confused by the simultaneous mix of caring and discipline. Also, there was a Grand Canyon sized chasm between workers' perceptions of the young women they were attempting to help and the young women's insights about their own lives. Often the discrepancy centred on the evaluative meaning that each group gave to bearing and mothering children, without the advantage of marriage and at a young age. On the one hand, mostly white liberal workers often asked why these young women (frequently immigrants or women of colour) became pregnant and kept their babies, implying that traveling that particular road had often been unwise for the young women. On the other hand, the women, who were the clients, at times did not view their circumstances in the same perilous fashion their workers did. Concurrently, for clients, fears and anxieties revolved around the risk of losing their babies through the potential apprehension by the Children's Aid Society (CAS), the child welfare organization in Ontario, Canada. Even workers in agencies not designated as direct child welfare organizations had a hand in those apprehensions. Frequently the quintessential issue for the workers was the protection of the child from a mother they perceived of as inadequate.

Like Mies (1983, p.123), I believe, that research "must be brought to serve the interests of dominated, exploited and oppressed groups, particularly women." Feminist ethics is fundamentally about the exercise and distribution of power (Walker, 2001). The single teenage mothers, whom workers see as clients, are an important category for the exploration of the problem of ethical practice as they are at the nexus of a number of marginalized categories: they are young, female, usually poor, working-class, often non-white, mothers (from my perspective, another marginalized group) and raising children outside of the institution of marriage. Thus these women occupy a particular social location. Social location refers to the cluster of social demographics and the meaning ascribed to them in a society. Because of the social location of this oppressed group, to understand how front-line workers either perpetuate their marginalization and/or contribute to their emancipation is particularly relevant. The young women who come to the attention of social workers are discursively framed as problematic by the larger public and the media, and are currently the focus of a great deal of punitive legislation in many Euro-Western countries. In the work with young single mothers, the paradoxes of attempting to 'help' when one is also an agent of surveillance, regulation and discipline are especially acute.

I assumed that the workers in my study would articulate and adopt some of the primary discourses about young single mothers that I have outlined above. While I did not form formal hypotheses, I did speculate that generally, practitioners would have fought against the reactionary discourses of single teen mothers (Lessa, 2006; Rains, Davies, and McKinnon, 2004). At the same time, I thought they would have been forced, at times, by their mandated roles, to subscribe to and implement policies that emerged from these tropes. This, I felt, would set some of the foundations for the dilemmas that the front-line workers might confront. I anticipated that a more radical revisionist discourse would not be frequently applied, but might signal moments of resistance. I conjectured that liberal explanations would be the primary discursive framework for the workers in my study.

The Research

Originally I intended to start this inquiry from the viewpoint of the young single mothers. But I felt I could not answer even basic questions about what the perceived terms of the helping relationship were, as the workers, rather than the moms, understood them. This seemed to be a necessary starting point for exploratory research. Thus, my question became what actually constituted the helping relationship from the standpoint of the practitioners and how did workers understand the clients and themselves? What did they take to be ethical practice?

I was interested in the front-line practitioners who had to confront the daily realities of practice and yet might have more limited opportunities to actually influence the constraints and enablers that shaped the work than the managers in their agencies. Being closest to the construction of 'help,' I believed they held a great deal of practice wisdom to be tapped (Sherman and Reid, 1994). Since there has been a dearth of qualitative research on ethics from a critical feminist perspective, examining the work of front-line social workers with young single mothers, I felt a qualitative inquiry would be appropriate because clarity about social phenomena must precede the generation of hypotheses for the purposes of prediction (Mandell, 1997).

The research occurred in Ontario, the most populous province in Canada, having the largest city and as well as the capital of the country. In Ontario, social service agencies whose primary focus is young mothers and fathers operate under an umbrella organization. I met with senior managers from this organization to apprise them of my intended research. They believed that a sample based solely on individuals with social work degrees was too restrictive because, despite being understood as 'social work,' few of the front-line workers actually held degrees in the social work field. The administrators also identified that there were limited opportunities for diversity of sample; since most of the individuals working in this area were white, middle-class, and female. Based on their critique, I broadened the sample. I also contacted agencies that had mandates to work specifically with diverse populations. The sampling was designed as "typical case" sampling to provide a profile of the practice of conventional representative agencies (Patton, 1990, p.173).

The research involved interviews with five front-line social workers. Four participants worked in agencies under this encompassing organization. The fifth operated out of a community health centre that had a specific programme for young single mothers. One interviewee worked in a rural setting, while the other four were in urban environments in Ontario, Canada. While this is small number, the intended depth and length of the interview process was designed to generate information-rich data (Patton, 1990). Each participant will be introduced individually in the specific chapter where I discuss a case of one of their clients.

All five social workers identified themselves as white and female. Three were married, two single. Two of those married had children of their own. All of them had been in the field for a significant length of time, working in multiple settings. They were born between 1961 and 1971, being approximately between 30 and 40 years of age at the point of the interviews. I knew none of these individuals personally.

The interview schedule included questions about the nature of the helping relationship and the workers' understanding of it, their own positionality, their beliefs about the young women and the tensions they experienced in ethics.[4] To move away from theory to actual practice, I asked workers to tell me about

---

4   Interview schedule is attached as Appendix A.

particular cases. Questions were open-ended and exploratory, based on a semi-structured format that changed with time. While I was interested in studying what *was* occurring in their work, particularly the enablers and constraints of and on helping relationships, I was also concerned about what workers thought *should be* and *could be*.

I was aiming for redundancy as a technique to determine the adequacy of the data obtained and to enhance credibility (Lincoln and Guba, 1985). I also had the goal of providing 'thick description' to increase trustworthiness. Therefore, I used the later interviews to pursue enigmatic aspects of the interviews or to deepen my understanding about important themes that had emerged. This prolonged engagement potentially contributes to the trustworthiness of the research. In the one instance when a worker (Kristine) and her client agreed to make an audio-tape, I had an alternate source of information as well.

The interviews spanned a time frame of two years. While the plan was to have five interviews per person, with one participant there were six interviews, and with another seven. Some of these occurred in their homes, and some in mine. With all participants, there was access to the transcripts and a final meeting in which I shared summaries of my analyses. In one of these meetings, a participant expressed concern about the risks of the material she shared and none of that material was included in this book.

With each of the participants, I have begun the story of their client with a brief summary description of the workers' backgrounds. I believe that their earlier histories shed some light on their construction of 'client,' their understanding about a particular client, and what emerged for them as dilemmas. In the discussions that follow, at times, I have focused on parallels between their own personal stories and that of the service user, particularly any traumatic events (e.g. sexual abuse) or life experiences that the social workers described or identified as allowing them to more fully understand their clients.

The emphasis was an examination of the paradoxes of providing help in a liberatory fashion when one is positioned structurally in ways that demand regulation. My purpose was to untangle the complex web of what constituted practice from a social worker's standpoint; to obtain actual responses tied to particular concrete case examples, as a way to get past theories about practice to the 'realities,' regardless of the workers' professed principles.

Limitations of the Study

Of course every study has its limitations.

One was the choice of participants. They had a range of educational backgrounds with a variety of degrees and diplomas from Early Childhood Education to a Masters in Social Work. The fact that the workers had diverse educational backgrounds has implications in examining ethics in practice. Professions have been defined on the basis of traits that distinguish them, including a specific knowledge base, particular training towards an advanced skill set, and most importantly for this discussion, the values and ethics of that profession, including codes of ethics (Hugman, 2005b; McAuliffe, 2014; Weinberg, 2015). Thus, questions arise about how the responses of the workers might have been different had they all been trained specifically as social workers.

Conflicts can also arise as a result of those professional values but also due to the broad context workers find themselves in, the values of a particular organizational setting, the service users they are working with (Postle, 2007) or their own personal values. So, training into a particular profession is only one factor that influences how those values will be construed or acted upon (Kendall and Hugman, 2013).

Nonetheless, one function of professional groups is that of self-regulation of professional practice. The Ontario Association of Social Workers, that body in the province of Canada where this study occurred, could not discipline those participants who were not licensed social workers. Any disciplinary processes for those workers would either be via their employers, or their own discrete professional group. But, while they were not all formally trained as social workers, all participants were fulfilling 'social work' positions in their agencies, as it was quite common for non-credentialed social workers to perform social work jobs in the province of Canada at the time of the study. This state of affairs is anomalous when compared to other mental health professionals, such as psychiatrists or psychologists. However, because it was the case that 'social workers' often did not have formal credentials at the point that I conducted the research, and I was interested in on-the-ground current realities of practice, I have referred to them as 'social workers' and their practice was evaluated from the lens of social work standards and practices.

Of course, this situation is different in other countries that protect the title of social work and have stricter laws around registration and licensure. And in fact, in the last few years, some provinces in Canada that have the jurisdiction to determine title and licensure, have tightened up the requirements for people calling themselves 'social workers' as well.

Participants being self-selecting was another shortcoming of the study. I do not know how that influenced the material I obtained, although I would speculate that this group may have been more radical, dissatisfied or conceptually-oriented than others who did not volunteer. Despite attempts to obtain greater diversity amongst the interviewees, I was unsuccessful. While being white is a racialized position, I could not obtain the diversity of worker perspective on race or ethnicity that I might have unearthed had there also been workers of colour in my sample. Similarly, I do not know what having had other represented differences (such as sexual orientation or disability) might have brought to the research findings.

Also potentially problematic is that "what people do and what people say they do, and how people think in action and how people reflect on the way they think in action, are not necessarily the same things" (Parton and O'Byrne, 2000, p.32). The emphasis on discourse did not look at the materiality of what was accomplished, only workers' perceptions of what transpired. Furthermore, despite workers' desires to be honest, most of us wish to frame ourselves positively, and that need may have influenced what was expressed. A related significant drawback was that this study does not examine the embodied experience of those acted upon; namely the clients. How they perceived the helping relationship undoubtedly would have diverged from either the workers' or my own perspective.

Also, in the way I made sense of their histories, these workers will become immutably fixed by these representations. I questioned how I could give a 'true' picture of each woman that was respectful, when I believe that subjectivity is fragmentary, fluid, and changing over time and space. My solution was to focus on case examples, rather than the overall practice of a worker, recognizing that even that solution, to some extent, totalized and essentialized both the workers and their clients. I have tried to demonstrate shifting subjectivity in the writing but recognize that there is no space of innocence for me as researcher. Moreover, key to the purpose of the research was not to provide a true, comprehensive portrait of any one worker, but to clarify paradoxes and contradictions in practice regarding questions of ethics.

Another restriction of the work was that it focused on a small population from the Canadian context. Social work in other parts of the world takes quite a different form and therefore the discussion may not be generalizable to these countries. Context, history, the role of government, professional status, the development of other helping professions, adoption of particular theoretical orientations (Healy, 2008), political, institutional, economic factors (Rossiter, Walsh-Bowers, and Prilleltensky, 2002), religion (Askeland and Døhlie, 2015) and culture are some of the influences that shape the profession in diverse ways. For example, the impact of Paulo Friere's theory of liberation theology has influenced the development of social work in Latin America in a manner that is more political and radical than North American social work (Healy, 2008). Also the breadth and depth of problems such as poverty change the nature of the work. Furthermore, since the development of the profession originated in Euro-Western countries and was exported to other regions, colonialism and "professional imperialism" (Gray and Fook, 2004, p.626) are threats to the practice of social work in other parts of the world (Healy and Link, 2012). The importation of values that disregard the local must be avoided. So, one should view this work as most relevant in the context of Euro-Western social work, and even then, there will be differences between the Canadian context and other countries.

Finally, in terms of limitations, I am acutely aware that there is no neutral arena for an author and every book is really a version of oneself. As a white, middle-class, Jewish scholar and former practitioner with this client group, I have the power to create a version of 'truth' by which workers and clients become the Other. In some ways, this monograph is a reconstruction of a white woman speaking for other white women on behalf of those marginalized. I am uncomfortable with the possible positioning of the white (literally) knight slaying the dragons of oppression on behalf of the subjugated client. In this way as an academic, I too am implicated in Othering practices.

Goals for the Book

This is not just an account about young single mothers and the workers who attempt to help them. This is also a tale of my anguish about the current state of social services, my anxiety about the possibilities of anti-oppressive applications in the field, and my passionate hope in the potential to edge towards more ethical practice.

There have been some authors who have argued that social work has lost its moral centre. Leslie Margolin (1997), in his text, *Under the Cover of Kindness*, formulates a damning critique of the field of social work, challenging the ethics of practitioners, and stating, "the problem *is* the core mission" (italics in the original, p.4). He attempts to "show how social work entails not only the imposition of surveillance and control in the heretofore closed space of the home but also the constant justification of this intervention as charitable and disinterested help" (p.8). He believes that the profession is rife with "that which must be hidden: power, self-interest, [and] hierarchical domination" (p.6). I found his book disturbing because so much of it on first reading seemed sound and, what is more, like my own theoretical perspective, he utilized a framework adapted from Foucault's work on disciplinarity to bolster his claims. In later chapters, I will be analyzing and disputing Margolin's argument. In part, this work will be my response to him and others whose opinions are comparable.

As mentioned, I concur with Margolin (1997) that there are far-reaching practices of domination inherent in the positioning of the helping professions. One goal for this book is to expose the extensive and, at times, injurious disciplinary practices enacted upon young single mothers by social workers who, for the most part, espouse a desire to contribute to liberatory practices on behalf of this client group. I wish to bring out the pain that accompanies the lives of these young women, as well that of the workers that, with the best of intentions, are trapped within disciplinary regimes that often perpetuate marginalization and punishment. At its most punitive, the work of help can lead to a crippling of the young women by social workers who view them as "at risk" rather than "at promise" (Swadener and Lubeck, 1995).

Such narratives have real material implications for these young mothers because often their suffering goes unrecognized and unseen in the official accounts and records. At the extreme, these young women become the recipients of a modern-day form of eugenics in which, while permitted to bear children, because they are often seen as unacceptable and unsuitable mothers, their babies are taken from their sides through apprehensions, and they can be barred from having one of the most fundamental relationships in our society, that of a mother to her child. Simultaneously, however, as a society, must we not determine who is unfit to parent to ensure the protection of the most vulnerable in our society, such as young children? This work explores the complexity of this most painful of social processes.

A further goal is to delve into the possibilities for alternatives to the current state of practice with young single mothers. Given the inevitability of trespass, concepts of intentionality and individual responsibility, key ideas in liberal humanistic theory, may not be the most useful in understanding what can be done to practice more ethically.

Instead, I will examine what concepts are beneficial in the reduction of trespass such as the recognition of its inevitability, the problematization of power, and the possibilities of collaborative political action.

Consequently, this is also a story about resistances; those alternatives arrived at in small but significant ways by the workers in the field. I believe it is through these actions, in alternate acts of resistance that the potential for change towards more liberatory activity and more ethical practice occurs. Additionally, I will inquire: what facilitates or impedes those acts? It is my hope that this research will lead to knowledge that could be utilized in professional schools to refashion a more politicized and radical understanding of young single mothers and their children. Young mothers and their children represent the future. They also symbolize how we, as a society, treat and should be treating those most marginalized.

Finally, I hope to provide an alternate view of how helping professionals should understand what constitutes the field of ethics and to offer some analytical tools such as the discursive field, ethical trespass, and notions of resistance to broaden their understanding. For practitioners, my aim is that this book will be a source of support through providing increased clarity about both the dilemmas and complexities they face in practice while suggesting some directions to move towards more ethical behaviour.

Bibliography

Abrams, L.S., and Moio, J.A. (2009). Critical race theory and the cultural competence dilemma in social work education. *Journal of Social Work Education*, 42(4), 245–61.

Aotearoa New Zealand Association of Social Workers. (2013). Summary of code of ethics. Available at: <http://anzasw.org.nz/social_work_practice/topics/show/158-summary-of-the-code-of-ethics> (Accessed May 5, 2015).

Arendt, H. (1958). *The Human Condition*. Chicago: University of Chicago.

Askeland, G.A. and Døhlie, E. (2015). Contextualizing international social work: Religion as a relevant factor. *International Social Work*, 58(2), 261–9.

Banks, S. (2004). *Ethics, Accountability and the Social Professions*. New York: Palgrave Macmillan.

Barsky, A.E. (2010). *Ethics and Values in Social Work. An Integrated Approach for a Comprehensive Curriculum*. Toronto: Oxford University Press.

Benjamin, J. (1995). *Like Subjects, Love Objects. Essays on Recognition and Sexual Difference*. New Haven: Yale University Press.

Bonac, V.A. (1996). Perception or fantasy? A new clinical theory of transference. Reprinted August 1998 from Electronic Journal of Communicative Psychoanalysis. Available at: <http://human-nature.com/articles/bonac.html> (Accessed June 24, 2003).

Breheny, M., and Stephens, C. (2010). Youth or disadvantage? The construction of teenage mothers in medical journals. *Culture, Health & Sexuality*, 12(3), 307–22.

Butler, A.C. (1992). The changing economic consequences of teenage childbearing. *Social Service Review*, 66(1), 1–31.

Canadian Association of Social Workers. (2005). CASW code of ethics. Available at: <http://www.casw-acts.ca/en/what-social-work/casw-code-ethics> (Accessed May 5, 2015).

Chambon, A.S. (1999). Foucault's approach: Making the familiar visible. In A.S. Chambon, A. Irving, and L. Epstein (Eds.), *Reading Foucault for Social Work* (pp.51–81). New York: Columbia University Press.

Chambon, A.S., Irving, A., and Epstein, L. (Eds.), (1999). *Reading Foucault for Social Work*. New York: Columbia University Press.

Christie, P. (2005). Education for an ethical imagination. *Social Alternatives*, 24(4), 39–44.

Congress, E.P. (2000). What social workers should know about ethics: Understanding and resolving practice dilemmas. *Advances in Social Work*, 1(1), 1–25.

Cornaccia, C. (1995, January 3). Babies having babies. *Ottawa Citizen*, p. C3.

Cornell, D. (1992). *The Philosophy of the Limit*. New York: Routledge.

Dean, M. (1994). "A social structure of many souls": Moral regulation, government, and self-formation. *Canadian Journal of Sociology*, 19(2), 145–68.

Dean, M., and Hindress, B. (1998). Introduction. In M. Dean, and B. Hindress (Eds.), *Governing Australia. Studies in Contemporary Rationalities of Government* (pp.1–19). Cambridge: Cambridge University Press.

Dryfoos, J.G. (1990). *Adolescents at Risk. Prevalence and Prevention*. New York: Oxford University Press.

Epstein, L. (1999). The culture of social work. In A.S. Chambon, A. Irving, and L. Epstein (Eds.), *Reading Foucault for Social Work* (pp.3–26). New York: Columbia University Press.

Fields, J. (2005). "Children having children": Race, innocence, and sexuality education. *Social Problems*, 52(4), 549–71.

Foucault, M. (1977). *Discipline and Punish. The Birth of the Prison* (A. Sheridan, Trans.) (2nd ed.). New York: Vintage Books. (Original work published in 1975)

Foucault, M. (1982). Afterword. The subject and power. In H. Dreyfus, and P. Rabinow (Eds.), *Michel Foucault: Beyond Structuralism and Hermeneutics* (pp.209–26). Chicago: University of Chicago Press.

Foucault, M. (1984). On the genealogy of ethics: An overview of work in progress. In P. Rabinow (Ed.). *The Foucault Reader* (pp.340–72). New York: Pantheon Books.

Foucault, M. (1988). Technologies of the self. In L.H. Martin, H. Gutman, and P.H. Hutton (Eds.) *Technologies of the Self: A Seminar with Michel Foucault* (pp.16–49). Amherst: University of Massachusetts Press.

Foucault, M. (1991). Governmentality. In G. Burchell, C. Gordon, and P. Miller (Eds.), *The Foucault Effect. Studies in Governmentality* (pp.87–104). Chicago: University of Chicago Press.

Fraser, N. (1989). *Unruly Practices: Power, Discourse, and Gender in Contemporary Social Theory*. Minneapolis: University of Minnesota Press.

Furstenberg, Jr., F.F. (1991). As the pendulum swings: Teenage childbearing and social concern. *Family Relations*, 40, 127–38.

Garn, S.M., Pesick, S.D., and Petzold, A.S. (1986). The biology of teenage pregnancy: The mother and child. In J.B. Lancaster, and B.A. Hamburg (Eds.), *School-age Pregnancy and Parenthood. Biosocial Dimensions* (pp.77–93). Hamburg. New York: Aldine De Gruyter.

Gasker, J.A. and Fischer, A.C. (2014). Toward a context specific definition of social justice for social work: In search of overlapping consensus. *Journal of Social Work Values and Ethics*, 11(1), 42–53.

Gil, D.G. (1998). *Confronting Injustice and Oppression. Concepts and Strategies for Social Workers*. New York: Columbia University Press.

Gray, M. and Fook, J. (2004). The quest for a universal social work: Some issues and implications. *Social Work Education*, 23(5), 625–44.

Gray, M. and Webb, S.A. (Eds). (2010). *Ethics and Value Perspectives in Social Work*. New York: Palgrave MacMillan.

Guttmann, D. (2006). *Ethics in Social Work: A Context of Caring*. Binghamton, New York: Haworth Press.

Hardy, M. (2012). Shift recording in residential child care. *Ethics and Social Welfare*, 6(1), 88–96.

Harris, A. (2005). Discourse of desire as governmentality: Young women, sexuality and the significance of safe spaces. *Feminism and Psychology*, 15(1), 39–43.

Healy, K. (2005). *Social Work Theories in Context*. New York: Palgrave Macmillan.

Healy, K.M. (2008). *International Social Work. Professional Action in an Interdependent World*. (2nd ed.). New York: Oxford University Press.

Healy, L.M. and Link, R.J. (2012). *Handbook of International Social Work*. New York: Oxford University Press.

Hugman, R. (2003). Professional values and ethics in social work: Reconsidering postmodernism? *British Journal of Social Work*, 33, 1025–41.

Hugman, R. (2005b). *New Approaches in Ethics for the Caring Professions*. New York: Palgrave Macmillan.

Hugman, R. (2007). The place of values in social work education. In M. Lymbery and K. Postle (Eds.), *Social Work. A Companion to Learning* (pp.20–29). London: SAGE.

Hugman, R. (2010). *Understanding International Social Work. A Critical Analysis*. New York: Palgrave Macmillan.

Hugman, R., and Smith, D. (1995). Ethical issues in social work: An overview. In R. Hugman, and D. Smith (Eds.), *Ethical Issues in Social Work* (pp.1–15). New York: Routledge.

International Federation of Social Workers (2012). Statement of ethical principles. Available at: <http://ifsw.org/policies/statement-of-ethical-principles/> (Accessed May 5, 2015).

Irving, A. (1999). Waiting for Foucault. In A.S. Chambon, A. Irving, and L. Epstein (Eds.), *Reading Foucault for Social Work* (pp.27–50). New York: Columbia.

Jameton, A. (1984). *Nursing Practice: The Ethical Issues.* Englewood Cliffs, NJ: Prentice-Hall.

Jeffery, D. (2005). What good is anti-racist social work if you can't master it?: exploring the paradox in anti-racist social work education. *Race, Ethnicity and Education*, 8(4), 409–25, DOI: 10.1080/13613320500324011.

Jones, K.B. (1988). On authority: Or, why women are not entitled to speak. In I. Diamond and L. Quinby (Eds.), *Feminism and Foucault. Reflections on Resistance* (pp.119–33). Boston: Northeastern University Press.

Kelly, D.M. (1996). Stigma stories. Four discourses about teen mothers, welfare, and poverty. *Youth and Society*, 27(4), 421–49.

Kendall, S, and Hugman, R. (2013). Social work and the ethics of involuntary treatment for Anorexia Nervosa: A postmodern approach. *Ethics and Social Welfare*, 7(4), 310–25.

Klerman, L. (1986). The economic impact of school-age child rearing. In J.B. Lancaster, and B.A. Hamburg (Eds.), *School-age Pregnancy and Parenthood. Biosocial Dimensions* (pp. 361–77). New York: Aldine De Gruyter.

Knaak, S.J. (2010). Contextualising risk, constructing choice: Breastfeeding and good mothering in risk society. *Health, Risk & Society*, 12(4), 345–55.

Knights, D., and Vurdubakis, T. (1994). Foucault, power, resistance and all that. In J.M. Jermier, D. Knights, and W.R. Nord. (Eds.), *Resistance and Power in Organizations* (pp.167–98). New York: Routledge.

Kondrat, M.E. (2002). Actor-centred social work: Re-visioning "person-in-environment" through a critical theory lens. *Social Work*, 47(4), 435–48.

Lessa, I. (2006). Discursive struggles within child welfare: Restaging teen motherhood. *British Journal of Social Work*, 36, 283–98.

Leonard, P. (1994). Knowledge/power and postmodernism. Implications for the practice of a critical social work education. *Canadian Social Work Review*, 11(1), 11–26.

Lincoln, Y.S., and Guba, E.G. (1985). *Naturalistic Inquiry.* Beverly Hills, California: SAGE.

Luker, K. (1996). *Dubious Conceptions. The Politics of Teenage Pregnancy.* Cambridge: Harvard University Press.

Lundy, C. (2004). *Social Work and Social Justice.* Peterborough, Ontario: Broadview Press.

Macvarish, J. (2010). The effect of "risk-thinking" on the contemporary construction of teenage motherhood. *Health, Risk & Society*, 12(4), 314–22.

Mandell, D. (1997). *Fathers and Child Support: Discourse and Subjectivity.* Unpublished doctoral dissertation. University of Toronto, Toronto, Ontario, Canada.

Margolin, L. (1997). *Under the Cover of Kindness. The Invention of Social Work.* Charlottesville: University Press of Virginia.

Maynard, R. (Ed.). (1997). *Kids Having Kids.* Washington D.C: Urban Institute Press.

McAuliffe, D. (2014). *Interprofessional Ethics. Collaboration in the Social, Health and Human Services.* Port Melbourne, Australia: Cambridge University Press.

McTighe, J.P. (2011). Teaching the use of self through the process of clinical supervision. *Clinical Social Work Journal*, 39, 301–7.

McWhirter, J.J., McWhirter, B.T., McWhirter, A.M., and McWhirter, E.H. (1998). *At Risk Youth. A Comprehensive Response.* (2nd ed.). Toronto: Brooks/Cole Publishing.

Mies, M. (1983). Towards a methodology for feminist research. In G. Bowles, and R.D. Klein (Eds.), *Theories of Women's Studies* (pp.117–39). London: Routledge.

Mitchell, W.A., Crawshaw, P., Bunton, R., and Green, E.E. (2001). Situating young people's experience of risk and identity. *Health, Risk & Society*, 3(2), 217–33.

Moreau, M. [In collaboration with L. Leonard] (1989). *Empowerment. Through a Structural Approach to Social Work. A Report from Practice.* Ottawa: National Welfare Grants Program, Health and Welfare Canada.

Mullaly, B. (2007). *The New Structural Social Work* (3rd ed.). Oxford: Oxford University Press.

Nash, R.J. (2002). *"Real World" Ethics. Frameworks for Educators and Human Service Professionals.* New York: Teachers College Press, Columbia University.

National Association of Black Social Workers. (n.d). Code of ethics. Available at: <http://nabsw.org/?page=CodeofEthics> (Accessed May 5, 2015).

Oliver, C. (2013). Including moral distress in the new language of social work ethics. *Canadian Social Work Review*, 30(2), 203–16.

Ontario College of Social Workers and Social Service Workers. (2008). Code of ethics and standards of practice, Handbook, (2nd ed.). Available at: <http://www.ocswssw.org/professional-practice/code-of-ethics/> (Accessed May 5, 2015).

Orlie, M.A. (1997). *Living Ethically. Acting Politically.* Ithaca: Cornell University Press.

Parton, N. and O'Byrne, P. (2000). *Constructive Social Work. Towards a New Practice.* London: MacMillan.

Patton, M.Q. (1990). *Qualitative Evaluation and Research Methods* (2nd ed.). Newbury Park: SAGE.

Pearce, D.M. (1993). "Children having children": Teenage pregnancy and public policy from a woman's perspective. In A. Lawson, and D.L. Rhode (Eds.), *The Politics of Pregnancy, Adolescent Sexuality and Public Policy* (pp.46–58). New Haven: Yale University Press.

Phipps-Yonas, S.(1980). Teenage pregnancy and motherhood: A review of the literature. *American Journal of Orthopsychiatry*, 50(3), 403–31.

Postle, K. (2007). Value conflicts in practice. In M. Lymbery, and K. Postle (Eds.), *Social Work. A Companion to Learning* (pp.251–60). London: SAGE.

Rains, P., Davies, L., and McKinnon, M. (1998). Taking responsibility: An insider view of teen motherhood. *Families in Society: The Journal of Contemporary Human Services*, 308–19.

Rains, P., Davies, L., and McKinnon, M. (2004). Social services construct the teen mother. *Families in Society*, 85(1), 17–26.

Razack, N., and Jeffrey, D. (2002). Critical race discourse and tenets for social work. *Canadian Social Work Review*, 19(2), 257–71.

Rosenau, P.M. (1992). *Post-modernism and the Social Sciences. Insights, Inroads, and Intrusions*. Princeton, New Jersey: Princeton University Press.

Rossiter, A., Prilleltensky, I., and Walsh-Bowers, R. (2000). A postmodern perspective on professional ethics. In B. Fawcett, B. Featherstone, J. Fook, and A. Rossiter (Eds.), *Practice and Research in Social Work* (pp.83–103). New York: Routledge.

Rossiter, A., Walsh-Bowers, R., and Prilleltensky, I. (2002). Ethics as a located story. A comparison of North American and Cuban clinical ethics. *Theory & Psychology*, 12(4), 533–56.

Rousmaniere, K., Dehli, K., and de Coninck-Smith, N. (Eds.). (1997). *Moral Regulation and Schooling*. New York: Garland Publishing.

Sawicki, J. (1991). *Disciplining Foucault. Feminism, Power, and the Body*. New York: Routledge.

Sherman, E.A., and Reid, W.J. (1994). *Qualitative Research in Social Work*. New York: Columbia University Press.

Silva, E.B. (1996). The transformation of mothering. In E.B. Silva (Ed.), *Good Enough Mothering? Feminist Perspectives on Lone Motherhood* (pp.10–36). New York: Routledge.

Smith, D.E. (1987). *The Everyday World as Problematic. A Feminist Sociology*. Toronto: University of Toronto Press.

Stevens, J.W. (1996). Childbearing among unwed African American adolescents: A critique of theories. *Affilia*, 11(3), 278–302.

Swadener, B.B., and Lubeck, S. (Eds.). (1995). *Children and Families "at Promise." Deconstructing the Discourse of Risk*. Albany: State University of New York Press.

Valverde, M. (1994). Editor's introduction. *Canadian Journal of Sociology*, 19(2), vi–xii.

Walker, M.U. (1998) *Moral Understandings. A Feminist Study of Ethics*. New York: Routledge.

Walker, M.U. (2001). Seeing power in morality: A proposal for feminist naturalism in ethics. In P. DesAutels and J. Waugh (Eds.), *Feminist doing Ethics* (pp.167–83). New York: Rowman & Littlefield Publishers, Inc.

Weedon, C. (1987). *Feminist Practice and Poststructuralist Theory*. (2nd ed.). Cambridge, Mass: Blackwell Publishers.

Weinberg, M. (2007). Ethical "use of self." The complexity of multiple selves in clinical practice. In D. Mandell (Ed.), *Revisiting the Use of Self: Questioning Professional Identities* (pp.213–33). Toronto: Canadian Scholars Press.

Weinberg, M. (2008). Structural social work: A moral compass for ethics in practice. *Critical Social Work*, 9(1).

Weinberg, M. (2009). Moral distress: A missing but relevant concept for ethics in social work. *Canadian Social Work Review*, 26(2), 139–52.

Weinberg, M. (2010). The social construction of social work ethics: Politicizing and broadening the lens. *Journal of Progressive Human Services*, 21(1), 32–44.

Weinberg, M. (2015). Professional privilege, ethics and pedagogy. *Ethics and Social Welfare*. Online.

Weinberg, M., and Campbell, C. (2014). From codes to contextual collaborations: Shifting the thinking about ethics in social work. *Journal of Progressive Human Services*, 25(1), 37–49.

Wilson, H., and Huntington, A. (2006). Deviant (m)others: The construction of teenage motherhood in contemporary discourse. *Journal of Social Policy*, 35(1), 59–76.

Zembylas, M. (2003a). Emotions and teacher identity: A poststructural perspective. *Teachers and Teaching: Theory and Practice*, 9(3), 213–38.

Chapter 2
Discursive Fields And Ethical Issues

Introduction

My intention in this chapter is to present three distinct discursive fields that workers mobilized in order to conceive and implement a helping relationship with a particular client. I will demonstrate how the discursive fields of the workers led to very different framings of the quality of that relationship, of what constituted "help," and of different ethical issues (Keinemans and Kann, 2013). Specifically, I will investigate how these workers responded to the social process of evaluating mothering competency. I chose the task of workers' assessments of parenting skills because it is a primary responsibility for workers with this population and it is an undertaking that creates the most potential pain for clients and distress for workers. One clinical vignette each from three workers was selected to provide a range of discursive fields and subject positions available to and enacted by both workers and clients, and because these particular cases had emotional impact for the participants. The case examples illustrate all three discourses about young single mothers articulated in the first chapter: reactionary, liberal and revisionist. It seems that workers' significant experiences and early life events played a role in the take-up of positions and discourses in these vignettes. I will describe how each caseworker resolved the contradictions and dilemmas that arose in their case.

I have focused particularly on the enmeshment of the workers in practices of surveillance and discipline. All five participants, regardless of how radical their perspective, engaged in these practices. My intention in highlighting this aspect of the work is to expose the inevitability of disciplinary practices as part of the helping relationship, with the attendant potential of ethical trespass. I also wish to depict the extent of control to which clients are subjected. The prohibition against mothering and the loss of one's child generally lead to deep emotional pain for the women involved. I hope to make visible the grief that can disappear in documentary accounts. At the same time, as a society we have designated social workers as the protectors of children and as the agents responsible for determining the adequacy of a mother to safeguard those children, a necessary evil in our present society. Accordingly, the paradoxes inherent in this social process are significant, the implementation is complex, and the potential for trespass substantial, leading to it being a good illustration of the concerns explored throughout this book.

It would be an oversimplification to speak of the workers as just oppressors or clients as simply dominated. In Chapter 5, particularly, I will attempt to rectify this imbalance by portraying instances of workers taking action that was liberatory. The very attempt to 'fix' caseworkers' orientations through a delineation of these clinical sketches reduces those workers to portraits that are static rather than the fluid process that constitutes a worker's shifting subjectivity. None of the workers adopted one discursive position or practice with the young single mothers. Every participant, at times, attempted to ameliorate or avoid her positioning as an agent of domination. Furthermore, the story of the social workers' positioning does not take into account clients' forms of resistance.

Charlotte's Story of Violet[12]

The Worker

Charlotte identifies as a white woman and, at the time of the interviews, was approximately 40 years old. As a young person, she described herself as having low self-esteem. She felt she was told "lies" about herself and needed to discover that she did not have to follow the script provided by those who had little faith in her abilities. Originally, she did not have "a lot of direction" and her early years were difficult. As a youth, she was sexually abused and became promiscuous. The abuse occurred once, but she was unable to tell her parents. When Charlotte thought about her behaviours from that time, she stated that they were symptomatic of "who [she] needed to be to survive ... nobody else gave [her] any other options ... [she] did the very best with what [she] had."

I would speculate that she used the same reasoning to make sense of the young women who were her clients, leading her to see them in a sympathetic light. For example, when she heard "the harshness that [the clients] use[d] to describe themselves," it made her "go further past the words" to understand what trauma might underlie negative self-images. When clients were promiscuous, she would explore the possibility that there had been sexual trauma for them as well. But because she perceived herself as having healed from this experience, in part through counselling, she also believed others could reclaim those injured parts of themselves.

---

1   All names are pseudonyms

2   Transcription guidelines: (adapted from Mergenthaler & Stinson, 1992)

(-)	pauses representing approximately 1 second one dash for each second
(p:00:02:42)	pauses of longer than 5 seconds, in this case 2 minutes and 42 seconds
(/)	indecipherable utterances one slash for each utterance
(?: mother)	possible correct word, in this case "mother"
(!)	exclamation mark immediately follows words clearly emphasized by the speaker
(*)	in actual quotations, names are replaced with pseudonyms and an asterisk precedes the pseudonym

As a young adult, Charlotte was on social assistance and worked as a chambermaid. At the time of the interviews, she had two adolescent children. The same man had fathered both children, but his involvement was peripheral and they had not been married. Until a recent marriage to another man, she had always parented alone. Providing for her children had been a major motivator in her life and precipitated her return to school. During the research, she was studying towards a master's degree in social work. Charlotte did not perceive herself as "the most perfect parent" because, as a single parent who was in school, she felt she did not give her children the attention she would have liked.

"A very, very strong faith" and a "real personal relationship with God" were significant influences in her life and from her perspective, responsible for "a good majority of [her] success in [her] life." Her church was a fundamentalist Pentecostal assembly. Her belief had allowed her to think there was "nothing horrendous" in others, to see the humanity in everyone, and to attempt to be nonjudgmental of others. Similar to her own experience, she held that what defeated people was not believing in themselves and accepting the negative messages they had been given about their capabilities.

Charlotte was employed at a middle level in a maternity home in an urban setting. In this agency, she worked directly with clients. While she was "a salaried employee" and "not management" nor a supervisor, she did have some organizational and administrative responsibilities, unlike other line staff.

Client Behaviour – Absent and Unresponsive

Violet was an 18-year-old, white, young woman, pregnant with her first child, who had been in the residence for a month at the time of my interviews with Charlotte. According to Charlotte, Violet had been living in the community with her sister, but had had to move to her mother's when her sister ended up in a shelter due to domestic violence. The mother "had not raised *Violet for quite some time," and Violet was only "able to stay there two or three days" prior to her moving to the residence.

Charlotte's concern was that even with "prompts" to come down from her bedroom to eat a meal, Violet was "always in her room" or absent from the residence. Charlotte described Violet's behaviour: "she was isolating herself, she wasn't eating, she wasn't able to take care of herself." Attending the educational and information programmes was a requirement for her stay in the maternity home and even after having these expectations spelled out and agreeing to comply, Violet continued to absent herself and would "go out and not come back for a day." In addition, despite the maternity home supplying a layette list of items that clients were expected to accumulate in preparation for the arrival of the baby, Charlotte stated that Violet had "nothing in her room ... to identify that she [was] going to have a baby. She [had] no clothes, no bottles, no diapers." Additionally, Charlotte identified that Violet presented with a "very flat affect" and was "very non-responsive to questions."

Interpretation of Client Behaviour – Possibility of Foetal Alcohol Syndrome/
Post-partum Depression

Charlotte queried whether Violet might have "foetal alcohol effect (FAE) or foetal alcohol syndrome" which resulted in a "cognitive delay" that could explain the lack of connection and response to workers. According to Charlotte, the staff asked, "can you [Violet] manage a baby? Will you be isolated in a room and respond to the baby's needs to be fed, to be changed, to be … bonded with." Violet's lack of connection to staff and residents made Charlotte fear for her capacity to make an attachment with her own child. As an explanation for the subject positions Charlotte adopted with Violet, Charlotte stated, "we … had nothing to work with to [base a decision] … on whether or not she could do it [mother adequately]."

The most significant trepidation for Charlotte was, "Is there something bigger going on? Could she experience post-partum depression? Could we have a dead baby?" Without clarity in her assessment, Charlotte feared that since Violet was "due in three weeks … the baby could be apprehended."

In general, Charlotte believed that "the majority of the young women" had "come from places where they [had] … a need for the intimacy, for the love, for the connection, [and] for … validation." Charlotte argued that a very high percentage of these young women had had abusive or unsupportive relationships with their boyfriends. In explaining why a young woman would tolerate such a relationship, she proposed, a client "just wants a family, she wants to be loved." In discussing their sexuality, Charlotte argued that these young women were not necessarily making a "connection between their head, their heart, and their groin area" because if they did "really understand it, then they would make better choices in the partners that they're with." Her perception was that "there's this empty space in them that … isn't filled." She quoted one young woman as saying to her (and Charlotte concurring with this theory), "'it's not about that [being orgasmic], *Charlotte. It's about being nurtured and being held and being loved … .'" These explanations are examples of the liberal discourse identified in Chapter 1, of the young woman who needs protection and requires a psychological 'fix' to fill that empty space for appropriate nurturance and love that was not supplied either by families of origin or partners. It is also consistent with Charlotte's own experience of being a young woman who was promiscuous in order to fill her own need for care and validation. Additionally, Charlotte believed that, like herself, these young women had been given inaccurate messages about their adequacy. She thought she could correct those messages by saying, "I believe in you."

Strategies of Help – Connection/Diagnosis/Education/CAS involvement

Since Charlotte had two clients in this case, Violet and the anticipated new baby, the complexity of protecting the safety of that child at the same time as meeting Violet's needs to fill the empty spaces through "connection" and "validation" was apparent in the struggles Charlotte experienced. How should Charlotte meet these potentially conflicting needs?

Charlotte described her attempts:

> We have tried to support her in saying … "if there's any other special way you learn? We will incorporate that into your learning plan … have you ever had some difficulty in reading or anything like that?" … "do you know whether or not your mom had been consuming alcohol or drugs when she was pregnant? … we have to make a referral to Children's Aid because I'm really concerned. … we really need to see you make an effort in the next three weeks, be visible, because you cannot bring a baby back and be stuck in your room.

A primary strategy was to obtain an assessment to determine whether depression or FAE were operative. Multiple avenues were taken to ascertain Violet's diagnosis. The use of diagnoses is an important dimension in disciplinary power. In Foucault's theorizing, an emphasis is placed on the physical body as a means to discipline and control. Young single women's bodies are prime targets for modern society's scrutiny and particularly for the surveillance and intervention to 'rehabilitate' through the disciplinary power of professionals. Discipline is meant in two senses of the word here. The first is punishment, such as having one's child apprehended, but the second is the whole armamentarium of theories, methods and strategies employed by professionals as part of their branch of knowledge. Diagnosis is one of those strategies. By close observation and questioning, subject positions of 'the inadequate mother' or the 'at risk child' begin to be constructed and the dividing practices referred to in Chapter 1 are enacted. The process of classification is continually refined until a diagnosis is reached (Leonard, 1997), allowing for more specific treatments (and possible punishments) to be meted out. So for Charlotte, determining the classification of whether or not Violet had FAE or post-partum depression was a disciplinary tactic that worked on Violet's body and constructed her as a particular type of subject, as well as gave credence to Charlotte's interventions. In the process, Charlotte was constituted as an 'expert' subject, increasing the gap between the professional and the client on whom the surveillance was focused.

The importance of help as pedagogy is also seen in Charlotte's talk. Language of "learning plan," "difficulty reading," "prompts," and the "integration" of material taught are examples of help as teaching. Techniques to provide assistance also entailed providing supports in the way of educational programmes, attempting to respond to Violet's unique learning requirements, and providing concrete programmes such as "prenatal baby basics."

Foucault discussed "four strategic unities which … formed specific mechanisms of knowledge and power" (1978, p.103). Although Foucault examined these strategies in relation to sex, I believe they are the principal technologies in governmentality generally. One of these is education. Through mechanisms of pedagogy, subjects are made both productive and docile, argued Foucault. Social services assume that education, with its emphasis on rational thinking, is one of the most effective means of changing the individual and consequently society (Enns, 1997). This emphasis emerges from a liberal Enlightenment tradition that values rational judgment, believing it to be critical to human dignity. The emphasis is on the individual as the unit for change. Being open to the direction provided by instruction would have increased the likelihood that Violet would be inducted into the dominant discursive frameworks and would have accepted these strategies as her own. According to Rose and Miller (1992, p.188–9),

> by means of expertise, self-regulatory techniques can be installed in citizens that will align their personal choices with the ends of government. The freedom and subjectivity of citizens can in such ways become an ally, and not a threat, to the orderly government of a polity and a society.

Pedagogy also acts to socialize procreative behaviour, (another tactic that Foucault examined) (1978, p.104), by indoctrinating clients as to what is perceived of as responsible behaviour on the part of a mother. Violet resisted these technologies, leaving Charlotte in a quandary about Violet's willingness and ability to align with the ends of government.

Simultaneously, attendance at pedagogical programmes is, in part, designed to increase the likelihood of clients adopting, as self-government, middle-class values and expectations that the maternity home's programmes reflect. Not accumulating a layette was assessed as a potential sign of Violet's ambivalence about mothering. As well, the expectation of a layette reinforces a middle-class standard of conditions for the adequate performance of mothering. The classed aspect of these strategies of governmentality will be addressed further in Chapter 3.

Charlotte was unclear about how satisfactory the supports in the community were for Violet and consequently saw the unborn child as potentially at risk. However, instead of the emphasis being on ascertaining or increasing the sufficiency of those supports, the emphasis remained on the individual functioning of Violet and the consequent risk to the child rather than on a structural analysis. The ultimate strategy was the use of the CAS (The Children's Aid Society)[3] as a means to gain "some added support" and as "preparation" for Violet to go into the community. In this instance, the CAS was seen as back-up for Charlotte in her decision-making, as provider of additional supports for Violet, and as the ultimate arbiter of her mothering capacity.

Justifications for Those Responses – Risk and Utilitarianism Discourses

The primary justification for Charlotte's actions came from her fear for the safety of the unborn child. Charlotte posed the question, "Could we have a dead baby?" While Charlotte did not use the specific language of Violet's behaviour being

---

3   The child welfare agency responsible for the protection of children in Ontario.

'risky' or the baby being 'at risk,' it is a dominant discourse in modern social work and one might suggest it is implied by this question. In modern Euro-Western society, emphasis has been placed on the quest for safety with the resulting calculation, management, and attempts to reduce risk (Beck, 1992).

The risk discourse has emerged from the insurance industry, related to calculations of harm. The collective rights of citizens, a consideration for the general good and concern for the most vulnerable, have been replaced with expectations on the individual, a concern to avoid the worst and to govern oneself wisely (Adams, 1995; Stanford, 2011). "Ethical and moral concerns are 'screened out' of risk equations" (Stanford, 2011, p. 1527) despite the fact that there are ethical considerations to these issues. These anxieties have heightened with the erosion of the social safety net and the rise of neoliberalism. Mothers in particular, are seen as key managers of those risks (Knaak, 2010).

Using screening processes such as assessment and diagnosis, the intention is to locate both the intrapsychic and external factors that will predict who is at risk, with the goal of prevention or remediation. There are always political and moral components (Douglas, 1992; Hunt, 2003) to what are evaluated as 'risky' behaviours. The political dimension relates to the assigning of rights, responsibilities and punishments to ascribed risks (Fox, 1999). And risk discourse acts as means of moral regulation. Replacing language such as 'underprivileged,' 'dysfunctional,' or 'pathological,' the underlying the notion is still one of being "at risk for failure" (Swadener and Lubeck, 1995, p.2). Behaviour is evaluated as good or bad, locating responsibility and blame on individuals for the potential harm that can arise by the failure to avoid risks through carelessness or misconduct, particularly in relation to one's mothering. Values of self-control and self-improvement undergird the evaluations (Hunt, 2003).

But the emphasis on the individual in risk discourse does not take structural disadvantage into account and contributes to the maintenance of social stratification and the ongoing oppression of those already marginalized. There is a correlation between the risks identified and the targeted groups that are socially acceptable to blame (Swift and Callahan, 2009). The process reinforces current power structures between those assessed as involved in 'risky' behaviour and those mandated to assess (Swift and Callahan, 2009).

However, the assessors are not immune from concerns about risk, since there is the societal expectation that professionals will enforce risk management, leading to the responsibilization and governance of the professional themselves (e.g. Stanford, 2011). And risk experts, such as social workers, are charged with the responsibility to maintain vigilance against those who handle those risks poorly. Yet, professionals are on the horns of a dilemma: making too much of the risk can lead to claims of fear-mongering and perpetuating stereotyping and stigma; too little, and if the dangers are realized, professionals can be judged as negligent and held liable.

A further trepidation for Charlotte was that Violet "could abscond with the baby." The language suggests a kidnapping, as if this young woman was not entitled to take her child and leave of her own volition. If one is not comfortable in groups or is reclusive, refusal to be watched puts one at more risk to have one's child apprehended. The meanings of the term 'apprehension' are significant. The Oxford Dictionary gives it three definitions (1996, p.64). The one intended by the CAS is "to seize or arrest." The criminality that is ascribed to the young women whose babies are removed comes through in this use of the word. But equally significant are the other two meanings. One is to anticipate with uneasiness or fear, the constant state for the residents under the eye of the home and the CAS, and for the staff who must judge their suitability. The final meaning is, to understand or perceive; how the dominant discourses frame what are adequate mothering practices.

A lesser anxiety for Charlotte was the need for compliance to avoid inconsistency that could be construed as favouritism towards one client over the others. Charlotte stated, "It causes a really negative dynamic because she won't do it [comply with house expectations]. Because the other girls think she's just ... getting away with lots of stuff." Here Charlotte was articulating the utilitarianism argument from Chapter 1. Group participation, sharing the load in a residential setting, and being seen as a team player are all broader components of what constitutes the 'good' member of the community. They also become indicators of what can come to represent the 'good' mother. A maternity home is semi-institutional and teenage activities, such as being holed up in one's room, can be viewed as problematic. Clients were required to attend multiple educational programmes during the day, despite desire, interest, or ability, and if they resisted, they could be seen as deviant. At another point in the interviews with me, Charlotte recognized this structural difficulty for the young women generally but, with Violet, she was unable to support a challenge of these institutional expectations.

Ethical Issues

Drawing on her own personal history, as a consequence of seeing these young women as injured through no fault of their own, Charlotte wished to be an agent supplying information to aid her clients making better "choices" (for example in partners) and filling those "empty spaces" for nurturance through emotional support. (I will address the discourse of choice in Chapter 3). A preferred subject position for herself was as someone who would empathically present more positive interpretations of a client's capability. Charlotte used a metaphor of herself as a bodyguard for the client: "This person [the client] is ... a very important person and they're trying to make their way up to a stage ... . [I'm] ... making a way for this person ... and I'm just pushing them [others] back so that this person can walk through" but because of crowds, the important person does not necessarily "see the stage." The client is the very important person; the crowd represents the conflicts, stressors and other people who block the client's progress; and the stage is the goal of changing one's view about the choices available in one's life. She believed her skill was seeing what her clients could not understand or imagine and clearing a path through the problems so that clients could reach awareness and success. Charlotte's preferred subject position was as a bodyguard who protects clients from danger and helps them reach their ambitions.

At the same time, one of the positions Charlotte felt compelled to adopt was as an agent of the state, a voice of authority to "read ... the riot act" and act as a judge of Violet's parenting ability. Acting as overseer for the safety of the unborn child required that she be able to ascertain how Violet would perform as a mother. Charlotte's power was in interpreting Violet's behaviour. By Violet not revealing 'who' she was, whether she desired this child or was prepared to mother, Charlotte was left in a quandary about fulfilling her mandated responsibility to ensure safety for the baby. This is paradox 1 of care and discipline, at the heart of all social work practice, identified in the first chapter. The difficulty of making decisions is revealed, in this case, when the problems are unclear or when a client does not provide information on which to make a judgment. How does one know whether a child is at risk when the issues are subtle? What indicators are used and what constitutes risk? In these circumstances, the broader societal conflicts of privacy of the home, sanctity of the family, the state's responsibility to protect children, and agencies' culpability if a child is harmed are all being enacted within the context of these cases and the dilemmas they pose.

Charlotte did not want to be a source of condemnation, in part because she perceived society as having failed these young women. She reasoned:

> they [her clients] look at you because of the power that you have or they perceive
> you have ... why should I just be one more reflection of a society that in some
> ways has let them down? That's not what my role is to do.

Charlotte stated she, "really, really [did not] want to judge." Yet despite wanting to avoid the take-up of a subject position of judge, in this instance, Charlotte did in fact enact that subject position. Her explanation was she had the "responsibility and I know what's expected of me." This is paradox 3, non-judgementalism versus making judgments.

Here is a moment where Foucault's governmentality (outlined in Chapter 1) is apparent. Charlotte accepted the discourses about legal obligation for workers to report suspected abuse or neglect, and going a step further, determining the possibility for abuse or neglect. Risk identification, assessment and management present the professional with a whole series of obligations. Charlotte perceived needing to regulate not just her clients but also her own actions. Rose (1996, p.349) suggests that experts

> calculate and reduce the risk of their professional conduct, instruct the subjects
> of their authority in the riskiness of the practices and procedures in which they
> are engaged and manage their clients in the light of the imperative to reduce the
> risk they may pose to others.

Charlotte met this obligation through "being as clear as" she could with Violet about expectations and consequences, as well as providing educational opportunities for Violet to manage the risks.

Not just service users, but also professionals are disciplined when their judgments are found to be flawed. Workers must calculate the risk accurately or face consequences in multiple arenas: legal, professional, financial, and ethical. At the time of the interviews, it was stated in the Ontario Child and Family Services Act (1996, p.65) that if a professional in the

> course of his or her professional or official duties, has reasonable grounds to suspect that a child is or may be suffering or may have suffered abuse shall forthwith report the suspicion and the information on which it is based to a Society.

Contravention of reporting was a legal offense and a staff person in a social service agency could be fined $2,000 and even imprisoned for up to two years for not fulfilling this requirement. A director or officer of an agency, such as a maternity home, could also be penalized to the same degree, increasing the likelihood of surveillance of staff by administration. These penalties were twice those imposed for other breaches of this Act. Other scholars have examined the threats to the workers themselves (Stanford, 2011), highlighting the pressure of disciplinary practices.

Charlotte felt "desperate" that Violet herself understood the gravity of the situation. In part, this desperation arose from not wanting to be an agent of pain for Violet. She elaborated, "You want to always be able to be supportive and part of a healthy parenting process ... And ... what if I contribute to somebody else's pain?" This left Charlotte wondering, " ... how much longer I can do it ... (crying)." She worried, what "if I'm no longer being useful in what I do?" She felt like the "keeper of other people's pain."

Charlotte's desperation was also born from the paradox of having two clients whose needs were not the same. She explained, "You're looking at the client being the young woman but you're also looking at the client being the child." This is one of the paradoxes of practice that can lead to ethical trespass, namely paradox 2, having more than one client in a 'case.' While she was concerned about Violet's needs and the pain she would experience having her child apprehended, Charlotte perceived her first responsibility was to the child. In the protecting of a child, there is the potential of trespassing against the mother who may not perceive that child as being abused or neglected. While it may not be inevitable in every instance (since there is the possibility that a mother may ultimately agree that her child was at risk and should be protected from herself), the potential is quite high, making this one of the most difficult and painful of processes in which social workers play a part.

Charlotte also was aware of the power she could exercise in this position and the potential to be inaccurate in her assessment. She recognized the decisions she was required to make were not trivial but rather had an enormous impact on the lives of those whom she was judging. She said, "We are not deciding the interior colour of a car, we're deciding about people's ability to parent or not, or the safety of their children."

Because the cues about adequacy are not obvious, judgments are very subjective and intuitive (Chu, Tsui, and Yan, 2009). Much of Charlotte's own pain came from the anxiety around this lack of objectivity in evaluation. And objectivity is part of a dominant discourse in social work that privileges rational cognitive processes both in practice and in ethics, as we discussed in Chapter 1. Charlotte lamented, "If I'd ... been able to just feel we weren't being so subjective ... ." She queried, "What if you're wrong?"

She also was aware of paradox 4 in the concepts of empowerment and self-determination for the clients:

> And so in some ways they [the young women] don't really have a choice. They either meet our expectations or we do have the power to be able to say we're not sure if we can support it [a particular behaviour or need of a young woman] within our agency. So you're trying to encourage somebody ... without making them feel as if you ... have all this power over them.

Wise (1995, p.108) has suggested that an empowerment model is not viable for service users in some settings. Her rationale is that empowerment "involves the commitment to encourage oppressed people to understand how structural oppression in its various forms impacts upon them as individuals and to enable them thereby to take back some control in their lives" but this process is time consuming when sometimes the decisions that need to be made are immediate and do not allow for that flourishing of understanding. Also, worker and client may have discrepant definitions of the problem. Violet's definition of the problem was an inability to sleep and thus a wish to spend more time at her mother's house. Charlotte's provisional definition was that Violet was depressed or had FAE and consequently, perhaps might not adequately care for her newborn.

Social workers are in a very difficult position. They are mandated to assess and report those situations in which the safety of a child might be compromised. Yet the relationship they form is usually with the mother whom they are required to discipline. Swift has suggested, "help, in the form of authority, is provided *to* mothers but is actually *for* children" (1995, p.160, italics in the original). Furthermore, in the making of the social worker as expert and authority in current Euro-Western society, the subject position of the young single mother becomes one of vulnerable individual with reduced influence and control over her own destiny.

A contributing factor in the measures Charlotte took was her workload. In this instance, Charlotte felt that she'd been "harsh" due to the stress she personally was under managing three complex, serious, and stressful agency situations at one time. All the workers in my study voiced this worry. We will return to this problem in Chapter 4.

Charlotte's narrative of Violet suggests the following elements were in her discursive field: the efficacy of individual change; assessment and diagnosis as key technologies; power as both responsibility and burden; strategies of pedagogy, emotional nurturance, and validation; and discourses of risk and utilitarianism.

Jannie's Story of Shari

The Worker

At the time of the research, Jannie, a white woman, was in her early 30s, married, with a master's degree in education in counselling and an undergraduate degree (B.A.) with an honour's diploma in guidance studies.

Jannie's own mother was 15 when she became pregnant with Jannie. Due to the "shame" of this situation, her mother was shipped off to a maternity home and ultimately required to marry an unsuitable match. Jannie's own childhood was difficult with a mother she perceived of as "immature" and a stepfather who was an "alcoholic." Despite a lack of support from her parents, through dint of her own hard work, Jannie was able to make a success of her life, setting the stage for a belief that the same expectations could be applied to the young women with whom she worked.

Jannie had been employed as a social worker in an urban setting in a community programme for pregnant and parenting youth. She was responsible for students from a Section 19 classroom.[4]

Client Behaviour – Aggression

Shari, a white woman, was about 19 at the time of the interviews. She had two young children. Jannie described Shari's involvement in two altercations. In the first, Shari punched another student in the face and in the second, while she did not initiate the attack, she provoked it through "calling [the other student] names ... following her around, making phone calls to her home, harassing her."

Because workers had been told by senior clinicians to "leave her [Shari] be," Shari had been "running through the building yelling and swearing and threatening this ... young woman that she was at angry at ... ." Jannie felt, "You can't go around harassing, tracking people, calling them at home ... threatening to kill them, yelling and cursing and swearing in front of the daycare with the kids there." Jannie perceived Shari's presence as "toxic in the classroom ... creating a lot of tension, a lot of stress." Jannie was also concerned about Shari's "disrespect to staff and other clients" and saw her behaviour as "abusive."

4　In Ontario, Canada, Section 19 classrooms are multi-disciplinary settings provided when a student's needs are too great to be met in a regular or special education classroom.

Interpretation of Client Behaviour – Liberal, Reactionary, and Risk Discourses

Jannie explained Shari's behaviour as displaying "a lot of insecurity, a lot of trust issues ... and she ha[d] a lot of anger to begin with, very explosive." In her suggestion of insecurity and trust issues, Jannie's reading was one of individual intrapsychic problems, consistent with the liberal discourse delineated in Chapter 1. However, although these underlying causes for the anger were articulated, the emphasis for Jannie was on the explosiveness of the anger itself rather than highlighting causal factors as a critical explanatory framework, as it had been for Charlotte.

In this instance, Jannie referred to Shari as a "young girl." This designation gestured towards Shari as involved in out-of-time acts (Lesko, 2001). Jannie was suggesting that this young woman were taking on responsibilities before the correct time, inappropriately engaging in adult behaviours and consequently acting irresponsibly because she was unprepared for the tasks of adulthood. She speculated that the service users must "grow up fast. Because they have a child, they need to be responsible ... ." The problem, from Jannie's perspective, arose because "they need to evaluate what are their morals ... because ... they are going to be teaching these things to their children." But Jannie did not believe that "a lot of people consciously think about it [moral values and beliefs], especially at a young age, like a teenager." Jannie stated, "I don't think teenagers are ready." This characterization reflects a reactionary discourse, the irresponsible young woman, a child bearing children discussed in Chapter 1.

Jannie made comparisons between her mother and her clients. She said, "my mom was really(!) young when she had me. And ... I see a lot of similarity between how my mom is today and ... how I could foresee some ... of the students growing." She described her mother as "still very emotionally and socially immature ... . Everything revolves around her." In part, her explanation of her mother's immaturity was "having children at a young age." Implied is a perception of arrested development with these young women socially, emotionally, and morally immature. Having a child as a young single mother, according to Jannie, "kind of stagnates your growth."

Jannie saw Shari as willful and narcissistic. She claimed, "[E]verything revolves around her." For example, Jannie described Shari's attendance as not the best "but when she was asked to take a week off of school, she came to school every day." Her explanation of this discrepancy was "she doesn't want to be told what to do." Jannie believed that clients, and Shari in particular, were able to manoeuvre the managers by doing a "good song and dance." She described Shari "play[ing] on the heart strings," and having a manager "overrule any team decision and ... support the student [Shari]" rather than the team. Shari was not a "docile body" (Foucault, 1977). She was neither compliant nor remorseful about her behaviour. Those mothers who proceed in a contained and cautious manner were understood to be good clients (and I suspect good mothers as well), while those who did not, were seen as problematic and potentially pathological.

The reactionary discourse often elides with a risk discourse. Jannie deemed Shari a "really high risk mom." Jannie identified the risks to those immediately in Shari's environment as: injuring her child, harming another client, influencing other mothers and women to behave poorly, exposing other children to unacceptable or frightening behaviour, harming a worker, or endangering the legitimacy of Jannie's own expertise. Those adopting a reactionary discourse of young mothers may frame these mothers as the sources of risk and interpret their behaviour in moralistic terms when these mothers are seen to be engaged in behaviours that increase risks (Macvarish, 2010).

Out-of-control anger does present risks in our society. In Euro-Western society, there are constraints on the expression of anger, at the same time that the milieu continuously produces anger, particularly for those most marginalized, including women (Miller, 1991). Self-governing subjects are expected to monitor and contain their aggressive impulses. Consequently, anger must be suppressed and when it does leak out (for example, in yelling) it is often in forms that are seen as pathological. Being in a subordinate position evokes anger but others may not understand this anger as the outcome of oppression. What is missing from the discussion about Shari is the recognition of the possibility that anger is justifiable, given the circumstances of her life, even if its discharge must be moderated so as not to incur societal disapproval. This is especially true for women in a society that is intolerant of women's assertion or aggression. Bernardez, suggests that often there is censure from therapists for behaviours that do not conform to traditional role prescriptions of women, particularly in areas of anger or rebellion and this condemnation is "sometimes in moralistic terms" (1987, p.29).

Strategies of Help – Consistency/Zero Tolerance/Provision of Information

After Shari's second clash, the programme staff discussed suspension as a way to respond. Jannie believed that the possibility of suspension was "completely fair" because the school had a "zero violence policy" and a "three strikes, you're out rule." Her rationale was "you need to let her [Shari] know that we're serious." Jannie's preference was for a "consistent" response in which, after one incident, students would be discharged but connected to a therapist with the goal of "learn[ing] some anger management." Jannie expressed, "We don't (!) cut off services. We're just cutting her out of the classroom, taking her out of the students' public eye." She was disgruntled because the agency "did not follow these policies."

Jannie did not perceive that she could provide therapy herself. From her perspective, there was a discrete separation between her function as "social worker" and that of "counsellor" in the agency. She said social work is "more information giving, more helping her to fix things. And not counselling and asking … how are you feeling, getting at her deep-seated issues … ." She characterized social work as "a little bit of a cookie cutter formula … I know what kind of information to give. I know … where to make a referral … ." Jannie understood her positioning to be one that was formulaic, as information and referral, a subject position of the cookie cutter.

Justifications for Those Responses – a Behavioural Practice Discourse and a Consistency Discourse

Jannie's "greatest frustration" was how the agency handled the situation since she believed the women had "too many chances." She said, these "young women have not grown with structure. ... nobody to ... take them under their wing or to show them ... a way of life and I think as an agency we should be structured and organized and consistent" and that the agency "didn't ... meet those needs." Her explanation of why young moms have not had structure was that " they were born into ... families of young teenage moms, like that pattern is ... replicating itself."

Jannie's preferred positionality would have been to supply the missing structure, consistency, order and organization that she felt this young woman required, thereby correcting a deficiency and moving towards a disruption of the generational cycle of out-of-control behaviour. From Jannie's perspective, having given Shari a warning through an articulation of policy, then bending of the rules by not discharging her immediately, was more than fair and ample justification to discharge this client when she continued to disregard policy. In fact, to do otherwise was not to assist this young woman in plugging the gap of the lack of structure she might have experienced in her life. Reliability and structure were equated with caring and the means to show Shari a different way of living.

In Jannie's thinking, sound practice involved the provision of a homogeneous response to all clients. The danger of giving other students the message that it would be acceptable to hit someone and one could return to the classroom with impunity is that other clients "see the inconsistencies ... and then we operate based on emotion and feeling and who we like and who we don't like, rather than [basing it] on a clear, this is your behaviour, these are the consequences." Then students "see the favouritism."

One paradox in the helping relationship is that of providing consistency in group settings versus providing dissimilar forms of service to respond to the unique needs of individual clients who represent difference. This is paradox 6 from Chapter 1. Jannie came down on the side of consistency but did not articulate this as a conflict for herself.

Jannie was subscribing to a form of Kantian "impartial reason" because she wished to view individuals in a homogeneous way (Meyers, 1994). This rationale is an expression of utilitarianism, outlined in Chapter 1; namely, that the decision should rest on the greatest good for the greatest number, a concept which is central to modern democracy (Gray and Webb, 2010) and one of the key theoretical approaches on which the profession has evaluated ethical practice in current times. It is particularly complex and unwieldy to have dissimilar 'rules' for different clients, particularly in structured settings such as a classroom, because those discrepancies are visible to all and can appear as unfair and arbitrary to those not favoured, creating divisiveness and charges of preferential treatment. Charlotte, too, had identified the concern about favouritism. Also, inconsistent messages from varying staff make it impossible for clients to meet the expectations when workers disagree about what is required.

Yet a consistent response can also be a means to justify the status quo and the maintenance of the authority of workers, regardless of legitimacy. It privileges sameness over the unique circumstances and needs of individual clients. I will address this dilemma further in Chapter 5.

Equally important for Jannie was not positively reinforcing negative behaviours. She identified her practice as a "behavioural approach," saying she liked "to see action." Jannie subscribed to a method of reward and consequences to shape behaviour, in line with a cognitive-behavioural approach to the work. Behaviourists postulate that psychological difficulties can be corrected through reinforcing or extinguishing behaviours, irrespective of feelings. Jannie argued that to allow the children to remain in the daycare while Shari was suspended would allow her to create "a party for her[self], to be home with no kids for a week." Similarly, taking Shari "out of the students' public eye" was to prevent her being rewarded with attention from other clients when she was being aggressive. In turn, other clients would be given the message about what was considered appropriate behaviour.

Additionally, Jannie claimed, "[I]f we have a policy and we don't follow through with it and let's say a student does get hurt, we've got a lawsuit on our hands ... we are in big trouble as an agency." Part of this justification rested on considerations that went beyond individual clients to the status of the agency. In child welfare, there is increasing legalism and accountability to the court system as a means to reduce risk. Consistency of policy ensures safety from liability. Rose (1996, p.350) argued, "a new 'litigious mentality' ensures that 'the shadow of the law' becomes a means of managing professional activity through the self-regulation of decisions and action." Then the priority becomes the protection of the agency, rather than the client. And workers fall in line, accepting their individual accountability and obligation to avoid calamity (Weinberg, 2010).

Ethical Issues – Moral Distress – Inability to Provide the Help Shari Needed due to Managerial Constraints

Instead of Jannie's preferred way of operating, senior management suggested that Shari "take a week to think about it [her behaviour and the expectations of the agency]" and that "it was okay for *Shari to leave her child in the daycare." Jannie found this "irritating" because staff "weren't being supported" by the managers. Furthermore, while Jannie was expected to "monitor her [Shari's] attendance and her punctuality," she was instructed "not to approach her on anything." Jannie felt that she was "being kept out of the loop." For Jannie, her sense that she was impeded from doing what she felt was right was an instance of moral distress.

Shari was able to have a relationship with Jannie on Shari's "own terms." Management's actions, Jannie believed, "render[ed] staff impotent and [took] away the staff's credibility." Indeed, why should clients respond to a worker that they perceive of as having no authority or expertise? Jannie believed that other clients' needs were jeopardized, as well. The consistency and structure which were basic to her preferred positionality were undone, which ultimately led to Jannie believing that she was not providing the help that she should or could have offered, nor was she meeting Shari's needs.

Also, when management did not endorse the practices of workers, the ability to present a united front to clients to prevent splitting was eroded. Presenting a united front is a double-edged sword. It is helpful in avoiding the provision of confusing messages and mixed expectations, especially from authority figures. However, to side with the authority strictly because they are the authority, can maintain power at the price of justice. A united front can mask real differences amongst staff and can be used to protect cronyism.

Eventually Jannie felt so distressed by the discrepancy between her desired positionality and what management allowed, that she confronted the director, but she perceived her confrontation as ineffective and possibly damaging to their relationship.

Jannie perceived an ethical trespass against herself by the administration of the agency. Through the authority taken by a senior clinician to countermand a treatment strategy of Jannie's, her ability to fulfill her own understanding of help was compromised at best and invalidated at worst.

Rather than viewing a client whose behaviour is problematic as an indicator of deviance representing the raw material of the work to be accomplished, Shari's behaviour was personalized and perceived of as 'abuse' towards Jannie. What is missing from this interpretation is that these young women are troubled and in this setting precisely because they have been labelled as such. By the interpretation of 'abuse,' the subject position open to Jannie was one of needing to defend against being made a victim, perhaps requiring a more aggressive stance than might have been taken, had she not seen this behaviour as directed towards her personally.

In this analysis, I fear the possibility of my own trespass against Jannie. Workers, legitimately, should have limits to their sense of being undermined and rendered impotent by more senior staff. Also, by critiquing Jannie's notion of 'abuse,' I risk supporting a reproduction of social workers as all-giving, when, in fact, I believe there need to be appropriate boundaries around the work. We will explore this issue further in Chapter 4.

Two other significant factors in the ethical issue that arose for Jannie relate to her training and to supervision. In Chapter 1, I identified that not all the workers were trained as social workers. Jannie was one of those practitioners, having come to the field with a degree in education in counselling.

Education in ethics is one route to moral fluency. *Moral fluency* refers to "the capacity to consider the relationship between means, ends, and values, to grasp options and to be able to base practice on the morally conscious exercise of choices" (Hugman, 2005b, p.123–4). And in moral fluency and ethical decision-making, theoretical and practice frameworks are significant components (e.g.

Stanford, 2011), although only one element in the moral fluency of a practitioner (Banks, 2009; Hugman, 2005b; Sellman, 1996; Stanford, 2011). Nonetheless, social work as a profession places significant emphasis on moral fluency and has been referred to as a "value-laden" activity (Hugman, 2007, p.20).

I am not suggesting that Jannie's training lacked moral fluency. I do not know either the prominence or orientation of her training with regard to ethics. But one could question: had she been trained as a social worker would her educational training have led to different responses on these issues? How might her education have impacted her discursive field in this case?

With Jannie's discipline not being social work, one could speculate supervision as a vehicle for assistance in responding to her ethical conundrums from a social work perspective (although this did not emerge as a significant theme in the research interviews). Supervision is an important component for effective and ethical practice (Beddoe, 2012; Hair, 2014; Hardina and Obel-Jorgensen, 2009; Kadushin and Harkness, 2002) and I would suggest influences the discourses that workers take-up. Supervision in social work fulfills a variety of functions, including administrative, educational, support (Kadushin and Harkness, 2002), and advocacy towards social justice (Hardina and Obel-Jorgensen, 2009). However, while the complexity of cases seems to be rising (Hodge, Migdole, Cannata, and Powell, 2014), in a time of neoliberal constraints and with discourses of risk (Beddoe, 2010; Beddoe, 2012), one of the significant effects has been the increasing emphasis on administrative functions in supervision and particularly surveillance for the purpose of accountability (O'Donoghue and Tsui, 2013) rather than clinical and support functions (Beddoe, 2010; Beddoe, 2012; Noble and Irwin, 2009; Hodge, Migdole, Cannata, and Powell, 2014). And there is evidence that one of the consequences of this trend may be that workers do not necessarily turn to their supervisors for support around resolving ethical dilemmas, (McAuliffe and Sudbury, 2005). So again, a question that remains unanswered is: Might supervision have influenced Jannie's discursive field and her ethical practice, and if so, in what ways? This query could be posed for all the workers in the study, but it is particularly pertinent for those workers who were not professionally trained as social workers.

In the case of Shari, the key discursive field for Jannie included: a consistent and homogenous response, structure, the asynchronous development of Shari, a behavioural approach to treatment, the subject position of the cookie cutter, and primarily the use of reactionary and risk discourses.

Frieda's Story of Trina

The Worker

Frieda, a white woman, was single and in her early 30s at the time of the interviews. Her educational background was as a child and youth worker. She felt empathic for those who were poor, believing that privilege was tenuous. She thought her perspective also came from her own personal experience of having had very limited resources and being an incest survivor. She described this trauma as "a major catalyst" for her work. Regarding the lack of acknowledgement by her mother regarding the incest, Frieda felt, "judge[d]," not heard nor accepted, leading her to "believe in people and their stories and to give them as much credit for what they ha[d] to say and not to pass judgment." Counselling to cope with her own personal experiences had been helpful as well as providing "role modelling" for the manner in which she did her own work as a practitioner.

Frieda's employment involved the provision of outreach; i.e. outpatient contract services to a network of social service agencies for young single mothers in an urban area.

Client Behaviour – Attempts to Live in the Community

Trina, a 20-year-old white woman, had resided at the maternity home while pregnant, but unlike many young women who stayed through the birth and returned to the maternity home post-natally, Trina moved to her parents' home prior to her child's birth. Because the Children's Aid Society (CAS) had evaluated this as an unsafe place for the baby due to earlier allegations of abuse, the maternity home was required to inform CAS. Consequently, Trina moved into her boyfriend's parents' home as an alternative.

The acceptability for the CAS of this second plan was on the condition that the baby's father (who was also seen as abusive) was not in the home. However, despite promises, the boyfriend did not leave his parent's home. Also, welfare representatives threatened Trina that unless she moved back to the maternity home, they would charge her with fraud for taking money while she was living in the boyfriend's home. Frieda predicted that if she defied the authorities "more than likely" the "baby would be apprehended … ." Accordingly, Trina returned to the maternity home and after her stay there, the agency "kick[ed] her out into a motel" as no subsidized housing was available.

Interpretation of Client Behaviour – Revisionist and Strengths-based Discourses

Frieda had a different opinion from that of her superiors concerning this young woman's capabilities. Frieda stated that she did not agree with their belief that Trina "wouldn't be able to parent because of her history"; namely, "being a ward," and due to the diagnosis of Trina having a "learning disability or developmental delays." Frieda explained that managers "didn't think she'd be able to complete tasks: be able to feed the baby on time. And she wouldn't be able to protect the baby from … known sources of harm." Instead, Frieda's perception was that Trina demonstrated appropriate parenting skills. She argued, Trina "completed all programmes [in the maternity home] that she needed to do, she was insightful with some of the new information that she learned. She was very open to direction."

Like Charlotte, Frieda accepted pedagogical strategies and the layette as tactics of governmentality. They were means to both evaluate parenting and to produce what constituted the 'good mother.' Frieda thought Trina had "illustrated appropriate parenting skills" because "her layette was done three months before the baby was due." Her view was that

> the amount of money that they [the young mothers] get and most of them aren't motivated to do that [obtain a layette] until their third trimester ... So I thought she was very insightful to do that ... And just her interactions with the other babies in the house. Very appropriate handling.

As with the other workers in this study, Frieda subscribed to a developmental perspective of adolescence. She deemed this period as a time when most young people were not "motivated to plan and be future oriented." Trina's mothering behaviour was the antithesis of this norm. Therefore, Frieda was impressed, perceiving it as "insightful."

Addelson (1994) suggested that social scientists have conflated planning with both middle-class values and maturity. An individualist planning ethic suggests that the poor may be averse to planning because of internal obstacles, framing an inability to plan as a clinical problem, a medicalized model of deviance. This demarcation hides the structural disadvantage that makes planning difficult for some impoverished individuals. Furthermore, it equates virtuous mothering with the acquisition of material possessions, fostering a capitalist project. However, at times Frieda recognized the middle-class emphasis in the agencies in which she worked and resisted the imposition of those values on her clients. We will discuss aspects of this resistance in Chapter 5.

Fried also rejected the use of diagnosis that framed much of Charlotte's discursive field for Violet. Frieda's perception was that Trina

> ... might not understand something you say the first time, but if you say it in another way or describe it in a different way, she's going to pick it up. She's not stupid ... which is what I felt they [managers] were being by labeling her as such.

Instead, Frieda viewed Trina as "strong" and resilient. She described how Trina would get on the bus every day to attend educational programs. Frieda found her determination "incredible" because

> just to be able to get out of bed in the morning and get dressed and get the baby dressed and ... people talking down to her because she's a young mom or having difficulty getting the stroller ... on the bus ... .

Frieda felt that many of the problems stemmed from Trina's status as a ward of the CAS because her disabilities were more apparent due to her being "under a microscope." She felt the surveillance was "horrible" because it led to "re-victimiz[ing] the most horrifically victimized people in our society … and then, no matter what sort of strengths … they have, now bring[ing] up their past and us[ing] it against them." Frieda believed that "everyone" has "limitations" but Trina's were just more "visible."

Frieda's interpretation was that most of the difficulties in this case were structural and due to the unreasonable demands and expectations of service providers, rather than due to Trina's intrinsic intrapersonal or interpersonal difficulties. This is a radical, revisionist oppositional movement discourse identified in Chapter 1. She understood Trina's original decision to leave the residence as a sign of strength and maturity but believed that the reason Trina's decision was problematic to the officials of the maternity home was that they "get more money after the baby is born." Frieda argued that this strategy reinforced the power and economic base of social service providers in an unethical way.

Moreover, Frieda was also subscribing to a strengths-based discourse (Saleeby, 2006) in which resilience and the heroism of quotidian existence are recognized and celebrated. In this discourse, there is an emphasis on empowerment. Employing this discourse, practitioners attempt to be collaborative by recognizing clients as the experts in understanding their own lives. This discourse also stresses context as crucial to assessment and intervention, a key component in Frieda's discursive field.

Strategies of Help – Support/Access to Resources

The primary functions Frieda fulfilled were giving Trina "as much support as [she] could," and providing "access [to] resources." One support strategy was to allow Trina to "vent" about her frustrations regarding the system. Despite her own reservations about Trina moving back into her boyfriend's home, she held to Trina's right to make her own decision.

Frieda's preferred way of operating was for young women to be able "to open up and talk about all the stuff that they don't want to talk about … ." She believed there was a constructive power in the confessional aspects of the counselling bond. Honesty and trust were the bedrock of the counselling relationship for her. However, she understood that for Trina to be honest entailed a danger of being seen as dysfunctional with all the ramifications that were involved. Like the paradox about self-disclosure that Charlotte discussed, Frieda was aware of the dilemma of revealing the self. The 'good' client is one who confesses, however, the more clients disclose, the more likely they will reveal information that puts them at risk for disciplinary practices. This is paradox 5, self-disclosure as necessary but perilous. While Trina had "contact with her parents … she [was] very careful what she [said] about that contact." Frieda perceived this as "really sad" but she understood that these young women "don't open up because they know [the consequences] … ." Frieda found this paradox "horrible for everyone."

Justifications for Those Responses – Discourses of Rights and Basic Needs

Her understanding was that the clients are clients because they have basic gaps due to poverty and that social services should fill those inadequacies. Frieda perceived the priorities in the human services as contrary to what they should be, since clients are "starving" and therefore can't "listen." Instead she felt professionals should address fundamental necessities first. Frieda subscribed to "Maslow's hierarchy, right? Basic needs ... food, shelter, clothing." Maslow (Encyclopaedia Britannica, 1982) one of the patriarchs of humanistic psychology, formulated a personality theory based on a ladder of human needs, with physiological needs being on the bottom and self-actualization on the top.

According to Maslow, requirements at the lower end of the hierarchy dominate human concern until they are satisfied. By placing the goals of meeting basic needs as primary, Frieda was suggesting a subject position for workers that was ameliorative and redistributive. However, such a position is not generally viewed by those in the social service field as being as prestigious as counselling nor does it require individuals with the level of expertise that professional staff have or that funding sources require. Consequently, to define the problem for these clients in this manner would not carve out a terrain that would justify the requirement for professional social workers, which is perhaps one reason that this subject position has never been popular in social services.

Frieda also used a discourse of human rights. A discourse on human rights focuses on our shared humanity and what circumstances are required to meet our full potential as human beings (Ife, 2008). It tends to shift the emphasis to groups that have been marginalized, correcting for the individualist emphasis of conventional approaches to ethics and adding the importance of broader structural and political factors. Additionally, it supports putting the client back as a potential actor in ethical decision-making processes (Ife, 2008). This discourse frequently merges with that of a strengths-based discourse in the social services. Frieda argued, "that by forcing Trina to return," "any sort of support she had" was "taken away," a "human rights" violation.

Ethical Issues – Paradox of Judgement and Moral Distress of Being an Agent of Discipline

Generally, Frieda did not want to accept the societal expectation placed on social workers to appraise the parenting ability of this young mother. She criticized herself when she found herself making evaluative statements, pejoratively referring to herself as "omnipotent" several times. She said, "I can decide who can change and who can't change, who I can judge and who I can't judge. That's not very good." In Chapter 1, I identified paradox 3, of judgement and non-judgementalism. I will explore, in more detail in Chapter 5, strategies Frieda utilized to combat her subject position as judge but generally her articulated solution was not to use her ascribed power.

Frieda's stance about the maltreatment of clients by the social service system led to a preferred subject position of "devil's advocate." It entailed disputing taken-for-granted notions of "normal" and "healthy" and taking a contrary position. While she did attempt to discuss with the administrator her perceptions of Trina's return to the maternity home, the administrator's response was "if she [Trina] didn't come here, then she would have been charged with fraud, she wouldn't have any money, she, her baby would be gone" and that really the agency had saved her.

Two competing discourses are outlined in this exchange. The administrator perceived the help as saving the young woman from herself with the risk of losing her child, the reactionary discourse; while Frieda understood the problem as being the system, which had erected barriers Trina could not overcome, the revisionist discourse.

However, despite the potential take-up of 'devil's advocate,' Frieda did not warn Trina of the danger that she could lose her child if she left the maternity home pre-natally and returned to her parents' home. Frieda explained that she did not feel she could because she would be seen as "undermining the system," by not supporting the agency's partner, the CAS. Frieda's speculation was that the administrator would have asked, what if Trina "was a flight risk? What if she took off when she was pregnant and she went into hiding." Flight risks and going into hiding suggest a discourse of criminality. Frieda's response was, "I was thinking what's wrong with that" and she laughed, perhaps because she understood that this was a radical notion in an agency that was intent on keeping the young women in the home.

Ultimately Frieda feared that countering the administrator's authority could lead to her own "credibility" being compromised or even being let go from the agency. She felt like her "hands [were] tied" in dealing with the administrator who was "the be all and end all of the [agency]." It took "a lot to fight" to disagree with her and Frieda felt weary from the energy she had expended on other cases.

The ethical issue for Frieda was about the necessity of being an informant to those authorities who could apprehend Trina's baby, when her preferred positionality was to be more of a supporter and protector of Trina. This conflict is paradox 1 from Chapter 1, that of opposing responsibilities of care and discipline. Frieda's moral distress was that she had not warned Trina about the CAS potentially being alerted about the birth of her baby and that later she had not advocated strongly enough for Trina. Frieda believed that in terms of what was really important for this young woman, namely more adequate housing, she had not done "anything." In hindsight she declared,

I should have supported her. She deserved to have somebody stand up for her ...
and usually I'm the person that does the devil's advocate and I didn't. So I guess
I feel bad that she went through that ... Had I opened my mouth ... .

Frieda did not act in an ego-syntonic way, that is, in sync with her overall view of her best self. While an individual's subjectivity is not unified, people do have an internalized image of the ideal they would like to achieve (Benjamin, 1995). However, that preferred self is not always the one actualized and when it is not actualized, conflicted feelings may result (Weinberg, 2007).

The potential for ethical trespass here relates to which human being is privileged as the primary client for Frieda, paradox 2, having more than one individual as one's clients in a case. Not only in the case of Trina, but in general, Frieda allied herself with the young women, rather than their babies, a stance that may have related to triggers from her own personal history. As a consequence, she may have minimized the risks to the child that a worker like Jannie viewed as central.

The key elements in the discursive field in the case of Trina were problems as the inadequate structure of social services, the provision of emotional support, concrete services and advocacy, avoidance of judgment, developmental perspective on young single mothers and discourses of strengths, human rights, basic needs, and the radical revisionist discourse.

Comparison of the Helping Relationship in These Three Cases

Despite all three workers being responsible to monitor and evaluate the parenting ability of their clients, these three vignettes illustrate three quite distinct discursive networks of concepts, assumptions, beliefs and institutional demands that provided the discursive field in which help was enacted. For example, in these three narratives, the three workers adopted quite diverse responses to the social process of assessment. Charlotte saw it as essential to reduce the risk of making mistakes in her evaluation of Violet that could lead to disastrous and unfair consequences for her client. Jannie placed little importance on assessment, focusing instead on the value of a homogenous response to all clients and viewing non-compliance as problematic to all concerned. Frieda resisted assessment, seeing this social process as making her "omnipotent" and an ethical breach for her client.

These fields also led to different responses to the power they were able to exercise and varying dominant discourses to understand the young women. All three used metaphors of God. In the case of Shari, Jannie constructed her positionality as being consistent with the requirement to evaluate Shari's competence as a parent. She was relatively comfortable with the power of her position and did not question the dividing practices identified in Chapter 1, perhaps because she constituted herself within a bureaucratic rationality as an agency worker who was following orders through policies and procedures. However, she did question, "do I have this God complex?" when she realized that she was comfortable with her utilization of power but resented that of management's. Her distress came from being unable to actualize what she perceived of as her responsibilities due to organizational constraints and lack of support.

Jannie generally viewed Shari as a willful child, having an offspring before she was developmentally ready for such a task. This is the reactionary discourse that emphasizes personal accountability for difficulties, omitting possible broader structural factors that might contribute to a client's situation.

Charlotte was aware of the power inherent in her positioning and believed in the importance and necessity of making the judgments, but feared making the wrong decisions and the pain those decisions might cause. Her discomfort came because "we are playing God here and I'm not comfortable with this role." Young women's lives were at stake and she had the power to participate in the loss of their children. This is an example of Foucault's notion of power as constructive; namely, constructing identities of who are viewed as good or inadequate mothers. However, despite recognizing structural barriers, she still constructed her positioning with Violet as primarily focused on the individual client and the expectation that Violet (rather than the system) change, a liberal-discourse which focuses on the problems of young single mothers as primarily intrapsychic, rather than due to broader systemic factors.

Frieda resisted the power intrinsic in evaluating the parenting abilities of her clients. This position arose from a belief that the problems her clients encountered were primarily structural and outside of the self. This is an illustration of structural theory, as discussed in Chapter 1, that emphasizes the inadequacies at macro levels of society that maintain inequity and oppression. Consequently, the primary discourse Frieda took up to explain the young women was revisionist, viewing inadequate social conditions as the chief explanation for client difficulties. She was reluctant to make judgments, perceiving such action as God-like (language that she used on occasion). Her guilt arose from accepting her positioning as judge (paradox 3) and not advocating strongly enough for Trina.

These varying discourses and the broader discursive fields taken up by workers change the nature of the relationship with clients. The next chapter will look more deeply at some of those relational components.

Bibliography

Adams, J. (1995). *Risk*. London: University College Press Ltd.

Addelson, K.P. (1994). *Moral Passages. Toward a Collectivist Moral Theory.* New York: Routledge.

Banks, S. (2009). From professional ethics to ethics in professional life: Implications for learning teaching and study. *Ethics and Social Welfare*, 3(1), 55–63.

Beck, U. (1992). *Risk Society: Towards a New Modernity*. London: SAGE.

Beddoe, L. (2010). Surveillance or reflection: Professional supervision in 'the risk society.' *British Journal of Social Work*, 40, 1279–96.

Beddoe, L. (2012). External supervision in social work: Power, space, risk, and the search for safety. *Australian Social Work*, 65(2), 197–213.

Benjamin, J. (1995). *Like Subjects, Love Objects. Essays on Recognition and Sexual Difference*. New Haven: Yale University Press.

Bernardez, T. (1987). Gender based countertransference of female therapists in the psychotherapy of women. In M. Braude (Ed.), *Women, Power and Therapy* (pp.25–39). New York: The Haworth Press.

Child and Family Services Act: 1990. Revised. (1996). Toronto: Queens Park Printer of Ontario.

Chu, W.C.K., Tsui, M.-S., and Yan, M.-C. (2009). Social work as a moral and political practice. *International Social Work*, 52(3), 287–98.

Douglas, M. (1992). *Risk and Blame.* New York: Routledge.

Encyclopaedia Britannica. (1982). Chicago: University of Chicago Press.

Enns, C.Z. (1997). *Feminist Theories and Feminist Psychotherapies. Origins, Themes, and Variations.* New York: Harrington Park Press of Haworth Press.

Foucault, M. (1977). *Discipline and Punish. The Birth of the Prison* (A. Sheridan, Trans.) (2nd ed.). New York: Vintage Books. (Original work published in 1975)

Foucault, M. (1978). *The History of Sexuality. An Introduction. Vol.1.* (R. Hurley, Trans.). New York: Vintage Books. (Original work published in 1976)

Fox, N.J. (1999). Postmodern reflections on 'risk', 'hazards' and life choices. In D. Lupton (Ed.), *Risk and Sociocultural Theory* (pp.12–33). Cambridge, UK: Cambridge University Press.

Gray, M., and Webb, S.A. (Eds). (2010). *Ethics and Value Perspectives in Social Work.* New York: Palgrave MacMillan.

Hair, H.J. (2014). Power relations in supervision: Preferred practices according to social workers. *Families in Society*, 95(2), 107–14.

Hardina, D., and Obel-Jorgensen, R. (2009). Increasing social action competency: A framework for supervision. *Journal of Policy Practice*, 8, 89–109.

Hugman, R. (2005a). Exploring the paradox of teaching ethics for social work practice. *Social Work Education*, 24(5), 535–45.

Hugman, R. (2005b). *New Approaches in Ethics for the Caring Professions.* New York: Palgrave Macmillan.

Hugman, R. (2007). The place of values in social work education. In M. Lymbery and K. Postle (Eds.), *Social Work. A Companion to Learning* (pp.20–29). London: SAGE.

Hunt, A. (2003). In A. Doyle, and R.C. Ericson (Eds.), *Risk and Morality* (pp.165–92). Toronto: University of Toronto Press.

Ife, J. (2008). *Human Rights and Social Work: Towards a Rights-based Practice.* Revised edition. Cambridge University Press. Available at: <http://www.myilibrary.com?ID=194464> (Accessed May 14, 2015).

Keinemans, S., and Kanne, M. (2013). The practice of moral action: A balancing act for social workers. *Ethics and Social Welfare*, 7(4), 379–98.

Kelly, D.M. (1996). Stigma stories. Four discourses about teen mothers, welfare, and poverty. *Youth and Society*, 27(4), 421–49.

Knaak, S.J. (2010). Contextualising risk, constructing choice: Breastfeeding and good mothering in risk society. *Health, Risk & Society*, 12(4), 345–55.

Lesko, N. (2001). *Act your Age! A Cultural Construction of Adolescence.* New York: Routledge Falmer.

Leonard, P. (1997). *Postmodern Welfare. Reconstructing an Emancipatory Project.* London: SAGE.

Macvarish, J. (2010). The effect of "risk-thinking" on the contemporary construction of teenage motherhood. *Health, Risk & Society*, 12(4), 314–22.

McAuliffe, D., and Sudbery, J. (2005). "Who do I tell?" Support and consultation in cases of ethical conflict. *Journal of Social Work*, (5)1, 21–43.

Mergenthaler, E., and Stinson, C.H. (1992). Psychotherapy transcription standards. *Psychotherapy Research*, 2(2), 125–42.

Meyers, D.T. (1994). *Subjection and Subjectivity: Psychoanalytic Feminism and Moral Philosophy*. New York: Routledge.

Miller, J.B. (1991).Women and Power. In J.V. Jordan, A.G. Kaplan, J.B. Miller, I.P. Stiver, and J.L. Surrey (Eds.), *Women's Growth in Connection. Writings from the Stone Center* (pp.181–96). New York: Guilford Press.

Noble, C., and Irwin, J. (2009). Social work supervision. An exploration of the current challenges of a rapidly changing social, economic, and political environment. *Journal of Social Work*, 9(3), 345–58.

Oxford Dictionary and Thesaurus (1996). (American ed.). New York: Oxford University Press.

Rose, N. (1996). The death of the social? Re-figuring the territory of government. *Economy and Society*, 25(3), 327–56.

Rose, N., and Miller, P. (1992) Political power beyond the state: Problematics of government. *British Journal of Sociology*, 43(2), 173–205.

Saleebey, D. (2006).*The Strengths Perspective in Social Work*. (4th ed.). Boston: Pearson/Allyn & Bacon.

Sellman, D. (1996). Why teach ethics to nurses? *Nurse Education Today*, 16, 44–8.

Swadener, B.B., and Lubeck, S. (Eds.). (1995). *Children and Families "at Promise." Deconstructing the Discourse of Risk*. Albany: State University of New York Press.

Swift, K.J. (1995). *Manufacturing "Bad Mothers." A Critical Perspective on Child Neglect*. Toronto: University of Toronto Press.

Swift, K.J., and Callahan, M. (2009). *At Risk. Social Justice in Child Welfare and Other Human Services*. Toronto: University of Toronto Press.

Weinberg, M. (2007). Ethical "use of self." The complexity of multiple selves in clinical practice. In D. Mandell (Ed.) *Revisiting the Use of Self: Questioning Professional Identities* (pp. 213–33). Toronto: Canadian Scholars Press.

Weinberg, M. (2010). The social construction of social work ethics: Politicizing and broadening the lens. *Journal of Progressive Human Services*, 21(1), 32–44.

Wise, S. (1995). Feminist ethics in practice. In R. Hugman, and D. Smith (Eds.), *Ethical Issues in Social Work* (pp.104–19). New York: Routledge.

Chapter 3
Micro Relations: Power, Judgement, and Emotion

Introduction

Why are young single mothers such a focus for judgement by social workers, which young mothers in particular, and for what aspects of their identity? This chapter is concerned with answering these questions and with the relational aspects of practice with young single mothers by which these determinations are rendered. We begin by exploring the discursive field of a fourth worker, Kristine, in her story of Jessica. This case vignette will be used to concentrate on micro-interactions that influence ethical trespass or its attenuation.

Kristine's Story of Jessica

The Worker

Kristine is a white, single woman who was about 30 years old when we met. She described her family as economically successful but very unstable and emotionally problematic. Addictions, the institutionalization of her father, physical violence between her parents resulting in their separation and the chronic illness of her mother were the background of her upbringing. After the marital separation, her mother became "abusive" both verbally and physically to Kristine and a sister. Additionally, her mother's boyfriend sexually abused Kristine. Kristine "started drinking a lot" and her sister used hard drugs, ending up on the streets.

Throughout her childhood, Kristine had the support of extended family. Kristine argued that she was "lucky" to have people that could avert her street involvement but she believed, "it's not that far away … you can end up there very quickly."

Academia and intellectual pursuits provided stability for Kristine. She believed she went into social work to "look for answers to [her] own experience" and eventually received a Master's in Social Work. She wanted to make "a difference in the lives of … kids." She was diagnosed as having "a clinical depression and … anxiety" and found that her therapist was an important influence in her understanding of the helping relationship.

Kristine was employed as a social worker in a rural agency, serving pregnant and parenting young mothers. Although she provided a range of services, the priority was her work with clients in a Section 19 classroom.

Client Behaviour – Aggression/Drug Use/Minimal Family Support

Jessica, an 18-year-old, was finishing the first trimester of her pregnancy when she was accepted into the agency programme. She came from a mixed-raced family, with a black Caribbean father and a white mother. She was described as very angry, with "eyes ablazing ... gesturing and her hands moving everywhere and just swearing." A year earlier Jessica had assaulted her sister. For this attack, Jessica "was granted a year's probation."

The primary people in Jessica's life provided minimal support. Her relationship with her mother was rocky. Kristine explained that Jessica's "mother had told her that if she had an abortion, she [Jessica] would [have been] kicked out of the house so she didn't feel like she really had a choice in the matter." Finances in her family were a major stress. Jessica did not look to the birth father for help as she did not "like the father of the baby" and had not told him that he was expecting a baby because she wanted "nothing to do with him," according to Kristine.

Also, Jessica was "worried that her child might be foetal alcohol" because she had been "drinking daily ... and using drugs." She quit drinking "as soon as she found out she was pregnant," because she "really wanted to make a change for the baby."

Interpretation of Client Behaviour – Possible Foetal Alcohol Effect/Influences of Race and Class

Kristine concurred with Jessica's concerns about the health of the foetus, due to her drug use. Additionally, Kristine wondered whether some of Jessica's own behaviour was the consequence of foetal alcohol effect since Jessica's mother had "continue[d] to drink in" her pregnancy with Jessica.

Also, Kristine believed there were significant implications for Jessica being of mixed heritage, while living in a predominantly white environment, and working with a white clinician. She assumed that much of Jessica's struggle was related to racial and class dimensions. She described Jessica as a

> black woman in a very white community ... she's always making a point in front of other students in group how she doesn't like black men and ... how ... her father's side of the family refers to her as being too white ... there's an ongoing thing within her there and it's part of her identity and it sounds like she's struggling ... she associates being white with things that her mother taught her like ... listening to classical music ... drinking wine ... .

On the other hand, her father's family was described as "project people ... they don't work, they all drink and use crack ... a very rough violent ... life."

Due to Jessica's dark skin, Kristine speculated that Jessica may have reminded her mother of her ex-partner, Jessica's dad. Like Kristine's own history with her mother, Kristine conjectured, "when a mother has not a very good relationship with a father ... and then they break up ... she might take out her anger and frustration on the child of that father." Kristine feared the same dynamic could be repeated with Jessica's newborn child. She stated, that what Jessica

> finds upsetting is the circumstances in which she got pregnant and ... who she got pregnant with. ... she wants to be a mom but she wishes that it hadn't happened when it did. ... that the father of the baby, wasn't the father of the baby.

Discourses: Developmental Model of Normal Human Growth/Liberal and Reactionary Discourses of Young Women/Strengths

Like all the other workers in the sample, Kristine subscribed to a developmental model of normal human growth as an explanation for Jessica's behaviour:

> kids you know thirteen, fourteen, fifteen start to act out in certain ways and it is because they're testing out their new limits. ... they're immortal, they're indestructible, they're impregnable. ... teenagehood is that period where they're focused on their own needs ... on their independence ... and make ... probably not good choices but learning from them, hopefully.

Kristine's explanation of clients making regrettable choices was,

> they're experimenting with drugs or alcohol to the point of excess ... or engaging in relationships that may not be healthy. ... having to kind of ... fast forward ... your life, you can't really continue to develop that sense of who you are ... because now you're having to think about what's growing inside of you.

We will return to the discourse of choice later in this chapter. Despite the age concern, Kristine did not think these young women would be better off waiting until they were older to have babies since the pregnancy "actually helped them ... focus on their lives. It's provided a ... sense of structure where there was none before." Furthermore, "the pressure" on Jessica was to "figure that out before the baby's born."

Like Jannie, Kristine was implying asynchronous development, namely that Jessica had limited time to fulfill normal developmental tasks because with a child on the way, she would be propelled into the next stage of development, young adulthood, potentially before she had successfully accomplished the tasks of adolescence.

Generally, Kristine relied on the liberal discourses for young mothers. However there were elements of the reactionary discourse when she stated, "these are kids having kids" (reactionary discourse) and "they're doing it [to] ... have someone to love them or to have someone to love" (liberal discourse). Nonetheless, Kristine professed that sometimes a pregnancy would foster moving a youth to that next stage of development and could be constructive in terms of mental health, a view that differed from Jannie's in the last chapter.

The strengths discourse referred to in Chapter 2 is also evident in that, concurrent with her concerns, Kristine was also aware of the strengths of teenagers as a group. She admired "the energy and the possibilities for change" of adolescents and enjoyed working with this population because she thought that youth were "not set in their ways." Furthermore, she appreciated that "they can see almost through you ... so they always challenge you."

Kristine perceived Jessica specifically as bright, honest, insightful, and self-aware. For instance, she described Jessica as stating, "I worry about being a mom" or questioning "her decision to keep the baby" which Kristine found very "honest." Kristine was impressed that Jessica had acknowledged that she "resent[ed] how this all came about" because for Kristine, it demonstrated a

> lot of insight. ... it's really hard for the women to talk about ... being resentful of
> being the one who gets pregnant, has to maintain the pregnancy, and change her
> whole life, and raise a baby on her own, and fight for support ... .

Strategies of Help

I have only addressed those of Kristine's techniques that provide the material for the ensuing discussion about judgement, power and emotions.

Goal Setting
For Kristine, a key goal of the helping relationship was to aid young women "to make better choices about their lives, about their parenting." She felt she needed to counteract the impacts of "their environments [that] have not ... provided good role models around decision making." This is the reactionary discourse about young single women. She also stated, "I want to be part of her [Jessica's] process of learning who she is." Implied is a Euro-Western humanistic understanding of a unified self that evolves and is the primary task to be accomplished during adolescence.

Dealing with Clients' Emotions
One of Kristine's strategies was to support Jessica in dealing with angry emotions and in learning to express herself "safely ... that's not going to result in people getting hurt ... ." Kristine believed "if you bury an uncomfortable feeling ... the chances of it emerging at some time ... it's going to happen," often in hazardous ways. Like Jannie, the moderation of feelings was an indicator of problematic behaviour, requiring intervention.

Dealing with Sensitive Topics
Another significant strategy for Kristine was opening up sensitive topics. Kristine felt that racial issues were important for Jessica as she "brought [them] up herself"

and referred to herself as a "half breed." Despite this being a difficult and "anxiety" provoking issue for Kristine, she believed it was necessary to tackle. Kristine admitted:

> just addressing issues regarding being black ... being lesbian ... being of a different faith, they're always tough for me because sometimes I'm not sure whether bringing those issues up makes it sound like I (!) have an issue with them. And then I think, well maybe I do have an issue with them.

However, she also worried that focusing on it would stigmatize Jessica, despite her intent being the opposite. She elaborated, "if I address it [racial issues] then ... have I made an issue out of nothing? Am I seeing something and bringing up an issue that isn't really there?"

Kristine wanted to be "sensitive" and "accurate" in her handling of this subject, so she expressed concern about her use of terms. She said, "I struggled to figure out how do I address this issue and do I use politically correct terms?" When she discovered that she had used "mixed breed," rather than the term Jessica chose, she reflected, "I thought, oh my goodness ... have I given a message of bias or ... was there meaning attached to me saying 'mixed,' as opposed to 'half'?"

Using Educational Techniques and Information
Like the other participants in the study, Kristine utilized educational strategies, probably in part due to being in an educational setting. Kristine believed that pedagogical strategies such as workers providing 'factual' information could deepen the relationship and allow clients to make their 'own' decisions rather than having something imposed upon them. This is an illustration of discourses of empowerment and self-determination and of technologies of governmentality, which I will discuss below.

Selective Use of Confrontation
At times, Kristine was direct in her confrontation of Jessica. In conversing about Jessica's drinking, Kristine made a comparison between Jessica's sister, who "could become an alcoholic," and Kristine's suggestion that Jessica's own drinking could also lead to alcoholism. Kristine averred that alcoholism "could be something that's passed down."

Use of Disclosure and Worker's Emotions
Kristine discussed her use of disclosure and her emotions as components of her practice. When a woman addressed issues that paralleled her life she said:

> they don't come to me to hear about my life story and I'm very conscious of that. And yet part of why I think I'm able to connect with women the way I do ... is because ... I know what it's like to have feelings related to those kinds of comments or that kind of abuse ... that's not to say that my experience is

going to be the same, but ... I've been there ... and if she had asked ... did you have that experience or ... did that happen to you ... [if] they ask me questions directly, I will answer.

Generally, Kristine expressed that while she might share her personal history, she tried to keep her own emotions out of the helping relationship. Emotions could interfere with making appropriate and accurate judgements, according to Kristine. Personal disclosure could also be too personally painful as well. She elaborated, "I know that I shut the emotions off ... it's a lot easier to listen without starting to feel sad, and it just helps in terms of being able to keep a perspective." At the same time, Kristine expressed concern that she might have become emotionally numb to the pain of others: "I worry that maybe being too emotionally distant ... I've learned to accept(!) too much, you know?"

Justifications for Those Responses – Safety of Child/Maintaining the Therapeutic Bond/Self-determination

Primary justifications in Kristine's choices of interventions were the importance of the "safety for" and "health of" the baby, as well as Jessica's health.

An additional explanation for Kristine's strategies was the maintenance of the worker-client relationship and the avoidance of practices that might injure this relationship or result in Jessica choosing not to continue. This concern was also bound up in Kristine's wish to evade making judgements. She articulated, "There was just so many times where I knew that I chose the way I responded because I didn't want her to feel judged." For instance, on her thoughts about Jessica's use of marijuana and why she chose educational strategies rather than more direct confrontation, she elaborated that if Jessica felt judged, Kristine was "going to feel useless and she's going to stop seeing me." Furthermore "as soon as I start judging ... and saying no, you shouldn't be doing this or that, then I might close a very important discussion that we need to have." At times however, this justification ran counter to the need to maintain the health and safety of the foetus, creating dilemmas in how she should proceed, an illustration of paradox 3, judgement versus non-judgementalism.

The avoidance of hurt and pain were also critical for Kristine, yet at times, inescapable. Therefore, the use of confrontation was difficult for Kristine. She expressed, "I don't like to feel like I've hurt someone. ... I don't think anybody does."

In choosing less direct methods, Kristine drew on the importance of encouraging self-determination, making decisions for oneself, an underlying principle of casework practice and a key discourse adopted by the workers in this study. Her rationale was that she would not always be around for these young women and ultimately they would be making significant decisions on their own. She expanded her reasoning in the following exchange:

give her ... the opportunity to make different choices? And I think that as much as my own values about how I think a woman should ... maintain her own ?: health about her pregnancy, I think that it's more important that she make some decisions because she's going to have to make some bigger decisions once the baby is born and once this child grows ... .

The following are several of the key factors in Kristine's discursive field from her narrative about Jessica: belief in asynchronous development, self-determination, and the importance of safety. Also, she wished to avoid judgement and utilize educational interventions. Discourses included liberal and reactionary discourses about young moms and a strengths discourse.

Discussion

Given the complex challenge of power, judgement and emotions in the helping relationship and using Kristine's case as the primary illustration, but with reference to the other workers' case material, let us now explore the push and pull of these factors.

Power, Discipline, and the Process of Making Judgements

One's comfort with judgement, a component in the exercise of power, is a key feature in the construction of the helping relationship. With the exception of Jannie, all the workers denied that they made judgements in their practice, often even while making such evaluations. For example Kristine stated, "It's not my job: to judge a parent." Nonetheless, regarding Jessica's drug use, internally Kristine "scream[ed] sometimes no(!) don't do this. ... That's wrong. How could you do that to your baby?" While in that instance, she held off expressing those opinions aloud, because she speculated that Jessica might think, that she was "going to judge" her; at other times, she directly confronted Jessica about her drug use.

Foucault (1978) raises questions about judgement and power that are useful in examining the helping relationship in social work. He compared counselling to a confessional relationship, suggesting that it was one of the key mechanisms of governmentality in modern times. According to Foucault, the helping relationship is understood to free the confessor by releasing the hidden and secret "truths" of the individual (p.60). The judgements of the person to whom one confesses are central in this process. Foucault suggested (1978, p.67), "The one who listened was not simply the forgiving master, the judge who condemned or acquitted; he (sic) was the master of truth." What is taken as truth emerges from the confession and from the interpretation that the one with authority, the social worker, places on those revelations. Then, that individual intervenes by prescribing actions and must "judge, punish, forgive, console, and reconcile" (1978, p.61–2).

On an audiotape that Kristine had made of a session with Jessica, a 'confession' occurred when Kristine showed Jessica a booklet about the impact of caffeine on the foetus. Earlier, Jessica had substituted hot chocolate for caffeine. Kristine described that Jessica "was laughing saying 'here I thought I was doing something friggin' great by ... not drinking coffee and now they're telling me that it's [hot chocolate is] wrong.'"

Here the connection between knowledge, power and discipline are clearly apparent. The knowledge of the effects of caffeine on a foetus is an example of a disciplinary technique that, rather than being repressive, 'produced' a norm. It guided Jessica's desire to meet that standard, working on her body and her identity, all productive (rather than repressive) aspects of power discussed in Chapter 1. In part, its effectiveness comes from addressing a real concern; namely, the health of the baby (Sawicki, 1991).

Consequently, Kristine "wanted to reassure her." Kristine said to me, the interviewer, "this is a good part actually" before playing the audiotape. What follows is from that counselling session:

> Jessica: Substituting coffee for hot chocolate and it's under the caffeine [in written material] well that was friggin' pointless (laughs).
>
> Kristine: (Laughs) see what you learned already?
>
> Jessica: You know, I was thinking I was doing something great / / a hot drink and whatever.
>
> Kristine: Mm-hmm, well I assume it's got a lot less caffeine than coffee. But there you go, it's a perfect example of making better choices, right?

In this instance, Kristine 'absolved' Jessica in her use of hot chocolate while pregnant and in fact went further, supporting and suggesting that she was making "better choices." Here Kristine both forgave and consoled Jessica, telling her, "it's got a lot less caffeine than coffee." The very act of such a confession regarding consuming caffeine, albeit unintentionally, "exonerates, redeems, and purifies him (sic)" (Foucault, 1978, p.62). Kristine, as the benevolent pastor in the confessional relationship, is the one with the power and authority to establish the "better choices." And in this instance, she determined that hot chocolate was better for the foetus than coffee.

Nonetheless, Foucault argues that judgements are "intended to correct, reclaim, 'cure' ... In modern justice and on the part of those who dispense it there is a shame in punishing, which does not always preclude zeal" (1977, p.10). I concur with Foucault and believe that a component in the denial of this essential aspect of workers' practice is workers' shame at being positioned as judges. The imagery of the judge is a hierarchical one: an individual who looks down from the dais, harshly evaluating truth, and meting out punishment. Both in this case example and more generally, I think a component of the denial of judgement was gendered; the discrepancy between the positioning as judge and the positioning of workers as women.

Representations of judging are antithetical to the essentialist notions of womanhood – mutuality, emotional receptivity, and nurturance. With one client, Kristine felt "like her mother" and with others she stated "sometimes they see me as kind of the older sister." In discussing the court system, Kristine made comparisons between male and female judges. She stated that the female judges took "pregnancies and the children into consideration" while the male judges "lecture and they're very stern and ... judgemental." In other words, in her view, justice offered by female judges was tempered with gentleness and concern for contextual realities while judgement by men was uncompromising and severe. The workers repeatedly expressed wishing to avoid injuring their clients, yet judgement carries the potential to be hurtful, the opposite of the succour and care envisioned by these women professionals.

Workers also wanted to avoid "bias" and prejudice that judgement potentially could reinforce. Generally, workers perceived clients' marginalization and wished to avoid contributing further to their oppression by stigmatizing or replicating inaccurate mainstream views. This concern was one of the issues behind Kristine's anxieties regarding Jessica's mixed race. The fear of wrong evaluations also fuelled their concerns, an apprehension spelled out by Charlotte regarding Violet.

Judgement entails making decisions at a moment in time and assessing without knowing the 'whole' person. Yet every clinician is responsible to determine who is 'fit' and who is not. Analysis, by its very nature requires thematization, which totalizes, simplifying that which is too complex and unknowable ever to be grasped in its entirety. Using a part for the whole does not acknowledge the gaps, shaping what is seen but obscuring what is not. Any system of classification misses nuances, complexities, and changes over time and space, acts of reduction that ultimately are a trespass in one's relationship with the Other.

Consequently, the therapeutic process bumps up against the limits of representation. "We cannot know the 'outside,' the 'beyond,' of any system of objectification, for the world that appears to us is the world represented to an objectifying consciousness" (Cornell, 1992, p.68). This paradoxical dilemma was what Frieda alluded to when she argued that she did not want to judge because, "I don't know everything about them [the clients]." Consequently, "we can never fully meet the promise of fidelity to otherness inherent in the ethical relation" (Cornell, 1992, p.90) and are bound to be implicated in ethical trespasses.

Yet, a value-free practice in which power and judgements do not operate is neither desirable nor possible. In Euro-Western society, social workers are one professional group that has been assigned the responsibility and authority to safeguard those who cannot fend for themselves. Walker (2001, italics in the original, p.13.) claims:

Many "powers over" are indispensable "powers for," that is, on behalf of, the infant, the immature, the frail, the ill; occasionally, developmentally, or permanently dependent; the mildly or severely incapacitated. These are not different (kinds of) people. *They are all of us at some times – and necessarily.*

I believe there must be checks and balances to ensure that the strong do not thrive at the cost of the weak. To judge assumes the authority to render determinations both about what is and also what ought to be, which is the ethical component of the work (Robertson, 2002). Despite workers' disavowal, normalization and dividing practices are at the root of the profession, representing fundamental components of the subjectivity of helper.

Non-judgementalism, Self-determination and Empowerment

Another concern about judgement relates to discourses in social work that delineate the importance of being *non-judgemental* in the therapeutic process. For those theoreticians, the interest in judgement is less about the production of truth, as it was for Foucault, and more about the effectiveness of being change agents. According to Carl Rogers (1942), the grandfather of humanistic psychology, judgements should not to be formulated by practitioners in the counselling relationship. By being totally accepting and non-directive, the unacknowledged emotions and attitudes of a client are thought to be released, and clients' goals for counselling achieved. This was the approach that Kristine took when she encouraged Jessica at the beginning of sessions to vent her feelings. Also, Kristine proposed that being overt with one's judgement might damage the potential of the helping relationship as a space of safety and support.

Kadushin and Kadushin (1997, p.104), in a classic social work textbook on practice state, "the interviewer is not concerned with praise or blame but solely with understanding." In another text, the basic social work practice principle of non-judgementalism is outlined as one of the central values to empower service users (Miley, O'Melia and DuBois, 2013, p.54). Being non-judgemental is defined as workers neither blaming nor evaluating clients as good or bad (p.54). Instead, practitioners should "let clients make their own value decisions" (Miley, et al., 2013, p.54). Supporting the discourses of non-judgementalism, the skilled worker should allow clients to come to their own conclusions and make their own choices, the discourse of self-determination, another key discourse for social workers (p.55).

Here is an example of the importance of seeing this study as specific to the Canadian context. The value of self-determination is quite culturally specific (Healy, 2008). While it is very strong in a country such as the United States and to a somewhat lesser degree in Canada (given its more socialist roots), in a more communitarian-oriented country such as Denmark, and even more so on the continents of Asia and Africa, self-determination is de-emphasized or viewed as a problematic value (Healy, 2008).

Kristine subscribed to the importance of clients' self-determination in her explanation of the provision of educational information as a helping strategy and in her discourse of 'choice.' Her rationale concerned an "ethic around self-determination." Frieda, too, justified her positioning in relation to Trina on the basis of self-determination. Self-determination refers to "a belief in the capacity and right of individuals to affect the course of their lives" (Wong, 2000, p.104).

Through self-determination, clients are empowered, or at least that is a pervasive discourse in social work. In its liberal-humanist manifestation, the two discourses, self-determination and empowerment, can overlap when they emphasize individual responsibility (Pease, 2002). Although Kristine did not use the language of empowerment, both Charlotte and Heather did. In this empowerment model, the locus of change is still the individual; exposing an underlying assumption that a person can alter her circumstances through her own increased self-awareness. This model does not zero in on structural constraints (such as poverty) that may severely limit a client's real freedom to be empowered (Wendt and Seymour, 2010).

Discourses of self-awareness and self-determination act as tools towards self-government and the "creation of the moral subject" (Chambon, 1999, p.68). Self-determination was Kristine's goal for Jessica. In the above interaction about the effects of caffeine, Jessica demonstrated burgeoning self-government by making the link between switching from coffee to hot chocolate in an attempt to protect the foetus, albeit ineffectively. That may be why it was the "good part" of the exchange from Kristine's perspective. Jessica's malleability in attempting to avoid caffeine represents both the empowered subject who is competent to conduct herself as a rational subject and Foucault's docile body (1977), one who is more politically obedient.

Pedagogy, as we saw in Chapter 2, is a perfect tool towards self-regulation because through the indoctrination of certain discourses, individuals take up as their own those normalizing discourses. It makes the young women productive, within approved bounds, by "creating desires, attaching individuals to specific identities, and establishing norms" (Sawicki, 1991, p.68) against which single teen mothers evaluate themselves and act.

McWhirter (1991, p.224) has identified four components of the process of empowerment. His third element, exercising control without infringing upon the rights of others, is problematic both in terms of empowerment and self-determination. Every time an individual asserts her rights, another's are affected. There is always a "third" in social relations, according to Emmanuel Levinas (1991), a French philosopher who was a pivotal influence in postmodern theory. The third is all the other human beings in a society (Critchley, 2002).

Levinas, (1991, p.150) stated, "justice begins" with the third person. This means that other parties are always in the background whether considered and/or physically present, or not: others in that client's social sphere, other clients with their needs, others not identified as clients but entitled to resources, other practitioners, and others who support the proffered services directly or indirectly through contributions and taxes. The human condition includes the fact of human plurality, namely that "men (sic), not Man, live on the earth and inhabit the world" (Arendt, 1958, p.7). Consequently, there are times when the needs and rights of one client may conflict with multiple other players: for example a mother with her child, her boyfriend, or other residents. Whose rights should take precedence? How can one support empowerment without infringing on the rights of others some of the time?

Also, in terms of empowerment, in settings where there are limitations of time and resources, a process modeled on the luxury of self-determination may not be safe or possible, leaving workers with the task of determining whose rights should be prioritized. A decision, no matter how enacted, potentially trespasses on the rights of the Other. Moreover, a model of empowerment is antithetical to the disciplinary component of social work, which is central to professional responsibility.

One of the underlying assumptions about the empowerment model is that it is collaborative (Wendt and Seymour, 2010). But empowerment implies a process whereby a problem is identified, a population is targeted that 'has' the problem and professionals are given the responsibility to provide 'help' to solve that problem, thereby setting up social workers hierarchically as the experts and stigmatizing the very groups social workers are attempting to empower (Parker, Fook, and Pease, 1999; Wendt and Seymour, 2010). Yet that too is an inadequate formulation since, while at times, clients may be 'indoctrinated' into the positions that their workers prefer, at others, clients exercise their power to reject those positions.

Judgement, Objectivity, Emotion, and Ethics

What is the connection between a worker's emotions and the judgements she is required to formulate? The place of emotions has not only been central in narratives about good clinical practice, but also in debates about ethical judgements (Houston, 2012; Keinemans, 2014). In an effort to obtain legitimacy and defeminize the profession, social workers historically adopted scientific principles of objectivity as a dominant discourse. Traditionally, the conventional narrative was that maintaining objectivity was necessary for making appropriate judgements. As was quoted earlier, Kristine claimed, "I shut the emotions off ... because ... it just helps in terms of being able to keep a perspective."

In Freudian theory, objectivity and the nondisclosure of the workers' affect were viewed as supporting the maintenance of a *tabula rasa* on which the client could project unconscious and symbolic fantasies. This unconscious material was assumed to be the key to unraveling 'pathology.' In this model, "the personhood of the therapist is seen as an unwanted intrusion in the therapeutic process" (Greenspan, 1986, p.6). Objectivity ensured, according to this premise, that one was not imposing one's own needs/wishes/emotions onto the client, but allowing the unconscious to emerge, untrammelled by suggestions from the clinician. Discourses about objectivity are discourses of control and a form of governmentality (Niesche and Haase, 2012). Kristine's statement illustrates the belief that control of her emotional responses and keeping those responses out of the therapeutic relationship were required actions for good clinical practice.

The traditional model of objectivity has been viewed as a prototypically masculine, emotionally dispassionate expert who observes, diagnoses, and treats (Greenspan, 1983). Feminist practitioners have disputed the notion of the effectiveness of the distant expert who does not disclose affect and stays emotionally detached. They suggest that the worker's emotions are being revealed all of the time, whether deliberate or not (Brown, 1994b). The question for feminist theorists then becomes, how do workers divulge affect "explicitly and intentionally rather than covertly and indirectly?" (Greenspan, 1986, p.9).

Not just sullying the clean slate for the unconscious, but concerns about boundary violations have also buttressed the emphasis on objectivity. The primary theme in understanding such violations is "that they often occur when the relational nature of therapy is forgotten, and work begins to center around the ...person of the therapist" (Brown, 1994a, p.37). Kristine averred, "they don't come to me to hear about my life story," demonstrating her sensitivity to keep her needs out of the therapeutic relationship. However, there have been critiques about the traditional notion of boundaries in social work; suggesting that a more relational and inclusive model is needed to meet the spirit of social work as a political and moral activity (e.g. O'Leary, Tsui, and Ruch, 2013).

And while there is legitimacy to concerns about boundary violations, discourses on objectivity and emotions collide with another dominant discourse in social work; namely, the importance of empathy as a key strategy in engagement. Objectivity requires workers to keep emotions controlled while maintaining a stance of non-judgemental detachment and neutrality, but empathy, a component that is viewed as crucial to the helping process, requires emotional connectedness and responsiveness. The topic of empathy will be developed in Chapter 5 as one route to trespass reduction.

There is a history to the debate about emotions in ethics. David Hume, Scottish philosopher in the 1700s, proposed that one's passions underlay one's ethical judgements (MacIntyre, 1966). He believed that pleasure and pain were the feelings that motivated one to act. Morality was felt, rather than reasoned, according to Hume. However, a contemporary of Hume's, Immanuel Kant, refuted Hume's position, positing the primacy of reason in ethical decision-making. As a key theme in the Enlightenment, Kant's rationalism was taken up as the prevailing approach and has continued to predominate in discursive debates about reason versus emotion in ethics today.

However, there are now theorists in modern philosophy and psychology who recognize the intuitive, non-rational influences and biases that are components in ethical decision-making (Keinemans, 2014; Monin, Pizarro, and Beer, 2007; Rogerson, Gottlieb, Handelsman, Knapp, and Younggren, 2011). Emotions provide useful functions in ethical deliberations. They may signal the need to make judgements about some matter of ethical significance and highlight the moral aspects of that situation (Keinemans, 2014). Furthermore, they both reveal one's values and are motivators toward ethical action (Keinemans, 2014). Some would go so far as to say that the reasons provided by individuals are *ex post facto*, after the fact, justifications for actions taken in ethical deliberations (Haidt, 2001). Others suggest that both the rationalists and emotionalists bring important insights into an understanding of the processes of ethical decision-making and that both are required for ethical action (Craigie, 2011; Monin, Pizarro, and Beer, 2007). Consequently, a dual-process account that recognizes the importance of both emotions and reasoning has developed (Craigie, 2011; Haidt, 2001; Houston, 2012) outside of post-structural theorizing.

In post-structural and feminist theory, emotions have had an important place in ethical considerations. "Ethics is not about obeying fixed moral precepts; rather, a subject's own life and his or her thinking about that life is the stuff of ethics" (Infinito, 2003, p.160). Foucault stated that in modern societies, the aspect of the self that was most relevant to ethical formation was that of feelings (1984, p.352). Because subjectivity is understood as always in flux and an ongoing process in which the boundaries of the self are constantly being redrawn and repaired, it is "fraught with emotions" (Zembylas, 2003b, p.108). For example, in order to look like the competent and ethical subject who keeps her feelings out of the therapeutic relationship, Kristine needed to work on herself. She expressed this as thinking it important to shut her emotions off, but at the same time she then wondered if she was being too emotionally distant. Foucault identified four aspects one has with oneself to be an ethical being. One of these was the *determination of the ethical substance* (1990, p.26, italics in the original). By that he meant "the way in which an individual has to constitute this or that part of himself (sic) as the prime material of his moral conduct" (1990, p.26). In other words, what aspects of the self does a person view as needing to work on in order to be ethical? For Kristine it was her emotions that were a component of the ethical substance she viewed as prime material for conduct on herself.

While emotions are experienced as arising from within the individual and having a physiological component, they are constructed within a societal context and are not separate from the narratives of that culture. Consequently, emotions always occur within political contexts and have political implications. But currently, the management of one's emotions is viewed as an individual responsibility, even while many of the ethical stressors arise from the broader organizational or environmental context in which a worker is functioning (Williams, 2015). For instance, Charlotte's stress about her client's ability to mother was directly related to her both mandated agency responsibilities and also significant time pressures that constrained her from taking up a preferred self.

Emotions can provide signals of "fault lines among competing social explanatory schemes" such as the place of objectivity with which Kristine was struggling (J. Nelson, 2001, p.180). "Out-law emotions" (Jagger, as cited in J. Nelson, 2001, p. 180), those one is not supposed to feel, can operate as indicators of one's discomfort with narratives that predominate and offer opportunities to resist, a thread we will pick up in Chapter 5.

Also, emotions are performative. By this I am not implying they are manipulative, but in their expression, certain functions are performed nonetheless.

When Charlotte in Chapter 2 cried about her concerns regarding her power with clients, while I have no question it was a genuine reflection of her distress, it also served the function of her appearing caring, self-reflexive and analytical to me as an interviewer. Emotions are a highly 'flexible' resource in the type of interactional business they can accomplish (Edwards, 2001), including being accountable, or answering the question of why someone behaved as s/he did. Thus, Charlotte crying at that point in the interview could be interpreted as being answerable as an ethical human being, despite enacting disciplinary processes.

To summarize, workers are required to perform a complex balancing act between the avoidance of judgement that can create shame and interfere with the therapeutic bond, and being required to judge, given their positioning as agents of normalization. Objectivity, while viewed as essential for judgement in the dominant discourses of social work, is problematic in the paradox it creates regarding engagement and empathy for one's clients. And the utilization of one's emotions, while a subjugated discourse in social work, is in fact an important component in one's ethical deliberations and actions.

But who and what behaviours in particular were the foci of judgement's gaze in this particular study?

Judgement of Whom and What?

Who is Being Judged Today?
There is an underlying tension of whether it is feasible to view ethics as universal or whether they are always relative to the culture in which they are embedded (Healy, 2007). This is especially apparent in the discrepancy between countries that are more communal in orientation and those that are more individualistic (Ross, Rossiter, Walsh-Bowers, and Prilleltensky, 2002; Healy, 2008). The debate is particularly pertinent with regard to the role of women (Healy, 2007; Healy, 2008; Hugman, 1996). Thus, the discussion about ethics and young single women and social work in this monograph should be viewed from the cultural lens of post-industrial Euro-Western societies.

Both historically and now, in Euro-Western welfare states such as Canada and the United Kingdom, the emphasis on parenting has been gendered, with expectations for care of children resting almost entirely on mothers, rather than fathers. This gender disparity has a profound influence on the lives of these young primarily single impoverished mothers, as we will see in the next chapter.

These women are also marginalized in multiple other categories. Earlier, we saw how workers appraised age as contributing to the 'problems' of mothering for these young women. A high number of clients came from environments in which they had been abused, abandoned, neglected, or exposed to addictions. And the issue of clients with disabilities arose with Frieda and Trina, and I would speculate with many other service users as well. Any of these categories could be investigated further to understand the discourses that lead to the construction of 'clienthood' (Hall, Juhila, Parton, and Poso, 2003). However, I will restrict this next section to an examination of how class and race relate to who is judged and on what grounds.

In social work, the standards that are set usually come from the perspective of white, middle-class professionals. These standards operate to stabilize white and middle-class privilege and identity, maintaining relations of power by producing narrow normative standards that are generalized to parents living in very different material and cultural circumstances (Phoenix and Woollett, 1991).

Through professional status and expertise, the notion of the 'good' mother that is constructed by social workers sets up a hierarchy of inequality that has significant influence on both the way young women who are clients live out their embodied existence and the way that hierarchy reproduces itself. At times the workers in this study were cognizant of the inequalities and biases of class or racial-ethnic positioning and other structural inequities, and fought against these inequalities; while at other times they contributed to the maintenance of systems of oppression and discrimination. We will start by investigating social class.

Social Class

When we speak about poverty such as many of these young women experience, we are referring to a socio-economic perspective of class, a Marxist conception of the relationship between modes of production and other social relations. Max Weber added the dimension of social status which is a "cultural rather than an economic source of social inequality" (Barbalet, 1987, p.136), proposing culture as an alternate basis of inequality (p.148), an ideological, values-based component. For instance, Kristine identified Jessica's mother as "listening to classical music … drinking wine" – cultural designations usually associated with the middle-class. Cultural versus economic constructions can be discrete or can overlap, such as when individuals with limited economic income aspire to middle-class dreams thus suggesting "contradictory class locations" (Waters, 1991, p.147).

In the liberal and reactionary discourses about young single mothers, there is an assumption that poverty leads to difficulties mothering, since single working-class mothers cannot supervise their children in the manner consistent with middle-class norms (Kasinsky, 1994). Jannie explained that working-class mothers are "not present in the family. They're not able to do the parenting … because they're having to work so many hours and to be out of the home." Consequently, from her perspective, children are "bringing themselves up" without a lot of "consistency." She elucidated, when a mother states, "you're grounded," because she is out working, she "can't enforce" it. This type of reasoning results in all working-class mothers potentially being unfit to mother, ignoring material conditions. Upper middle-class or upper-class mothers may have significant work or volunteer responsibilities that take them out of the house for long hours (and perhaps have nannies or babysitters doing much of the parenting) but they do not tend to come under the same scrutiny as working-class mothers.

Additionally, lack of resources can become a sign of inadequate mothering. Frieda railed against this when she contended her agency "manipulate[d]" clients with "middle-class standards." She gave the example of an expectation that the young women obtain a "change table" to demonstrate their readiness to parent, but she argued that "those change mats that are portable that come in diaper bags" were "all they need." Yet she still judged the completion of that layette as one component of Trina's adequacy to parent.

In her work, Kristine acknowledged that she subscribed to middle-class values as a route out of cycles of poverty. Her thinking was that middle-class values:

> open up a lot more doors for them and their kids. I think that if you grow up and you're not expected to do better than your parents ... or your parents don't help you maybe get to where you want to go, I mean your choices are going to be that much more limited, as are your children's choices.

Note her conflation of working-class values with parents without ambitions for their children or support for their dreams. Also, what is absent from this analysis is the potential that working-class values are in fact just as constructive, or even preferable to middle-class norms, for raising healthy and productive children.

Some revisionist theorists have questioned the dominant perspectives on 'adequate' mothering and particularly the links between poverty and class. For instance, in a study about mothers and daughters, Walkerdine and Lucey (1989) proposed that middle-class and working-class mothers socialize their daughters in different ways, each with its own merits. Working-class mothers were more likely to give direct messages that their daughters should not interfere with mothers accomplishing domestic tasks, thereby supporting more individualized play and self-reliance (Walkerdine and Lucey, p.78). Similarly, in studies where race and ethnicity were examined along with class (e.g. Chaudhuri, Easterbrooks, and Davis, 2009; Elliott and Asseltine, 2012), parenting styles were related to the needs that mothers saw for their children's safety and survival, reflecting the divergent proximity of dangers and threats such as racism and sexual exploitation for different classes. Yet the need for divergent mothering styles may not be understood by middle-class workers or may be viewed as lacking (Walkerdine and Lucey, 1989, p.103).

Intersection with Race and Ethnicity
In addition to poverty, some of the young women who were clients in the settings for this study were pathologized due to their race or ethnicity. While there are differences between the struggles of black women and those of other racial or ethnic groups, I will primarily focus on the issues for young black mothers in this discussion.

Feminists (Bryan, 1992; Dickerson, Parham-Payne, and Everette, 2012; Elise, 1995; Mantovani and Thomas, 2014; Merrick, 1995; Stevens, 1996) have explored theoretical paradigms that explain the causes of single pregnancy and parenting for poor adolescents of colour. Stevens (1996) distinguishes between models that emphasize individual deficits and group pathology, from those that examine this social phenomenon as adaptive. These writers argue that stigmatizing models fail to examine historical and social context (Dickerson et al., 2012), blaming individuals for social arrangements that dominate and exploit the poor (Stevens, 1996, p.282). Instead, these theorists argue that structural barriers and racism have required young single black women to find alternate means of coping.

Stevens (1996) proposes mothering for these young people as an alternative life-style when more traditional pathways to adulthood are blocked. Childbearing may be interpreted as a career choice that offers the best option amongst limited possibilities (Merrick, 1995), rather than the dysfunctional acting-out articulated by some dominant discursive frameworks. Mothering may be an adaptive strategy to poverty and/or racism (Furstenberg, 2003) or provide one of the few opportunities to receive respect and be viewed as adults (Salusky, 2013). Kristine, for one, supported the idea of childbirth being productive for some of her clients, when she stated that becoming a mother provided a focus that acted as a conduit to maturity.

Young single poor black mothers themselves both accept the dominant discourses and resist them (Anamoor and Weinberg, 2000; Kelly, 1996; Klaw, 2008; Mantovani and Thomas, 2014; Salusky, 2013). Some young mothers have articulated motherhood as a turning point (Salusky, 2013) and as bringing meaning to their lives (Mantovani and Thomas, 2014), despite the stigma experienced, including from helping professionals who at times framed them as morally defective (Mantovani and Thomas, 2014). Notwithstanding the challenges, these young women are able to draw on alternate social institutions and cultural traditions, such as extended family and the church (Dickerson et al., 2012; Este and Bernard, 2003), to provide the supports necessary to sustain and nurture themselves and their offspring.

Valverde (1991), in a historical treatment of moral reform in English Canada around the turn of the century, argued that those of British descent were thought to have the most character because they appeared better able to control their instincts than other 'races.' And controlling one's impulses and sexuality were central to an understanding of moral 'character.' The educated white middle-class Protestants of the period viewed immigrants as 'savages' who could not control their sexual desires and therefore required coercive external controls. Valverde stated (p.104) that "the ruling group saw 'the regulation and control of instinct and emotion as the basis of civilization.'" Now, in a liberal democratic state, internalized control, suggests Valverde, is the best foundation for a social order built primarily through consensus and respect for authority (p.105). She contends that these sexual and moral issues undergird the racism in the Euro-Western world today.

Yet, different cultural groups have very diverse norms around the expression and intensity of allowable emotion. This is not necessarily a sign either of poor impulse control or of inadequate 'character.' When Anglo-Saxon white middle-class workers make judgements, how often do they evaluate intensity as 'excess' and/or as signs of pathology? Charlotte spoke about "our expectation of what [appropriate] behaviour is" and it being "based on the fact of upbringing and a class." She gave the illustration of "a Somali young women who … [was] very gregarious and outgoing" but was perceived as "very loud in the way in which she talks but she's not upset, she's not mad … but she irritates some workers sometimes because of her loudness." And is it not the corollary that the potentially more subdued responses of the white middle-class are then perceived as 'normal?'

Rarely did the workers in my study question their own whiteness and the privilege attendant with their race. At times, the practitioners seemed to view themselves as bystanders in the issue of race, using the racial card to claim a space of innocence, at the same time that it contributed to seeing themselves as helpful. For example, when Kristine stated that she did not want Jessica "to feel that she needs to be white for me," this statement on one level could be viewed as sensitive and responsive; on another, however, it allows for a distancing and blamelessness from the advantages that accrue to Kristine through her whiteness. I will return to this issue in Chapter 5 when we look at routes to the reduction of ethical trespass.

In examining the "colour of neglect," Swift (1995, p.126) stated in attempting to determine what is appropriate mothering, "the question of whether a clear and standardized definition, even if claimed to articulate only the most minimal standards, could still be used to impose the values of the dominant culture on minority groups" (p.135). Even when culturally and racially sensitive, practitioners are left with the dilemma of needing to recognize the unique and special needs of marginalized groups, while using concepts "invented, defined and enforced by the dominant culture" (Swift, 1995, p.136).

Now let us look at what is spotlighted for judgement.

What is Being Judged?

Prior to the birth of these young women's babies, there is intense scrutiny and assessment. It has been theorized that "what the mother does with her body – what she eats, where she goes, how and when – is open to public scrutiny" (Pillow, 1997, p. 351). Pillow goes on to argue that the mother, is a "legitimate target of moral concern" (Diprose, as cited in Pillow, 1997, p.351) and thus "subject to very direct state control" (Wilton, as cited in Pillow, 1997, p.351). Where a mother's body ends and the child's begins confounds notions of the unitary self, increasing the likelihood of the moralization "of the pregnancy as an ethical practice" (Weir, 1996, p.373). Programmes, such as 'Kick Butt for Two,' a smoking cessation programme, are common fare for young single mothers in Ontario, working on the notion of not just the regulation of the mother, but the unborn child as well. 'Good' mothers protect the health of their babies both *in utero* and out, meaning that what mothers ingest or smoke is cause for surveillance and discipline. Additionally, virtuous mothers ensure 'good citizenship' both by not adding to secondary smoke and ensuring healthy babies as future citizens for the state.

For the workers, once a child was born, safety was the primary consideration. Workers described scenarios that alerted them to concerns about potential abuse and neglect. Children's exposure to domestic violence was a key factor. When asked about indicators of poor parenting, Frieda gave the example of a client "not protecting their child" because the mother was in a "violent situation. They're getting beaten up on a regular basis" and the mother was "not seeing ... it as abusive and the child [was] at risk," of "either being caught in the cross fire or just witnessing" the whole incident. A very high percentage of the women in the workers' caseloads had both struggled in relationships of abuse and continued to confront domestic violence in their personal lives making this a major emphasis for the work.

Addiction was another significant red flag. Frieda asserted, "people with severe addictions ... couldn't physically take care of their child. [They] wouldn't be able to bond." And the impact of drug abuse on the next generation was a serious threat. This was a component of Kristine's concern with Jessica. Kristine explained, "decisions about what's right and wrong, like moral decisions ... that's really compromised ... in foetal alcohol syndrome."

A third highlighted area was mental illness. Frieda asserted that clients with "severe" mental illness "can't remember to feed the baby or to change [him/her]."

But how severe is severe? How does one determine adequate safety? The signs of addictions, for example, may be subtle, yet the consequences for the child may be grave. Workers ranged widely in their expectations and methods of evaluating safety. Jannie supported a "zero drugs, zero violence" policy. One guideline she incorporated was that any use or even suspicion of mind-altering drugs constituted a rationale not to return a child to his/her mother at the end of the school day. And the kinds of behaviours that constituted suspicion for Jannie were, "your eyes look red, your speech is slurred, you look like you have a dry mouth." But other workers had more lenient expectations about what, in addictions for example, represented unacceptable behaviour.

Excesses in general put young single women at more risk for being seen as unfit mothers. This was particularly true in group settings where the needs of one client came into conflict with those of others. As was described in Jannie's narrative, Shari's level of anger was perceived as dangerous, not just for her child but for the other participants and staff of the school programme.

However, the issues that lead to intervention extend way beyond physical needs to the emotional and psychological requirements of the child. Generally, in this study, the social workers adopted the discourses of maternal bonding and sensitivity regarding 'good' mothers. When I asked Frieda, "*what, for you, would be indicators of good parenting?*" her response was "bonding." When I pursued what the markers would be, she answered

> the mother and the child ... they're really connected. ... [the] child ... checks in with mom ... makes sure she's around ... feels confident to go and explore things ... and mom is ... *always, like not always* (italics added), but talking positively about [the] child ... .

There is an extremely high level of availability and emotional responsiveness implied in this view that was generally consistent with the other workers as well.

Emphasis extended to more wide-ranging requirements for nurturance, stimulation and education. Jannie's answer to what constituted good mothering was, "the ... better mothers were the ones who were there for their child and meeting their child's needs, like *all of their child's needs* (italics added)." She explained, "they're the ones who are actually spending the time with their children ... taking their kids to the park ... reading to their children at night."

But how realistic are these demands on impoverished single young mothers whose emphasis may be on survival needs? Returning to the Walkerdine and Lucey study identified above, (1989, p.74) they found that middle-class mothers transformed domestic labour into an opportunity for pedagogy and through this strategy were judged "sensitive." The power dynamic in their mothering was hidden through these manoeuvres whereas, because working-class mothers are more explicit in their demands to be left alone to fulfill domestic chores, they can potentially appear as less sensitive to the psychological needs of their children by middle-class workers. Yet the 'attunement' of middle-class mothers was at the expense of overt expression of a mother's power, an alternate lesson of life learned by working-class children.

Moreover, those young women who require 'help' with their mothering skills were evaluated at micro levels of functioning, from how a mother pumps breast milk to the adequacy of a brand of stroller, as we shall see in Chapter 4. Kristine expressed concerns that they might "not make the best (!) decisions around parenting ... giving them solid foods too early, or not breast feeding, or ... being really sometimes irresponsible with not changing diapers as often as they should." Charlotte spoke about needing to assess whether Violet was "sterilizing [bottles] properly."

And appraisal extended beyond interactions with children to the young mother's functioning in virtually every arena of their life: from budgeting to a willingness to participate in group activities. Of course, none of these behaviours in isolation would constitute poor mothering for the workers. And the caseworkers must ascertain, from concrete indicators, issues that, while subtle and abstract, do have serious consequences for the well-being of the child. The problem is that the composite picture is both highly subjective and variable and is based on norms that may be classist, racist, or ableist; intruding into the private sphere of the lives of these women. Also the women's mothering is often evaluated outside a structural analysis. Who would be seen to mother adequately with the level of expectation and surveillance that is a constant for these young women?

I want to revisit the discourse of choice articulated above by Kristine. Generally, workers suspected that the young mothers in their caseloads did not make "good choices" for a range of reasons: for example, the assumed narcissism of their developmental stage, cycles of familial or community dysfunction, and/or emotional vulnerability because of poor self-esteem. However, we cannot talk about true 'choice' when structural inequities and oppression so limit the actual choices open to these young women. Indeed, the workers in this study at times identified this dilemma. Charlotte, for example, commented on the restrictiveness of her clients' lives. She asked, "how many choices do they really have?" Furthermore, at times, it seemed that workers viewed 'choices' as good when they coincided with their own sense of what a client should be doing. This was the case when Kristine evaluated Jessica as making "better choices" by drinking hot chocolate rather than coffee. Compliance and attitude, like that of those judged as "fallen women" at the turn of the century (Kunzel, 1993), continue to be evaluated. While there were moments when resistance was viewed as constructive and appropriate (as we will explore in Chapter 5), often receptivity to other points of view and acquiescence to the input of the worker were judged as signs of being the good client. Margolin (1997, p.96) has argued, "[t]o resist is to announce one's need for a visit" from a social worker.

Although instruction results in more compliance and self-regulation, education also potentially does open up more options around subject positions. These strategies, according to Frieda, give clients a "broader knowledge base so that they can pick and choose different coping skills." Workers were trying to provide that entrée to opportunity through an emphasis on education about alternatives. A person who chooses is active, "her desires and reasons are increasingly integrated; she is less self-deceived or ignorant, more knowing" (Ruddick, 1993, p.129).

While we have looked at what constitutes the 'good' mother, the converse is one who puts her own needs first, and therefore is viewed as egocentric. In terms of Jessica's decision to stop her use of marijuana, Kristine stated, "she's not … being selfish, she's already got an awareness that this baby is growing inside of her … and making decisions for that baby."

But where do desire and pleasure fit into life for a young single mother? In another case of Frieda's, the young mother as evaluated as having "a lot of difficulties with parenting the baby." Frieda described the 'problematic' behaviour:

> the way we set up the living room, it's like a … horseshoe of chairs and in the middle is where we put the mats and the toys … . And some moms … end up sitting in the chairs and the babies are on the mats but we really (!) strongly encourage the moms to get down on the mats with the babies. She was one of the moms that would sit in the chair and her child would just [be] … crawling over things and just getting into a lot of dangerous situations and mom wouldn't even be watching the child to make sure that she was safe … .

Clients were encouraged to join the babies on the mats to reinforce "interaction" and "mother-baby bonding."

I later queried whether it was possible that the mom perceived this as a chance for "*social time or some kind of relief?*" Frieda acknowledged that the possibility of "respite" or "socializing" was "one of the biggest catalysts for the program" but the aims of the programme were "to augment the family relationship" and "modelling appropriate family sort[s] of activities."

I will address this example further in Chapter 4 when I examine the wider structural limitations in the work. My point here is that there is a subordinating of concern for the needs, pleasures and desires of women, apart from their positions as mothers. This has been a continuous theme in the historical construction of mothering work (Silva, 1996) and persists in the helping professions. A mother's own requirements for nurturance are minimized, yet how is it possible to have healthy children without care for caregivers? Apart from the argument that ultimately it is not good for children to have mothers whose own needs are not met, must the interests of mothers always be secondary to the needs of their children? Pleasure, as an important and legitimate aspect of a young mother's existence, is sorely absent from the discourses.

And desire, especially sexual desire, is often overlooked in the discourses except from a cautionary perspective. In 1988, Fine (1988) identified three discourses of sexuality for adolescents in school settings: sexuality as violence, as victimization, and as individual morality. These discourses were dominant in the interviews with the workers in the social service agencies as well, especially the workers' views of clients' sexuality as damaged by the perpetration of sexual abuse against them. Fine's (1988) argument was that a discourse of desire was missing, as it generally was with my participants as well.

While there has been a sea change in the discourses of young women's sexuality in the intervening decades (Harris, 2005; Tolman and McClelland, 2011), the impacts on the most marginalized has not changed. In Fine and McClelland's (2006) review of Fine's 1988 article, despite a concern for those populations served by social workers, no mention is even made of *mothering* adolescents and their desires. Because desire is "spoken into existence" through discourse (Davies, 1990b), it is crucially important that these women's needs, desires and pleasures be part of the collective discourses offered by workers as normative and healthy.

How Judgement is Rendered

Since judgement is a constant in the helping relationship, *how* judgement is exercised is significant in responding to the complexities of power as a productive force, in the success of the therapeutic enterprise, and in ethical practice. My observations were that when judgements were rendered, workers attempted to do this respectfully and gently, with honesty and transparency. Sensitivity and accuracy were important for Kristine. Clarity was a central operating principle for Charlotte to reduce the pain of judgement. Workers attempted to avoid shaming their clients in their judgements.

Shame is "the ongoing premise that one is fundamentally bad, inadequate, defective, unworthy, or not fully valid as a human being" (Fossum and Mason, 1986, p.5). It is not regret about particular actions, but a primary overriding sense of pain about the self, more difficult to undo or repair. Jannie suggested that to judge "brings [to the client] too much shame with it" and shame, according to her, was not helpful because "it just kind of pushes [a client] down even more," working against the very change that is intended.

Margolin (1997) would suggest that all of these negotiations are merely tactics that are part of a process of self-mystification and deceit towards clients by social workers. His central premise is that the profession of social work labours under what he perceives as a fundamental contradiction of desiring to do good, while simultaneously being required to scrutinize the activities of clients and impose mainstream values on the poor (p.ix). According to Margolin (p.60) since "awareness of manipulation, self-interest, or hierarchical domination represents for social workers an 'ontologically fatal insight' into their activities, social work survives only insofar as it hides from itself any awareness of what it is actually doing." This is accomplished through a process of Orwellian "doublethink" by which workers know and do not know, simultaneously, giving people "confidence while holding them under suspicion" (p.35).

Kristine expressed:

> being nonjudgemental doesn't just simply mean absorbing everything they are telling you, but at some point, when they give you an idea and say ... this is what I believe in, saying, okay, why are you trying to convince me that you believe in it? ... and being able to challenge.

Is this a form of doublethink or simply the complexity of challenge when one is attempting to balance judgement with non-judgemental engagement and empowerment discourses?

One component of the mechanism of doublethink that supports Margolin's claim (1997, pp.130–31) is the denial of the power to make judgements. He contends that workers need to blindly fool themselves about their power in the helping relationship. While there were moments of repudiation on the part of the workers I interviewed, their disavowal was neither comprehensive nor all encompassing. Rather, I believe it was a product of the workers' ambivalence around power that they grappled with moment to moment, at times acknowledging and at others denying. It also reflected the fluctuating, fluid nature of subjectivity in which individuals respond to shifting contexts, amongst many factors. Margolin's position seems to diminish the intense psychological struggle of the workers, underestimating their insight, and overstating their denial.

Nonetheless, he does raise important ethical concerns about the line between manipulation and "politeness, between harmless social lubrication and harmful deception, and between the 'use of self' and dishonesty about the nature of the professional relationship" (Wakefield, 1998, p.563). But no human being can tolerate bombardment of painful insights without any sensitivity to timing and pace. Who, even in their most intimate relationships, discloses every judgement immediately without reservation? Would that be humane or effective?

Wakefield (1998, p.566) suggests that every profession has rituals that help to reduce anxiety and ameliorate the discomfort of violating the customary boundaries of human interaction, whether it is medicine or psychotherapy. Since social workers are authorized to create change, it would be a ridiculous premise to then suggest that the field be constructed in ways that utterly reduced the potential to exercise power to be successful as change agents. The vignettes of this and the previous chapter demonstrate the awareness and, at times anguish, of the problematization of power for the workers.

Margolin's premise also assumes that clients are pawns without any power, oblivious to the possibility of being deceived and manipulated. While it is not the subject of this book to concentrate on clients' use of power, it is mistaken, I believe, to see them as weak victims without any ability to contend with disciplinary practices. While power may be between unequal players, the relations are "mobile" (Foucault, 1978, p.94) and social workers cannot usually accomplish their functions without some cooperation and acceptance on the part of their clients. There are infinite instances of reversals in the helping relationship. As an illustration, Kristine was well aware that if Jessica had been dissatisfied with the relationship, she could choose not to continue. Foucault suggests that power is "exercised rather than possessed" and is "not univocal" but defines "innumerable points of confrontation, focuses of instability, each of which has its own risks of conflict, of struggles, and of an at least temporary inversion of the power relations" (Foucault, 1984, p.174).

Margolin (1997, p.122) argues, "apparently, social workers have it both ways. They claim the moral imprimatur of client self-determination, continuously describing their interventions as 'empowering,' but retain their prerogative to plan and strategize, direct and control." While I agree that workers have it both ways, that reality is part of the complexity of the work. Margolin's tone suggests that it could or should be otherwise. However, I believe there is both a need for those social processes (empowerment, but also direction and discipline) as well as the possibility that, at least some of the time, clients desire for social workers to operationalize those strategies. For instance, there is the potential that Jessica, in order to protect the budding development of her baby in utero, may have wanted the information about caffeine that Kristine evaluated was necessary to impart and was able to share. Healy (2000) found that the young women in her study were ambivalent about workers' technical power and knowledge, but, at times, were frustrated when the practitioners took less active stances and did not provide these. Similarly, there are times, given ethnic and cultural orientations, that clients expect and seek more directive responses from practitioners, finding the norms of non-directive interventions problematic. Judgement seems a necessary, notwithstanding problematic, condition of the helping relationship.

I have explored the helping relationship at the micro-level, particularly the inevitability of judgement as a component of that relationship. In Chapter 4, you will meet the final participant in the study and we will examine the structural factors that influence how help is constituted.

Bibliography

Anamoor, A., and Weinberg, M. (2000). Fighting shame: A Somali single teen mother in Canada. In S.A. Inness (Ed.), *Running for their Lives. Girls, Cultural*

Identity, and Stories of Survival (pp.97–112). New York: Rowman & Littlefield Publishers, Inc.

Arendt, H. (1958). *The Human Condition*. Chicago: University of Chicago.

Barbalet, J.M. (1987). Marx and Weber as class theorist and the relevance of class theory today. In C. Jennett, and R.G. Stewart (Eds.), *Three Worlds of Inequality: Race, Class and Gender* (pp.136–52). Melbourne: MacMillan.

Brown, L.S. (1994a). Boundaries in feminist therapy: A conceptual formulation. *Women and Therapy*, 15(1), 29–38.

Brown, L.S. (1994b). *Subversive Dialogues. Theory in Feminist Practice*. New York: BasicBooks of HarperCollins.

Bryan, A. (1992). Working with black single mothers: Myths and reality. In M. Langan, and L. Day (Eds.), *Women, Oppression, and Social Work. Issues in Anti-discriminatory Practice* (pp.169–85). New York: Routledge.

Chambon, A.S. (1999). Foucault's approach: Making the familiar visible. In A.S. Chambon, A. Irving, and L. Epstein (Eds.), *Reading Foucault for Social Work* (pp.51–81). New York: Columbia University Press.

Chaudhuri, J.H., Easterbrooks, M.A., and Davis, C.R. (2009). The relation between emotional availability and parenting style: Cultural and economic factors in a diverse sample of young mothers. *Parenting: Science and Practice*, 9, 277–99.

Cornell, D. (1992). *The Philosophy of the Limit*. New York: Routledge.

Critchley, S. (2002). Introduction. In S. Critchley, and R. Bernasconi. *The Cambridge Companion to Levinas*. Cambridge University Press (pp.1–32). Available at: <http://www.myilibrary.com?ID=42090> (Accessed 15 May 2015).

Davies, B. (1990b). The problem of desire. *Social Problems*, 37(4), 501–16.

Dickerson, B.J., Parham-Payne, W., and Everette, T.D. (2012). Single mothering in poverty: Black feminist considerations. *Social Production and Reproduction at the Interface of Public and Private Spheres. Advances in Gender Research*, 16, 91–111.

Edwards, D. (2001). Emotion. In M. Wetherell, S. Taylor, and S. Yates (Eds.) *Discourse Theory and Practice. A Reader* (pp.236–46). London: SAGE.

Elise, S. (1995). Teenaged mothers: A sense of self. In B.J. Dickerson (Ed.), *African-American Single Mothers. Understanding their Lives and Families* (pp.53–77). Thousand Oaks: SAGE.

Elliott, S., and Aseltine, E. (2012). Raising teenagers in hostile environments: How race, class and gender matter for mothers' protective care work. *Journal of Family Issues*, 34(6), 719–44.

Este, D., and Bernard, W.T. (2003). Social work practice with African Canadians: An Examination of the African-Nova Scotian Community. In J.R. Graham and A. Al-Knenawi (Eds.), *Multicultural Social Work in Canada: Working with Diverse Ethno-racial Communities* (pp.306–37). Don Mills, Ontario: Oxford University Press.

Fine, M. (1988). Sexuality, schooling, and adolescent females: The missing discourse of desire. *Harvard Educational Review*, 58(1), 29–53.

Fine, M., and McClelland, S.I. (2006). Sexuality education and desire. Still missing after all these years. *Harvard Educational Review*, 76(3), 297–338.

Fossum, M.A., and Mason, M.J. (1986). *Facing Shame. Families in Recovery.* New York: W. W. Norton & Co.

Foucault, M. (1977). *Discipline and Punish. The Birth of the Prison* (A. Sheridan, Trans.) (2nd ed.). New York: Vintage Books. (Original work published in 1975)

Foucault, M. (1978). *The History of Sexuality. An Introduction. Vol.1.* (R. Hurley, Trans.). New York: Vintage Books. (Original work published in 1976)

Foucault, M. (1984). On the genealogy of ethics: An overview of work in progress. In P. Rabinow (Ed.). *The Foucault Reader* (pp.340–72). New York: Pantheon Books.

Foucault, M. (1990). The use of pleasure. Volume 2 of *The History of Sexuality.* New York: Vintage Books.

Furstenberg, Jr., F.F. (2003). Teenage childbearing as a public issue and private concern. *Annual Review of Sociology*, 29, 23–39.

Greenspan, M. (1983). *A New Approach to Women and Therapy.* Blue Ridge Summit, Pennsylvania: Tab Books.

Greenspan, M. (1986). Should therapists be personal? Self-disclosure and therapeutic distance in feminist practice. In D. Howard (Ed.), *The Dynamics of Feminist Therapy* (pp.5–17). New York: Haworth Press.

Haidt, J. (2001). The emotional dog and its rational tail: A social intuitionist approach to moral judgment. *Psychological Review*, 108(4), 99–111.

Hall, C., Juhila, K., Parton, N., and Poso, T. (Eds.). (2003). *Constructing Clienthood in Social Work and Human Services.* New York: Jessica Kingsley Publishers.

Harris, A. (2005). Discourse of desire as governmentality: Young women, sexuality and the significance of safe spaces. *Feminism and Psychology*, 15(1), 39–43.

Healy, K. (2000). *Social Work Practices. Contemporary Perspectives on Change.* London: SAGE.

Healy, K. (2007). Universalism and cultural relativism in social work ethics. *International Social Work*, 50(1), 11–26.

Healy, K.M. (2008). *International Social Work. Professional Action in an Interdependent World.* (2nd ed.). New York: Oxford University Press.

Houston, S. (2012). Engaging with the crooked timber of humanity: Value pluralism and social work. *British Journal of Social Work*, 42, 652–68.

Hugman, R. (1996). Professionalization in social work: The challenge of diversity. *International Social Work*, 39, 131–47.

Infinito, J. (2003). Ethical self-formation: A look at the later Foucault. *Educational Theory*, 53(2), 155–71.

Kadushin, A., and Kadushin, G. (1997). *The Social Work Interview. A Guide for Human Service Professionals* (4th ed.). New York: Columbia University Press.

Kasinsky, R.G. (1994). Child neglect and "unfit" mothers: Child savers in the Progressive Era and today. *Women and Criminal Justice*, 6(1), 97–129.

Keinemans, S. (2014). Be sensible: Emotions in social work ethics and education. *British Journal of Social Work*, 1–16.

Kelly, D.M. (1996). Stigma stories. Four discourses about teen mothers, welfare, and poverty. *Youth and Society*, 27(4), 421–49.

Klaw, E. (2008). Understanding urban adolescent mothers' visions of the future in terms of possible selves. *Journal of Human Behavior in the Social Environment*. 18(4), 441–61.

Kunzel, R.G. (1993). *Fallen Women, Problem Girls. Unmarried Mothers and the Professionalization of Social Work, 1890–1945*. New Haven: Yale University Press.

MacIntyre, A.C. (1966). *A Short History of Ethics*. New York: The Macmillan Co.

Mantovani, N. and Thomas, H. (2014). Stigma, Intersectionality and motherhood: Exploring the relations of stigma in the accounts of black teenage mothers "looked after" by the State. *Social Theory & Health*, 12(1), 45–62.

Margolin, L. (1997). *Under the Cover of Kindness. The Invention of Social Work*. Charlottesville: University Press of Virginia.

McWhirter, E.H. (1991). Empowerment in counseling. *Journal of Counseling and Development*, 69, 222–7.

Merrick, E.N. (1995). Adolescent childbearing as career "choice": Perspective from an ecological context. *Journal of Counseling and Development*, 73, 288–95.

Miley, K.K., O'Melia, M., and DuBois, B. (2013). *Generalist Social Work Practice. An Empowering Approach* (7th ed.). Boston: Pearson.

Monin, B., Pizarro, D.A., and Beer, J.S. (2007). Deciding versus reacting: Conceptions of moral judgment and the reason-affect debate. *Review of General Psychology*, 11(2), 99–111.

Nelson, J.L. (2001). Jane Austen and Naomi Scheman on the moral role of emotions. In P. DesAutels, and J. Waugh (Eds.), *Feminist Doing Ethics* (pp.167–83). New York: Rowman & Littlefield Publishers, Inc.

Niesche, R, and Haase, M. (2012). Emotions and ethics: A Foucauldian framework for becoming an ethical educator. *Educational Philosophy and Theory*, 44(3), 276–88.

O'Leary, P., Tsui, M.-S., and Ruch, G. (2013). The boundaries of the social work relationship revisited: Towards a connected, inclusive and dynamic conceptualisation. *British Journal of Social Work*, 43, 135–53.

Parker, S., Fook, J., and Pease, B. (1999). Empowerment: The modernist social work concept *par excellence*. In B. Pease, and J. Fook (Eds.). *Transforming Social Work Practice* (pp.150–57). London: Routledge.

Pease, B. (2002). Rethinking empowerment: A postmodern reappraisal for emancipatory practice. *British Journal of Social Work*, 32, 135–47.

Phoenix, A., and Woollett, A. (1991). Introduction. In A. Phoenix, A. Woollett, and E. Lloyd (Eds.), *Motherhood. Meanings, Practices and Ideologies* (pp.1–12). London: SAGE.

Pillow, W. (1997). Exposed methodology: The body as a deconstructive practice. *International Journal of Qualitative Studies in Education*, 10(3), 349–63.

Robertson, S.M. (2002). *The Non-judgmental Attitude in Feminist Social Work Practice* (Unpublished manuscript). Carleton University, Ottawa, Ontario, Canada.

Rogers, C.R. (1942). *Counseling and Psychotherapy: Newer Concepts in Practice.* Boston: Houghton Mifflin Co.

Rogerson, M.D., Gottlieb, M.C., Handelsman, M.M., Knapp, S., and Younggren, J. (2011). Non-rational processes in ethical decision-making. *American Psychologist*, 66(7), 614–23.

Ross, E. (2008). The intersection of cultural practices and ethics in a rights-based society. Implications for South African social workers. *International Social Work*, 51(3), 384–95.

Rossiter, A., Walsh-Bowers, R., and Prilleltensky, I. (2002). Ethics as a located story. A comparison of North American and Cuban clinical ethics. *Theory & Psychology*, 12(4), 533–56.

Ruddick, S. (1993). Procreative choice for adolescent women. In A. Lawson, and D.L. Rhode (Eds.), *The Politics of Pregnancy, Adolescent Sexuality and Public Policy* (pp.126–43). New Haven: Yale University Press.

Salusky, I. (2013). The meaning of motherhood: Adolescent childbearing and its significance for poor Dominican females of Haitian descent. *Journal of Adolescent Research*, 28(5), 591–614.

Sawicki, J. (1991). *Disciplining Foucault. Feminism, Power, and the Body*. New York: Routledge.

Stevens, J.W. (1996). Childbearing among unwed African American adolescents: A critique of theories. *Affilia*, 11(3), 278–302.

Swift, K.J. (1995). *Manufacturing "Bad Mothers." A Critical Perspective on Child Neglect*. Toronto: University of Toronto Press.

Tolman, D.L. and McClelland, S.I. (2011). Normative sexuality development in adolescence: A decade in review, 2000–2009. *Journal of Research on Adolescence*, 21(1), 242–55.

Valverde, M. (1991). *The Age of Light, Soap, and Water: Moral Reform in English Canada, 1885–1925*. Toronto: McClelland & Stewart Inc.

Walker, M.U. (2001). Seeing power in morality: A proposal for feminist naturalism in ethics. In P. DesAutels, and J. Waugh (Eds.), *Feminist Doing Ethics* (pp.167–83). New York: Rowman & Littlefield Publishers, Inc.

Walkerdine, V., and Lucey, H. (1989). *Democracy in the Kitchen. Regulating Mothers and Socialising Daughters*. London: Virago Press.

Waters, M. (1991). Collapse and convergence in class theory. *Theory and Society*, 20(2), 141–72.

Weir, L. (1996). Recent developments in the government of pregnancy. *Economy and Society*, 25(3), 373–92.

Wendt, S., and Seymour, S. (2010). Applying post-structuralist ideas to empowerment: Implications for social work education. *Social Work Education*, 29(6), 670–82.

Williams, N. (2015). Fighting fire: Emotional risk management at social service agencies. *Social Work*, 60(1), 89–91.

Wong, M.-K. (2000). A new look at self-determination. In L. Napier and J. Fook (Eds.), *Breakthroughs in Practice* (pp. 104–15). Concord, Mass: Whiting & Birch Ltd.

Zembylas, M. (2003b). Interrogating "teacher identity": Emotion, resistance, and self-formation. *Educational Theory*, 53(1), 107–27.

Chapter 4
Macro Relations: Broader Structural Issues In Practice

Introduction

Charlotte asked, "how do you really effectively support young women when you have such a constricting structural - - - - - box that you have to work out of?" In this chapter, I will elaborate on worker's notions of this "constricting structural box" and on how this box changes the nature of practice generally and the notion of ethics specifically. By structural factors, I am referring to both organizational arrangements and to social signifiers such as race, class and gender as they contribute to structuring an individual's social relations. Kondrat (2002, p.436) suggests that structure refers to "social regularities and objective patterns external to individual action, intentions, and meanings, and not reducible to the sum of those meanings or actions." In Chapter 3, I explored social signifiers, so the emphasis in this chapter will be on patterns in organizations and the broader macro structures of Euro-Western society, including the emphasis on neoliberal policies and processes that emerge from this perspective.

While the focus is on macro structures, it is important to remember that individuals are not separate from these structures. Kondrat (2002) provides a useful metaphor of dancers in a ballet. While a ballet is greater than all the individual dancers, without the dancers, there would be no dance. Similarly, without distinct discourses and action, there would be no structures. This theoretical understanding is significant to counter the helplessness that can pervade workers' subjectivity regarding these structures.

The chapter begins with the final participant, focusing on those details that illustrate structural factors.

Patricia's Story of Kelly and Marshall

The Worker

At the time of the research, Patricia, white and middle-class, was in her early 40s and married with a young child. She was trained as an Early Childhood Educator.

Growing up, she perceived herself as a "tough kid," "hanging out and ... doing drugs and being a wild teenager." She had lived in squats so felt sympathy for street youth. She had been sexually assaulted as a teen and had sought counselling, believing these factors contributed both to her ability to maintain an appropriate stance with clients and to her practice approaches. As a single woman, due to a birth control failure, she became pregnant. She stated that her pregnancy and subsequent mothering gave her a different perspective on her work.

Her father had always taught her to speak up and not "sit on the fence!" Patricia saw herself as an "anarchist." She thought it was possible to live a middle-class life-style and still be "politically active," "standing up for what's wrong."

Patricia worked in a large urban city at a community health centre as an outreach worker for street-involved youth who were pregnant or mothering. At the time of the interviews, her job entailed providing support, education, and advocacy.

Client Behaviour – Drug Use/Street Involvement/Attempts to Be Viewed as Adequate Parents

Kelly, was a white 19-year-old woman at the time of the interviews. She had a history of drug and alcohol use. She had a child previously but lost custody after six months when her father alerted the CAS about her drinking. The baby was apprehended and put up for adoption. According to Patricia, "that's when [Kelly] left and hit the streets." She resisted the shelter system and had been living on the streets for two years.

Kelly became pregnant a second time and in her seventh month began to obtain prenatal care, which was the start of her involvement with Patricia. She was living with her boyfriend, Marshall, 20 years old, who although not the biological father, was "taking … the role of the father." Originally, she intended to give the baby up for adoption, because with her previous history of CAS involvement and living on the streets, she assumed the child would be apprehended. However, towards the end of her pregnancy, she decided that she did want to mother her child. She discussed with Patricia whether anything could be done to help her keep her newborn.

When Kelly was 3½ weeks overdue to deliver, she was admitted to the hospital. Patricia perceived Kelly as suffering a series of unsupportive and harsh responses from hospital and social service personnel. For instance, medical staff decided to induce Kelly on a Friday, at 4 PM. Patricia was appalled by this plan as the beginning of the weekend reduced the possibility of any kind of agency support or planning.

After the baby was born, Kelly wanted to breastfeed. Despite a drug and urine screen, a hair sample, and a blood sample all coming back negative for drug usage, the hospital staff still did not allow her this request. They kept the baby in the intensive care unit (ICU), and every time Kelly asked again if she might be able to breastfeed, the staff had a reason why she could not. Patricia detailed that Kelly "had something like thirty stitches, she ripped" but "nobody (!) came in to see her." The nursing staff did not give her any pain medication and the staff left the food tray in the hall rather than bringing it to her, justifying that decision because they said she was asleep.

CAS apprehended the baby and the couple went into two different shelters after Patricia could not find a shelter that would accommodate both of them. However, the couple worked very hard to prove their adequacy to parent. While they were still in the shelter system, they "made all their visits with the baby." During this period, Kelly pumped her breast milk using an inadequate manual pump, according to Patricia, and took the milk to the CAS office for their child. Patricia was "sure they [CAS staff] just pitched it." Rather than being cooped up with the baby in a little receiving room, Kelly and Marshall asked if CAS had a stroller that they could use to take their child for a walk. The CAS worker said there was no baby carriage. They asked if they could use a carrier they had been given by Patricia and the intake worker said it was inadequate.

The parents managed to obtain an apartment and both got jobs. Support services were provided, which included Patricia, a high-risk nurse, and the family support worker doing home visits. Marshall expressed his interest in attending parenting groups and anger management groups. He acknowledged the dramatic change of life-style. Patricia's recollection was that he declared, "it's warm, we have a place, we have an address and we are going to get the baby back" but also, "I can't think of ... any more better, boring kind of life than to be a family."

Kelly and Marshall were required to do drug screens, which came back negative, but it was a full year before the CAS returned the child to them.

Patricia was "pleased" but "shocked" because she had not seen a young couple be successful "in a long time." When Patricia asked Kelly if it was worth it, she said, "yes, but I'm so tired." She had been doing drug screens every other day. Patricia assumed that this practice would continue for another year. Additionally, Kelly was required to keep separate appointments with a public health nurse, her Children's Aid worker, and Patricia as well as attending a parenting group.

Despite the child "doing really well," the relationship between Kelly and Marshall began to "fall apart." Kelly "was stuck at home with this baby all the time" while Marshall was "using" drugs. Kelly stated that "he wasn't a support for her anymore" and she felt "there was a lot of pressure on her to take care of this baby." Kelly "started working at night as an escort" to make ends meet. Patricia ascertained there was someone babysitting during these hours.

Kelly tried to move out of the apartment she shared with Marshall and he contacted the CAS to inform them she was hooking. The CAS stated that her prostituting was "not grounds for removal," "providing the baby [was] safe" and that she was "not using drugs." Patricia stated that Kelly was finding the escorting "really difficult because she had been a survivor of sexual abuse." She started using drugs again.

After a couple of weeks, Patricia said, "Kelly was in the front lobby crying." She asked to speak to Patricia who said, "let me drop my stuff off" but when Patricia "turned around" Kelly "was gone." Patricia "went to their apartment ... banged on the door" and got no answer. Patricia "managed to look through the window" and she "could see the baby asleep in the crib and [Kelly] ... asleep on the bed." Patricia felt she needed to contact the CAS about her perception that

Kelly was using drugs and that the child was at risk. She left a message for Kelly explaining what she was doing, and that she was worried about her and the baby.

For "about a week nobody saw the child, nobody saw Kelly, [and] nobody saw Marshall." Marshall called saying that "he was taking care of the baby" and he was going over to his parent's house. At that point, Patricia perceived that Marshall had "started using again because his urine screens were coming back positive." The CAS found out where Marshall's parents lived "and showed up ... with police and a warrant."

After the baby was back in care, Kelly said, according to Patricia, "'I've just been out using' ... I couldn't do it. It was too hard.'"

Marshall went into the hospital to detoxify. After he left, Patricia described that "he was clean, he looked good, [but] he had a lot of regrets around what happened. He still carried a picture of the baby in his wallet." He had asked Patricia if she knew what happened to the child because they had not made the court dates and did not know the outcome of custody. The child was "with a foster family" and was "going up for adoption." When Patricia last saw Kelly, Patricia reported that Kelly said the child was "'just going to hate [her]'" for having failed to keep her.

Interpretation of Client Behaviour – Hard Core Homeless/Unstable Histories

Patricia referred to Kelly as one of her "hard core homeless" clients. She believed that a lack of trust was central for these youth and engaging them in a helping relationship was critical for success. She described a chaotic lifestyle that could not be easily accommodated within the parameters of traditional outpatient treatment. She explained, "half the time, they don't even know what day it is ... they're just all over the place." She said one could go for months without seeing them and they were "a hard group to connect with."

Patricia explained, that both Kelly and Marshall, as children, had been "sexually ... and physically abused and ... in and out of foster care themselves and they never really got the help that they needed." When Kelly began escorting and the case deteriorated, Patricia explained that she thought "the flashbacks [were] just too much for her."

Patricia did not condemn them for their drug usage and instead sought to understand why they might use. She was somewhat tolerant of this behaviour, saying on one occasion that they looked like they were "smoking crack" but "given the circumstances of what they were going through ... as long as it's not constant."

However, behind Patricia's decision the day she contacted the CAS was her concern that Kelly was using drugs:

> I thought she's probably been using because she had this very kind of doe-eyed look and she ... looked at me and her eyes kind of rolled back and she went back to sleep. Now ... I could see the baby sleeping beside her in the crib but I thought, this isn't good and then just thinking why was she there [at Patricia's

office] that early in the morning? Why was she crying? You know, what was wrong?

Discourses: Strengths/Liberal and Radical Discourses

Despite her acknowledgement of the difficulties of these clients, an attitude that was central to Patricia's discursive field was a belief in the strength of the young mothers with whom she worked. Her philosophy was articulated in the notion that "they were the expert of their child. That they knew their child the best and that they were doing the best job they could as a parent and above all … they … wanted … the best for their kid."

Nevertheless, Patricia made a distinction between wanting to do the best for their children and the adequacy of those attempts. Her speculation of what motivated these young mothers was that they were "really looking for that unconditional love and … they're hoping … that this baby's going to give them everything that they've lacked in their whole life," the liberal discourse. However, she recognized that "whether they can do it [parent] or not is one thing but I think in their heart of hearts," "every women who is pregnant wants the best for their baby."

For Patricia, a significant explanation for the difficulties for Kelly and Marshall was the inadequacy and punishment of the broader system. This is the radical discourse of the "wrong society" frame. Throughout, Patricia was aware of structural dimensions. From her perspective, these factors contributed to, if not were responsible for, the difficulties Kelly and Marshall encountered. By illustration, she argued, "I'm finding women are losing their babies because they're poor, they don't have stable housing, they're in the shelter system themselves." In general, she felt, "the system really screwed this kid [Kelly] over."

She believed the likelihood of success for these clients was minimal. She argued that the CAS was having Kelly "jumping through hoops … it is a test obviously but it's almost like how can you win?" She continued that Kelly "got the baby back, she's got the supports in place but then … this other piece … makes it really hard for her to access the support she needs for herself … it's a whole new battle … she's facing." The "other piece" referred to extensive and intrusive expectations, which transformed the relationship into a "policing entity."

Strategies of Help

Supporting and Emphasizing Strengths

One strategy that Patricia employed was trying "to support them the best" she could. She believed that even with "the … worst mothers" there was "always something they [did] right" and she would try to find those strengths, and build on them in the counselling process. This is the strengths discourse referred to earlier. For example, she declared, "for these two to get an apartment, it's huge … ." And when the baby was apprehended, she remarked, "I was amazed by the amount of dignity [Kelly] showed."

Building Trust/Provision of Concrete Services

Due to Kelly and Marshall being perceived as "hard core homeless" youth, Patricia saw her first task as building trust. The provision of concrete resources was a primary method to achieve this.

At the beginning, when clients came to Patricia for "stuff," such as diapers, pads and formula, it "bugged" her "a little bit." She had heard that the designation "diaper lady" had been used by the medical staff to refer to the previous worker and Patricia thought, "that's totally insulting" because she perceived herself as "so much more." She saw concrete resources as a "means to an end." Her metaphor was "putting the food out to the wild animal."[1]

Over time, her attitude shifted dramatically. She had "come to embrace" the term. She remembered her own experience of being poor, and came to the conclusion that supplying that kind of a service was "equally as important" because "it's ... what they need" and she was "able to provide it."

There was minimal money in the agency budget for material goods. Patricia described how resource allocation was handled amongst colleagues:

> We get two hundred dollars a month in food coupons to split between the four of us to give to clients for emergencies ... If somebody's desperate for diapers, you can give them ten dollars and I'm thinking ten dollars isn't going to buy diapers. It's like twenty-five to buy a pack of diapers or some formula ... I try not to hog the food coupons. My coworkers are very generous and say ... feel free. But I try and just stick to my ... fifty dollars' worth, which doesn't buy much.

Patricia described her strategy for supplementing these resources: "Half a day every couple of weeks, I'm on the phone wheeling and dealing and trying to make contacts," writing to diaper companies, "really pouring it on thick," going to a warehouse for spoiled goods, and checking out "different shelters" because "sometimes they'll get a big load of diapers and ... if they have too much of one size ... they'll pass them on to me or vice versa." When her own friends' children outgrew diapers, the mothers would pass them along and even "women whose babies have been apprehended and they've had big stocks of diapers" would "bring them in for other clients."

Not just diapers, but most services were in short supply. Patricia had to wheedle others to obtain a spot in a shelter for Kelly because there was "such a humongous waiting list." Consequently, if potential clients "didn't show up," because of her relationship with the shelter staff, "then the spot was mine." But she also "upped the ante by offering a case of formula (laughs) and some diapers as well." Patricia acknowledged that there was a "whole network of ... people that work with young moms that are wheeling and dealing in ... the back rooms and supporting each

---

1   For an elaboration of the use of metaphors, see Weinberg, M. (2005). The mother menagerie: Animal metaphors in the social work relationship with young single mothers. *Critical Social Work*, 6(1).

other." She explained that "it's kind of like, you scratch my back and I'll scratch yours."

Advocacy

Patricia took an active stance to protect and campaign for her clients. When Patricia heard about the planned induction of Kelly on a Friday night, she "just showed up at the hospital," and "went down to labour and delivery." Patricia stated she "was furious" about the timing of it. She obtained Kelly's agreement for her to involve the hospital social worker who was "equally ... appalled and disgusted that they [had] decided to induce her at [that] point." The two of them tracked down the CAS intake worker regarding his plan, but it was to no avail.

At three months, when the baby was returned to Kelly, Patricia advocated a reduction of the intended level of intervention, saying, "that's a hell of a lot for somebody to do with a young baby, no money for [public] transportation ... and somebody who is probably ... really tired." Consequently, Patricia negotiated that Kelly would come to the group once a week and Patricia would stay in contact with her by phone and do a home visit every other week.

In her efforts to expand her advocacy beyond the individual to the broader system, Patricia wanted to enlist for the homeless committee at the hospital. To take on that position, she had to negotiate with her manager. Despite the resistance she met, she was able to join the committee.

Confrontation and Limit Setting

At the same time as Patricia advocated, she also would set limits, confronting clients on their behaviour and being direct about how she saw the system working. While she said, she "hated" doing "that awful 'well this is your situation, this is what they're [the authorities are] going to do'" routine, in fact she was straightforward about the roadblocks she perceived clients being up against. In the case of Kelly, the ultimate setting of limits came the morning when Kelly appeared at the office asking to speak to Patricia and then disappeared.

Patricia's confrontation extended to agency personnel with whom she liaised. To exemplify, Patricia felt she needed to draw a line about the positioning the CAS wanted her to take with Kelly and Marshall. Patricia understood that CAS workers had "humongous" caseloads and liked "rely[ing] on" other workers "to go in and do" the monitoring because CAS had "a very antagonistic relationship" with clients and assumed that Patricia's relationship would be more positive. However, Patricia was clear she did not want to "do their job for them." She made a distinction between "reporting any concerns to them" and going into a client's house and doing "a check."

Surveillance

However, due to CAS involvement, her practice was to provide instrumental needs, parenting education, and monitoring through home visits, such as "checking if the bottles [were] clean." She ambivalently took on the positioning of "watchdog" of

Kelly and Marshall, while trying to minimize and, at times, deny this aspect of the helping relationship. Her fluid and changing subjectivity is illustrated in her explanation:

> ... it almost turns into like a bit of a policing role which I am not comfortable with and I won't do it for the Children's Aid. ... I try and do it ... in a way that ... she [Kelly or the CAS worker?] wants me to do it ... it is so hard sometimes ... it's a real balance.

She explained her 'duty to report' by saying to Kelly, "you can tell me ... your feelings and what's happening for you but if you tell me that you went out three nights in a row and got blasted and left the baby alone, that's something I have to report."

This quotation is an example of paradox 5 listed in Chapter 1, namely self-disclosure as risky but necessary. The way in which it is dangerous is overt in this context – Patricia would need to inform the CAS about Kelly's unacceptable behaviour of drinking, an intervention that carried the risk of potential apprehension of Kelly's baby. But the other side of the paradox is covert. Through disclosure, a worker is able to be more effective in providing the needed help since she will know what is required. Additionally, a client who is open about what is happening in her life will more likely be perceived as the 'good' client. Despite the injunction, to be fair to all, it is human nature to favour those who are compliant and viewed positively. Consequently, it is more likely that clients who reveal their difficulties will obtain what they want from the relationship with the practitioner. Patricia stated that this form of surveillance was "very different from the work" she wanted to do, as "advocate" or "support," her preferred subject positions.

Justifications for Those Responses

Mandated Responsibility, Professional Obligation and Children's Safety
Despite her discomfort with the positioning of "watchdog," because Patricia saw these young mothers as "high risk," she accepted her statutory responsibility and would enact this positioning when necessary. To some extent, she relied on, or accepted that, if the CAS had significant concerns in these cases, they might be legitimate. Ultimately, she determined, "I do have to do the job" namely, "being responsible for the well-being of their children" because "somebody has to watch out for the little ones when they [parents] can't do it themselves." With Kelly and Marshall, she stated that she ultimately contacted the CAS "because it [was] part of making sure that the baby [was] okay."

When I enquired how she brought this positioning together with her belief in mothers wanting the best for their children, she replied, "a lot of the work I did with those moms was getting them to realize that ... what was best for their kids was to let them go, at that point." In making sense of why they could not mother, Patricia circled back to a stance of the problems being beyond her clients' control, part of the revisionist discourse. She stated, "their circumstances haven't allowed them to ... be ... the mother that they want to be."

Ameliorating the Effects of a Punitive System

Because Patricia asserted that these young people did "have hopes and dreams" which a lot "could very easily attain ... if we had a better government," her strategies, especially advocacy, were often attempts to ameliorate the punitive effects of that system and to bring those dreams to fruition.

For this case, Patricia's discursive field included: both revisionist and liberal discourses about young single mothers, activism and advocacy to reform a faulty system, a strengths discourse, the building of trust and the provision of concrete services, while at the same time, a reluctant acceptance of the positionings of "watchdog" and limit setter. Ultimately, she used the discourse of protecting the most vulnerable.

Discussion

Social Services in an Environment of Austerity/Social Inequality – Impacts on Clients

In Canada, the delivery of social services is occurring in a shifting environment characterized by globalization, economic restructuring, and debt reduction. In the post-war period, there had been an assumption on the part of the electorate of the importance of the government's responsibility to provide a social safety net for its most at-risk citizens (Evans and Wekerle, 1997). But since the mid-1980s, taxpayers have been "persuaded that social wellbeing was being harmed by state regulation, high taxation and welfare programmes" (Midgely, 2000, p.22). There has been a transfer of power and redistribution of funding to the provinces in Canada (Armitage, 2003; Evans and Wekerle, 1997), and beginning in 1995, spending cuts at both the federal and provincial levels of government (Aronson and Sammon, 2000). In Ontario, the province in which this study occurred, the cuts were in line with the government's political philosophy of neoliberalism. Neoliberalism is an economic and political philosophy that favours debt reduction, restricted public spending, and curtailed obligations to the welfare of citizens (Chappell, 2014).

These trends are not unique to Canada and can be seen in many Euro-Western countries such as the United Kingdom and the United States (Armitage, 2003; Chappell, 2014; Dunlop, 2009). Changes have included reductions in public services, re-privatization to the private sector for the responsibility for social welfare, the institution of tax systems that lower taxes but sustain the wealthy, and a deconstruction of the welfare state. Now social welfare institutions have only a 'residual' function. The strategies have promoted a "politics of scarcity" (Bakker, 1996, p.5) generating an increasingly unresponsive, inadequate, and punitive approach towards public expenditures in welfare, its recipients, and often those who administer or support those costs.

These social policy directions have resulted in increased income inequality across Canada. In a study of 17 countries, Canada was positioned twelfth in measures of inequality (Chappell, 2014). And of the provinces in Canada, Ontario has the greatest inequality of income, with the gap reaching proportions not seen since the Depression (Chappell, 2014). Lightman and Riches (2009, p.46) argued, that Canada is "a great place to live, but not for the poor or marginalized." For example, since statistics have been collected in 1989, there has been a 118 percent increase in usage of food banks and 41 percent of consumers were children and young people, the very population of this study (Lightman and Riches, 2009, p.62). Relative to other Euro-Western nations, it has "relatively high levels of child poverty and gender inequality" (Chappell, 2014, p.113) and was ranked in 2005 by the Organisation of Economic Cooperation and Development as the third-worst country for its poverty rate among working adults (Chappell, 2014).

One group that has fared particularly badly are the clients who were the sample for this study, namely young single mothers, generally impoverished, and often women of colour. Therefore detailing some research about the barriers to clients' capacity to thrive is pertinent.

The feminization of poverty in Canada is a well-established fact (Armitage, 2003; Brodie and Bakker, 2007) and it has been getting worse (Rice and Prince, 2013). Women are "more likely than men to live in deep poverty and for longer periods" (Brodie and Bakker, 2007, p.19) and the rate for marginalized women, such as Aboriginals, women of colour, recent immigrants and those with disabilities, is even higher.

Women head over 80 percent of all single-parent households in Canada (Rice and Prince, 2013, p.219) and are especially vulnerable to poverty (Armitage, 2003). In 2001, 90 percent of female-headed single-parent families lived in poverty (Brodie and Bakker, 2007), despite the numbers of women who are entering the labour force, even with young children. In Ontario, single mothers had at least double the average rate of poverty (Maxwell, 2009). Women generally have lower incomes than men and are more reliant on government assistance, and that gap is growing (MacArthur, 1997).

Although there was almost no difference in the rate of labour market participation for teenage mothers and adult mothers of the same educational attainment, teenage childbearing has "been shown to have negative and long-term effects on women's socioeconomic outcomes" (Luong, 2008, p.11). According to Workfare Watch (1997, p.8), "single mothers face an extraordinary high risk of poverty … to a near certainty for young mothers. This age-based polarization is increasing."

Additionally, structural disadvantages make women's poverty distinct from men's. Women are more likely to work in part-time jobs, with fewer benefits and weaker job security (Rice and Prince, 2013). In 2008, women earned 64.4 percent of men's rates of pay (Cool, 2010). Lack of available childcare (Armitage, 2003;

Imada, 1997), poor maternity benefits (Baker, 1992), and grossly poor payment of child support by non-custodial fathers (Mandell, 2002) are all examples of the circumstances that distinguish women's poverty. Yet, in Canada in the last 30 years, gender, as an analytical category, has virtually disappeared in social policy development (Brodie and Bakker, 2007).

While this study focused on Canada, many of these trends can be seen throughout the world and in fact, in some countries may be even more pronounced than in Canada. The United Nations has identified that "although women perform two-thirds of the work in the world, they receive only 10% of the income and own less than 1% of property" (cited in Mapp, 2012a, p. 249). The feminization of poverty worldwide is a documented fact with 70 percent of the world's poor being women (Nadkarni and Dhaske, 2012).

Additionally, "violence against women is widespread around the world, occurring in all countries and to women of all classes" (Mapp, 2012b, p. 260). Intimate partner violence affects one in three women with between 20 percent and 30 percent rates in the Global North (Mapp, 2012b). Many of the young women in this study had also experienced domestic violence. And while the health and well-being of single mothers as a group varies enormously across the world, one study suggested that being a lone mother led to the highest odds of having poor health outcomes (Witvliet, Arah, Stronks, and Kunst, 2014).

The service users in this research were young women. Children and youth are also high-risk groups. In 2006, UNICEF reported that over 100 million children were living on the streets (Ferguson, 2012). One of the workers in this research, Patricia, worked primarily with young women who were street involved. In order to survive, these "children are commonly involved in high-risk behaviors to meet their basic needs" (Ferguson, 2012, p. 161) and are consequently vulnerable to greater health problems, limited education and poorer work skills (Ferguson, 2012). While the causes of child abuse and neglect vary considerably in parts of the world, "child maltreatment exists in every country of the world" (Rock, 2012, p.143). Also, children born of non-marital relationships are more likely to experience instability and may have more negative outcomes both behaviourally and scholastically according to one study (Mapping Family Change, 2014).

Additionally, racism and ethnic hatred are global problems that operate on social, cultural, institutional and structural levels, notwithstanding variability as to which groups are Othered from country to country (Razack, 2012). Many of the service users in this research were racialized youth, people of colour or indigenous. Indigenous groups are significantly overrepresented as clients in welfare systems throughout the world (Hugman, 2010). In every continent, Indigenous people have seen their numbers dwindle and have experienced the appropriation of their land, culture, and resources by colonizing groups (Johnson and Bird, 2012).

Of course there are vast differences as well. For example, while one in four individuals live in poverty, there are significant discrepancies on rates of this social ill between the Global North and South (Nadkarni and Dhaske, 2012). A further difference is that "the number of young people at risk varies enormously across the world" (Williams, 2012, p.269). Another interesting finding is that "customs, attitudes, and laws regarding marriage and cohabitation, divorce and union dissolution, and widowhood, vary widely across cultures" (DeRose et al, 2014) so being a single mother in some countries may actually be a more privileged position, despite the earlier cited research which suggested a gloomier picture.

However, what is consistent internationally is the unequal treatment of women, the risks to children and youth, and those of colour, leading to the necessity of social work as a profession to undertake steps to reduce discrimination based on gender, age, race, and ethnicity given its mission of social justice and human rights.

We will now look at two illustrations of the consequences of these macro factors for the workers and clients in this study; housing and respite.

Resource Inadequacies

Canada has not recognized shelter as a primary right and a responsibility of the state, despite its wealth. The urban workers in this research repeatedly identified acute affordable housing shortages as one of the most pressing problems for their clients. Charlotte stated, "Housing is just horrendous ... now it's like a hundred people that [are] trying to get a one bedroom that's over-priced and poor, poor quality." Contingent on location, waiting lists for public housing ranged from 5 to 21 years (Maxwell, 2009). Without adequate housing, clients' chances of any kind of normal life or ability to parent were limited. Patricia expressed the belief that the lack of subsidized housing was the death knell in Kelly's attempts to be seen as fit to parent. She said:

> One of the reasons why this young woman went back into working as an escort was because she couldn't afford the apartment by herself. It was ... a dumpy little gross apartment that was eight hundred dollars a month. ... [F]or her that was really kind of the beginning of the end, having to go back into sex work.

Given the insufficiency, workers frequently had to place young women in a hotel system, described by Patricia as "no tell, motel." Frieda portrayed these settings as creating enormous obstacles to parenting. She explained that often these hotels had no fridges or hot plates. She judged that the hotel was "not a secure environment" and that "a lot of criminal activity" occurred there. She elaborated, "prostitution, drug dealing, that sort of thing, so ... being in that environment is scary, especially if you're ... sixteen years old, brand new baby." Frieda believed her clients were, "scared shitless ... so they move back(!) to dysfunctional relationships." No phones, no fixed address, and dangerous neighbourhoods diminish the potential of successfully accomplishing the very tasks that would allow these young women to mother effectively and 'prove' their ability to parent. Additionally, these inadequacies increase the isolation and the likelihood of staying in abusive relationships for economic survival.

As well, according to several of the workers, there were "huge waiting lists" for maternity homes. Even if a space was available, Patricia professed, for some of these young women it was difficult to stay there "because of the rules and the regulations."

Other alternatives were problematic as well. Scarcity of options, rigidity of rules and limitations of who can access those options abound. Homeless shelters were scarce. And living in a shelter was often seen by the CAS as an inadequate environment in which to bring a child. This was the case for Kelly. Also, actual neglect and abuse have been perpetrated in the very institutions that have been set up to protect these clients (Raychaba, 1993), which was illustrated in my own research, but due to a confidentiality agreement, has not been included here.

Often the available shelter services infantilized clients. Patricia described the system:

> people aren't allowed to collect welfare. They get … a daily allowance of … three dollars, or something ridiculous like that, if they're staying in a shelter … . This is also to last them for the day for lunch and anything else they need … .

The structures were often rigid and the settings neither comfortable nor usable as a home base, even to leave a phone number for possible job or apartment searches. Patricia stated that clients "have to be there at a certain time for their meals and a lot of times they're not allowed to stay there during the day. They have to leave." Consequently, Kelly resisted it, preferring to live on the streets until she became pregnant.

Patricia stated there were few, if any, shelters that allowed couples to stay together. Patricia described a situation where a young woman had been on a public housing list for single mothers for seven years. During that time she developed a relationship with a young man. Despite a willingness to move into a smaller apartment than they would have been eligible for as a couple, had authorities been told the truth about her changed situation, this young woman would have been required to start over and be at the end of the queue of the list for families. She would no longer be eligible for the list for single individuals, even though she and her partner were willing to be in a smaller unit. Might this be an example of the "socialization of procreative behaviour" (Foucault, 1978, p.104), a disciplining of young women as sexual beings or for having progeny without the benefit of marriage?

The other example of limited resources is respite. Generally, in the system there were few alternatives to give these isolated women a break from their children. In Chapter 3, Frieda spoke about a client with a very active baby who would have profited from some respite, but that was not the nature of the provided programme. Frieda's opinion was that her clients

> have [their children] twenty-four, seven … It must be so difficult to … not get any time on their own and … a lot of them don't have partners or social supports that will take their children for them for any length of time.

In many maternity homes, contact with families of origin was reduced or restricted and there was no possibility of boyfriends living with the young women. Generally, the young men were either discounted altogether or seen as problematic. Kristine stated, that "most" of the young women "don't end up staying with the fathers of their children ... . [U]sually he leaves or they break up."

The workers judged that a significant proportion of the young women in their caseloads had been sexually and/or physically abused by the men in their lives. This was the case for Kelly. Kristine stated that *all* of the clients on her caseload had reported sexual assault by male extended family members. Consequently, reducing contact with a natural family is viewed as being for the protection of either the children or the young mothers. This fact appreciably complicates how professionals could increase the supports available to the young mothers in a manner that is both effective and safe. Thus, the availability of another person to provide respite and support is truncated for these young women.

"Isolation is a material condition which is implicated in the practice of mothering," states Rossiter (1986, p.244). Charlotte judged one client with the flu as "very, very sick. Well not very, very sick ... she was not feeling good ... which can be very, very sick because when you're parenting alone, there's no support there." In this instance the client's isolation led to a redefinition of the severity of her condition. Since respite was not identified as an appropriate function for the residence in which Charlotte worked, when this client became ill, there was no one to look after her baby. Therefore, the client contacted her boyfriend with whom the CAS had forbidden her to have contact and the child was apprehended. The mother's lack of supports coupled with a lack of material resources became constitutive of 'clienthood' and even more problematically, of poor mothering, which led to the removal of her child.

In a world of limited resources, some means must be found to determine who receives and under what circumstances. The operationalizing of dividing practices is not simply designed to reproduce the status quo or just to punish those who are marginalized. With insufficient resources to give indiscriminately, dividing practices are the strategies to separate those eligible to receive and at what level, from others. Consequently, dividing practices are, in part, aimed at redistributive justice; to tip the balance of resources towards the have-nots. However, the pool from which this determination is made tends to be between those with very little and those with even less, and comes at the cost of significant scrutiny. And the redistribution is inadequate, perhaps maintaining rather than eliminating insufficiency. Nevertheless, the goal of preventing unfair advantage is a worthy objective. Wakefield (1998, p.550) states:

> Social control includes those processes of social regulation that allow for the continued existence of society. Social justice is the ultimate form of this kind of social control because, by reducing indignation and maintaining the perception of a fair social order, justice prevents a breakdown of social processes due to alienation or insurrection.

Complexity of the System

It is not just the inadequacy of resources, but also the complexity of the system that adds to the barriers clients and workers must negotiate. For clients, conflicting and changing expectations make governance according to desired 'standards' of mothering difficult, if not impossible. Frieda gave the illustration of expectations around the proper sterilization of baby bottles. She said, "Within the staff ... certain people ... feel you need to sterilize for ten minutes and then you have people that feel you only need to sterilize for five minutes."

These contradictions are compounded when different agencies take divergent stances about what constitutes appropriate mothering. In the case of Kelly, Patricia's support of her breastfeeding came in conflict with the assumptions and expectations of the CAS worker whom, according to Patricia stated, "well the baby is going to be apprehended ... Why would she want to breastfeed and bond with the baby anyway?" Accordingly, expectations are impossible to implement, even if a client wishes to comply.

The complexities of successfully negotiating the system extended beyond one worker or institution. For example, in the case of Kelly and Marshall, negotiations were with an intake worker, his supervisor, and a family support worker, all of whom had their own interpretations of how the case should be handled. This case also entailed collaboration and coordination with a variety of hospital personnel, a high-risk health nurse and ultimately, the police. Patricia's practice had to incorporate the discrete needs and wishes of Kelly, Marshall, the baby, Kelly's parents, and Marshall's parents. And the number of actors in this case was by no means unique.

Determining which system was appropriate for each need and negotiating the rules and regulations of those systems, particularly when they might be conflicting and require literacy, stamina, time, and resources, all worked against the clients. Frieda explained, "legal aid is sending them [clients] to duty counsel, duty counsel is sending them to legal aid and so they get jumped back and forth." Patricia spoke about doctors in her agency wanting her clients to take their children to the pediatrician despite the setting being a medical clinic. This scenario illustrates a game of hot potato in which no one wants to touch the clients.

Individualization/Less Eligibility

At the same time that there is a decrease in the quality and quantity of resources, there has been "an increasing emphasis on ... the centrality of individual responsibility, choice and freedom" (Parton, 1996a, p.10). Solutions have been framed as individualized, mothers in single-parent families have generally been viewed as the undeserving poor, and structural dimensions have been ignored (Brodie and Bakker, 2007). The history of social welfare in Canada is based on the principle of "less eligibility." This principle is that the assistance provided should be at a poorer standard than wages for the lowest paid labourer (Armitage, 2003).

Changes in programmes and even architecture support middle-class values, including the notion of 'choice' that we discussed in Chapter 3 and a restructuring of social services. For example, Kristine described the closing of local family resource programmes in 2001 and the development of an alternative model, touted by the government as an improvement. She stated that the old family resource centres were "local, they were very laid back, comfortable and very well known" to people in the community. She explained they offered "parenting programmes, drop in, just go borrow a video ... have a coffee with a mom while your kids play." On the other hand, the new centres

> do not offer a drop-in type environment. All their programming is structured ... There was pre-registration required. There is no transportation. ... They're very centralized. And they're very professional ... you walk in and you feel like you're walking into an academic setting ... everything is beautiful.

Kristine detailed that one of these centres was in same mall as the court building, using the "same writing, all the same décor." Consequently, "moms are ... so scared of being judged and they so hate ... going into institutions ... That's the last place they're going to go." The former family resource centres conveyed informality, warmth, and inclusiveness, while the space for the new centres suggested formality, disciplinarity, and exclusivity. Aronson and Smith (2010) described a similar scenario in their study. The values underlying these changes are dissonant for working-class or impoverished clients.

Yet clients are expected to cope under these conditions and are found wanting when they cannot. Struggles to cope with these structures were sometimes viewed by other agency personnel, the general public, and the workers themselves as indicators of poor parenting. Patricia argued that poverty is exacerbated by structural constraints and sets clients up for failure. She said, "if you don't have that [formula and diapers] you're really in trouble."

Disciplinarity and Surveillance

It is not just the dearth of services but the surveillance and disciplinarity that minimize the possibilities for practising ethically and the likelihood of success for clients.

Observation of service users is far-reaching and operates at micro-levels. Charlotte likened her clients to "tiny" "guppies" in a "little tiny fish tank" and her positioning as the person who "see[s] their every move." Her metaphor reflects her sense of their powerlessness and the constant scrutiny. It is comparable to the Panopticon (Foucault, 1977) in which inmates were surrounded by an architectural structure that permitted continuous scrutiny of them, but where they did not know whether they were being watched at any particular moment.

Surveillance can hinder the development of the tie between mother and child. Patricia suggested some of her clients "feel like they're being watched with their babies and I think … they're so worried about … the attachment they're going to have with their infants that they don't kind of let it come naturally." Professionals are there to strengthen that tie but through normalization, set the standards of adequate mothering. And the scrutiny surrounding poor mothers' attachments can interfere with meeting the benchmarks. This is yet another paradox in practice related to paradox 3. Workers wish to be non-judgemental, but must evaluate what is acceptable parenting. Furthermore, it is an example of ethical trespass. Despite the wish to do no harm, the very act of scrutinizing a mother's interactions with her child can, in fact, lead to hindering that bond, with the potential serious consequences for both mother and child.

Surveillance contributes to yet another contradiction. Discussing one's difficulties enhances the potential of change but sharing one's struggles can jeopardize the possibility of being seen as an adequate mother. To adequately perform 'client' means: 1) knowing oneself; 2) being able to articulate that knowledge; 3) being willing to do that; and 4) to do it with someone who has the power to discipline you in some manner. But being a 'good' client requires openness about issues and concerns, putting clients at more risk for information coming to light that could result in discipline. At the same time, a young woman who demonstrates openness is more likely to be judged as making progress and being seen as fit, than one who refuses to divulge. Those who cannot or will not talk about what is going on, are not introspective, or have no analysis are viewed as less adequate or worthy by social services, regardless of the reasons for this behaviour.

This is paradox 5 from Chapter 1. Charlotte identified this conundrum for Violet. And Patricia explained, "a couple of times [Kelly] came in to see me and she said to me, 'you know there's stuff I really want to talk about, but I don't know whether you would report it or not, so I'm just not going to say anything.'" Consequently, like many clients, Patricia felt Kelly was "really caught between this rock and a hard place." While she wished service users could get support elsewhere, Patricia actually believed, "they don't [have other options] … so they're really getting set up almost."

For Patricia, ironically, the better the relationship between worker and client, "the harder it gets," perhaps because she felt more strongly the betrayal and trespass required in her own positioning.

The social workers generally perceived wards of the CAS as the most scrutinized of clients and more likely to fail in their efforts to meet standards of adequate parenting, due in part to the level of surveillance under which they functioned. Rather than being protected by the CAS, the workers felt that CAS input left clients more vulnerable to loss. With regard to Kelly and Marshall, Patricia said, "the system failed both of them. … they were let down twice. They were let down as parents and they were let down as kids." Like the historical bastardy laws, wards are punished for the 'sins' of their parents.

Additionally, there had been changes to CAS practice towards more punitive practices. Patricia said, the "Children's Aid have to investigate everything now, if anybody just called" once, even if it was perceived as a "grudge call." Furthermore, not only were children apprehended frequently, but the CAS was going for crown wardship[2] much earlier in a child's life. Historically, Patricia's experience was that "the Society wouldn't go for crown wardship until children were around two years old. Now it's three to six months." According to Foucault (1978, p.144), "the law operates more and more as a norm." Thus the default position for the CAS becomes surveillance rather than support, with the underlying assumption being the inadequacy and possibly criminality of the mothers involved.

These modifications were accompanied by a shift away from prevention. Patricia stated the CAS

> used to have a lot more preventative programs. They used to have ... workers [who] were pregnancy and aftercare workers that ... couldn't apprehend. ... they were strictly family support workers and prenatal support workers. They also used to have respite care programs ... All that stuff has been completely cut so what they've become is this kind of policing agency ... there isn't the nurturing piece anymore ... .

The requirements of statutory responsibilities for workers extended beyond the Child and Family Services Act (1996) to other social welfare policies. One illustration was "trusteeship" programmes in which workers were responsible for the distribution of social assistance cheques and for monitoring clients' expenditures of this money. Also, workers had to oversee their clients' involvement in programmes like the Learning, Earning, and Parenting programme (LEAP) in Ontario (2008). It mandated youth aged 16 and 17 who had not completed high school to be in an educational programme in order to receive public assistance. In discussing clients in the LEAP programme, Frieda claimed, "They have to get their high school in order to get their cheque. If they don't go, they don't get their cheque and they lose their child ... ."

The dominant discourse in public policy in Ontario is that young single mothers who do not participate in waged work are viewed by the state as welfare dependents (the reactionary discourse) and heavily penalized. However, this approach to expect mothers to be working outside the home removes working-class mothers from the care of their children, perpetuating the assumptions of maternal neglect due to absence; setting them up as inadequate mothers.

Patricia alleged that the young single mothers were "treated like criminals." Margolin, (1997, p.138), referred to a new social work credo of "guilty until proven innocent." While this may be too all-encompassing a statement, in the case of Kelly and Marshall, the overall effect did seem to be a starting assumption, on the part of the service delivery system, of their guilt and incapacity, which they had to prove as erroneous. The examples of punishment of Kelly and Marshall were not unique. Every worker described case situations in which clients were

---

2   This designation is for children who become permanent wards of the court.

abused, neglected and/or punished by the social service system. And to be proven as unfit and to lose one's child results in a further reduction of already meagre resources, both material and emotional, since those very services are predicated on being a parent.

The elimination of a network of support, the relegation of caring to the private sphere, the level of surveillance, and the valuing of self-sufficiency put an unreasonable onus on the young women, while making few, if any, demands on the men who have fathered these children. As a result, according to Frieda, there is a whole underground network of young women who "aren't getting contact anywhere" and refuse to use the social service system because they do not trust that it will help them, or worse, they see it as punitive and dangerous. Consequently a whole needy component of Canadian society is not receiving help at all.

Effects on Workers

Impact of Individualization

The emphasis on individual responsibility in the neoliberal context affects not just clients but professionals as well, including their construction of identity (Thomas and Davies, 2005a). Competence as a professional is equated with making independent judgments that isolate workers. The strong statutory imperatives regulate individual workers as agents of surveillance, imposing significant penalties for making the wrong decisions. There is scrutiny on the workers too, as they are held individually responsible. In the case of Violet, Charlotte spoke about "being on the line" to contact the CAS. She had a "responsibility" and knew "what's expected of [her]." Like being before a firing squad in this instance, she felt at risk and vulnerable if she did not discharge her legislative responsibilities.

Decisions are occurring in an increasingly litigious atmosphere. Workers have to walk the tightrope between harm to children versus unwarranted intrusion into the private sphere of the family (Parton, 1996a).

Ethics in social work in the neoliberal environment have been socially constructed in a manner that disciplines workers to be autonomous beings (Weinberg, 2010) and creates the category of what it is to be 'professional' (Rossiter, Walsh-Bowers, and Prilleltensky, 1996). Tactics of governmentality that operate through "regulated choices made by discrete and autonomous actors" (Rose, 1996, p.328) pull social work away from being a moral activity to a "rational-technical" one (Parton and O'Byrne, 2000, p.30). When Jannie referred to her practice as being "cookie cutter," she was describing her positioning to be one that was formulaic, as information and referral, veering towards being a technician rather than a healer. For other workers as well, there seemed to be a significant emphasis on the provision of concrete services and liaison to resources, at times supplanting, more traditional types of 'therapeutic' encounters.

Given the cutbacks and the swing to the political right, both social workers and their clients become easy scapegoats in a system that is precarious and inadequate. Media contributes to the scapegoating. For example, Patricia believed that the increased surveillance in Ontario was, in part, a result of the Heikamp inquiry. In 1997, Jordan Heikamp was born prematurely to a 19-year-old first time mother who was involved with the Catholic Children's Aid Society (CCAS). When Jordan was five weeks old, he died of starvation. In the investigation, the CCAS intake worker and the mother were accused of criminal negligence causing death but the case was dropped, due to lack of evidence (Jury rules, 2001). The risks of being held criminally or civilly responsible were highlighted for social workers as a result of this tragedy (Regehr, Bernstein, and Kanani, 2001).

Acceptance of Normalization

While subject positions requiring surveillance and disciplining were difficult for workers and interfered with the development of relationships, simultaneously, the mandates provided some relief in risk management. Nikolas Rose (1996) proposed that by behaving in a prudent fashion, individuals are provided with "certain guarantees against uncertainty" (p.343). Jannie stated, "I'm happy to call CAS because then if anything were to go wrong, I am not going to be one hundred percent liable or held responsible." Statutory expectations were also seen as providing back up, and confirmation in making complex and difficult decisions. Jannie argued, "I will not feel completely on my own." Charlotte had identified the same issue in the case of Violet.

Furthermore, there is a need for processes of normalization and surveillance. There are parents who are not capable of adequately protecting and raising children. As a society, we do have a responsibility to protect the most defenseless. Patricia stated that having a child of her own put "a different slant on it" because she began to think "if I couldn't cope, I would hope that someone would make that call for me to kind of take the heat off."

Location in Organizational Hierarchies

Pressures also come from where social workers are located in their institutions. Both Patricia's and Kristine's perceptions were that a social worker was "the lowest ... man on the totem pole" in the field of social services. Patricia's opinion was that the diaper lady subject position was "the only thing" her position was "good for," according to the medical staff. She believed they did not value her position because some held they could provide counselling themselves, and for others, that patients should "just take a pill and shut up."

Edelman (1988) suggests that the "diversity of meanings inherent in every social problem" (p.15) arises from the competing interests of different groups, "each eager to pursue courses of action and call them solutions ... The problem becomes what it is for each group precisely because their rivals define it differently" (p.150). Patricia was aware of the fighting for definition when she stated that she had often referred to her workplace "as like West Side Story because it feels like the Sharks and the Jets sometimes." She was referring to the Broadway musical in which rival teenage gangs duke it out to control a turf.

The lack of authority accorded to social workers may, in part, be gender biased. When Patricia stated that the doctors viewed talk as "a lot of hooey," we see doctors denigrating practice that is more affectively based. Jones (1988, p.120) argues that authority, "as a set of practices designed to institutionalize social hierarchies" is constructed as a binary, with the male voice "hierarchical and dispassionate" (p.121), while the female voice of emotional connection and compassion "non-authoritative, marginal pleadings for mercy – gestures of the subordinate" (p.121).

Also, Patricia felt that there was a moral judgment about the young women that 'contaminated' her own positioning. She questioned why her position was not full-time despite working "four or five hours overtime every week." She speculated that this was subtly connected to "this feeling that … these women aren't important and … that maybe they shouldn't be having children … and they shouldn't keep getting pregnant and they … shouldn't bring their babies here [to the clinic]."

Also, at times the inability to meet the needs of clients can appear to others as failure on the part of social workers, contributing to the scapegoating of the profession for much larger systemic problems and fostering lower status organizationally.

Many social workers are situated hierarchically with more emphasis on supervisory oversight than other mental health professional groups. Studies regarding worker relationships with management in the neoliberal environment suggest a contradictory picture of both support and censure (Aronson and Smith, 2010; Baines, Cunningham, and Fraser, 2011; Evans, 2011; Rogowski, 2011). There is an increased need for supervision, given the complexity of the systems, the rise in caseloads due to managerialism and the escalating complexity of cases (Hoge, Migdole, Cannata, and Powell, 2014). And while clinical supervision could be a support to workers struggling with the effects of managerialism, it requires a dialogical and collaborative approach that recognizes the inherent power in the supervisory position and allows for the time necessary for relationships of trust to flourish.

But in the current environment, the availability of regular clinical supervision within agencies has eroded in Canada (Hoge, Migdole, Cannata, and Powell, 2014) and elsewhere in the Euro-Western world (e.g. Noble and Irwin, 2009). For the workers in this study, it often was a source of stress in their ability to take up preferred subject positions. Their level of autonomy seemed dependent on the specific relationship with a supervisor, perhaps due to how small and flat the organizational structures were in the particular agencies of these specific workers. When organizations operate in a top-down model, a sense of impotence and anger may result for workers who do not believe they are able to exercise their power.

Jannie took a significant risk to promote her view of what was needed in the case of Shari. By pushing for dialogue and consensus, she experienced a deterioration in her relationship with her supervisor without the benefit of producing a plan that was more closely aligned to her understanding of good practice. Both she and Frieda feared their creditability was besmirched in one-up, one-down exchanges.

One research study found that in the prevailing climate, less than half of the workers turned to their in-house supervisors for support in dealing with ethical dilemmas (McAuliffe and Sudbery, 2005). What is taken as 'ethics' is produced within power relationships (Rossiter, Prilleltensky, and Walsh-Bowers, 2000), so a safe space is necessary in which to examine and resolve the complexities, paradoxes, and dilemmas of ethical practice. Contextual collaborations that focus on dialogue, a respectful openness to difference, and recognition of the place of emotions in ethical decision-making (Hair, 2014; Weinberg and Campbell, 2014), as well as trust, are needed to facilitate practising ethically for workers.

Regardless of the supervisory relationships, some theorists (L. Davies, 1990; Evans, 2010; Evans, 2011; Weinberg and Taylor, 2104) have argued that deterministic analyses of the welfare state, where workers are cogs in the machine with little control, are inaccurate and simplistic. In the classical research by Lipsky (1980) the complexity of organizations and the face-to-face interactions of front-line workers, outside the purview of supervisors, allowed for discretion in interpreting the myriad policies and procedures. While there has been a debate about the feasibility for discretion in the current socio-economic and political climate, scholars have suggested that street-level bureaucracy is still a factor (Evans, 2011) in part due to the complexity and contradictory nature of the rules workers must navigate (Weinberg and Taylor, 2014). Thus, workers do seem to exercise some power, regardless of the stances taken by their immediate supervisors.

Workers also struggle with their responsibilities to and relationships with other staff. Kristine described a case in which she felt a client had been poorly treated. Despite "wanting to validate [the client's] feelings about feeling disrespected" she did not see it as appropriate to create an alliance "making it ... me and her against the rest of the professionals involved." The need to present a united front had motivated Jannie in the case of Shari as well.

There are other organizational challenges to practising in a manner that seems ethical to participants. The organizational culture, specific mandate and programme options of the agency shape and limit what is possible in terms of practice, "constraining the type of information they [workers] process, limiting the range of alternatives available, and dictating the rules by which they will choose among alternatives" (Cohen, 1998, p.441).

Effects of Managerialism

Notably, social services have moved towards a more market-driven system. The restructuring of social services has led to a belief that the management systems of the marketplace should be adopted in the non-profit world. This philosophy and the technologies that accompany it are referred to as *managerialism* (Clarke, 2004). It is characterized by tight controls over spending, increased standardization, and the imposition of management structures and documentation to monitor for improved efficiencies (Banks, 2011; Clarke, 2004). As well as in Canada (Aronson and Sammon, 2000; Aronson and Smith, 2010; Baines, Davis and Saini, 2009), studies in other industrialized countries (Flynn, 2000; Rogowski 2011) have also found that there has been a narrowing of practice together with an intensification of workload responsibilities, leading to reduced quality of service. Kristine said, "there have been funding cutbacks recently. ... I feel angry about [it]." Staff in Patricia's agency had not had a raise in eight years and were in the process of unionizing. The effects of managerialism impacted on the caseworkers' ability to provide what they considered to be good and ethical practice.

Every worker identified the stresses of the pace and volume of the work. When the work was at a peak, Patricia identified that the atmosphere was: "so hectic and so crazy that (sigh) ... sometimes I just feel like I'm flying by the seat of my pants ... . Like it's one crisis after another and I almost don't even have time to ... sit back and reflect."

Short-term intervention rather than longer-term, more intensive practice is promoted as means to manage an insurmountable amount of labour. But, empowerment, as we have seen, is not feasible in situations where there is little time for the blooming of understanding and growth. Workers identified that, given how damaged their clients were, long-term relationships were often seen as necessary to allow young women who had been injured to develop trust and to potentiate lasting differences in their lives. Frieda judged that it had taken two and a half years for success with one client. Only at that point, could this young woman share "all these things that she [would not] tell other people."

However, Patricia stated at times, for workers, it was "self preservation" to "just do the crisis intervention." Her practice in those instances was as much a response to her own needs for survival as to her clients' needs for help. Yet it was clear that with Kelly and Marshall, significant expenditures of time were necessary to provide the support and advocacy required.

I asked Frieda, what was "*wrong with the way business is conducted in this field?*" She responded, "That's exactly what it is ... it's conducted as a business and this is social services." Her concern was that her agency was run like a commercial enterprise where "the bottom line [was] money." For example, she judged that part of the pressure on Trina to return to the maternity home was that the agency received "more money after the baby [was] born," as you may recall from Chapter 2. In this instance, Frieda felt that in order to maintain the finances of the home, the ultimate consideration was not the best interests for this young mother but rather the needs of the agency.

Both Frieda and Patricia relayed that they were accountable for establishing "a client base." Patricia found this stressful because without locating clients, she had no job. Prior to her arrival at the agency, her position had been vacant. She described the process of building up a caseload through "word of mouth with the ... girls." This got her name out "a little bit faster than having to do all the ... grunt work [herself] for a year." However Patricia was not entirely comfortable with this positioning because she felt she "was using" clients for her own needs.

Nevertheless, without a market share and funding, there would be no agency. Consequently, organizational survival ends up being an important consideration. Charlotte queried whether Violet might simply be relying on the residence for housing. From an agency perspective, that was an unacceptable use of the maternity home. The problem with this usage would be that it would have suggested a broader societal failure rather than an individualized need for psychological services for clients. It would have altered the potential positionality of workers to that of mere custodians, reducing the requirement of their expertise or the number of trained staff. Similarly, Frieda's explanation of why her agency did not provide respite was "you won't get funding to do respite" and it was "seen as babysitting." Since funding from government sources is, in part, predicated on the salary requirements of professional groups, an agency would not need the same financial resources for less qualified personnel. At the extreme, an agency could lose its designation as a social service agency since funding bodies might not perceive such an agency as falling under their mandate, potentially jeopardizing its future.

By discursively framing problems as necessarily relationship-oriented or intra-psychically oriented, workers were provided with subject positions of helper to improve or correct psychological problems, thereby maintaining their occupational terrain as needed experts and ensuring the survival of the agency as supplying necessary skilled mental health services. "The definition of the problem generates authority, status, profits, and financial support while denying these benefits to competing claimants" (Edelman, 1988, p.20).

Simultaneously, there is justification for an agency to pay attention to its own survival needs. If it provides a decent service, clients are not served well if it goes out of business. In one case, Kristine expressed anxiety about her organization's existence because, as a "small community agency, ... [it was] constantly having to fight for funding."

Stress and Burnout

All these factors lead to substantial tensions for workers in the field. And there may be a gendered component to these strains when the majority of workers are women (Baines, et al., 2011). The history of the profession of social work has evolved from the assumption that women are naturally caring. But caring *for*, namely the instrumental tasks of caring (Baines, Evans, and Neysmith, 1991), are compromised when the resources are inadequate and punitive, regardless of workers' caring *about* their clients, leading to tremendous stress and guilt for women who feel they cannot meet their preferred positions of self. Jannie stated, "I'm a social worker. You're not supposed to say no. You're supposed to be caring ... and give, give, give." It has been suggested that "social workers, belonging to a predominantly female profession, are notoriously bad at taking care of themselves" and meet their own needs, unconsciously, through nurturing others (Lawrence, 1992, p.40). If that is the case, then the inability to provide adequately for their clients would have a doubled impact. Jannie proposed, we're so trained and focused on the client that we're supposed to … really focus on the client and their needs, and forget about ourselves and our needs, and I think that's why social workers are way overworked and way underpaid and so stressed out and you know maybe don't take care of themselves enough.

Women have been socialized to be altruistic and to place others' needs before their own. This coincides with the professional ethical injunction that one's work must be free from personal gain. Patricia believed a helper was to be

selfless and … go above and beyond the call of duty in helping out clients and … we do it for all the right reasons … there's never kind of … [an] ulterior motive. … there's always that whole kind of Mother Teresa (laughs) saviour lady thing happening.

Consequently, the workers' positioning as self-sacrificing is problematic but well-suited for current market needs to do more with less.

Paradoxically, there is also an ethical imperative to look after oneself. Self-care is an articulated principle in codes of ethics due to the concern that individuals cannot practice effectively if they are burnt-out or experience compassion fatigue. So workers suffer the dilemma of both needing to subordinate self-interest and, at the same time, pursue self-care (Weinberg, 2014).

Three of the five workers described having some type of "breakdown," with two being hospitalized, and four of the five having either left the field or seriously considering it. While I do not want to imply that these personal problems were solely due to structural factors, generally, the workers expressed that these elements contributed to their personal distress and the potential for burnout in the field.

Burnout is an emotional numbing, akin to indifference, that may be quite pervasive for a practitioner (Newell and MacNeil, 2010; Weinberg, 2014). Margolin (1997) suggests that burnout comes from the "doublethink" of a belief in the clients' voluntariness, while silencing the recognition of power over clients. The danger of burnout may arise from the difficulty of being an agent of disciplinary practice and the pain that these judgements produce for the worker. But I think Margolin's statement omits structural causes of workers' distress, disengagement, and abandonment of the field. Sometimes I believe workers burn out and leave the field because of their perceived inability to exercise their power, given their own positioning in institutional regimes.

Conclusions

Depending on the discursive fields workers drew upon, structural deficiencies might or might not have been part of their understanding of practice and their attempts to engage in rearguard actions to minimize the impediments for clients. In a case example, Margolin (1997) argued that

[w]hatever system of rules and obligations is operating here originates neither in the social worker nor in the client but in the discourse itself – in the procedures that demand that certain things be said and repeated, and other things be unsaid and left forgotten. Both parties appear dominated but not by each other. Neither is to blame, yet each is a victim. (p.134)

But this delineation implies that there is only one discourse that informs how social workers practice, and that it is static and unchangeable. It leaves workers and clients as victims with no ability to effect or alter the discourses. However, practitioners contribute to the creation of competing discourses every time they speak or write. I have indicated that multiple, shifting discourses underpinned workers' understandings (or not) of the broader structures.

The location of workers in organizations, the complexity of the social service system, the political and economic environment with its politics of scarcity, the move towards a more market-driven system, and the emphasis on individualism and governmentality all significantly impacted on a workers' abilities to act in ways that they perceived as ethical. Those factors *are the very material* that results in the inevitability of ethical trespass. But workers are both a part of the creation of those structures and victims of them. They contribute to the creation of a social order which "*artificially* favors some makings and discourages or confounds others" (Orlie, 1997, p.18, italics in the original). Their discourses on macro structures influenced their understanding of 'ethics' and created what was taken as 'ethics.' Yet, with social justice as a key value, social work must be seen as both a moral and a political enterprise (Chu, Tsui, and Chan, 2009). Consequently, to move towards more ethical practice requires incorporating a full examination of workers' constitutions of these relations of power and the institutions in which they occur to begin to adequately address the reduction of trespasses.

Given the pervasiveness and strength of macro structures, their absence from workers' discourses is striking. Placing the onus on individuals rather than structural inequities allows the deeper structures that support dominant ideologies of capitalism and patriarchy to be maintained (Rossiter, Walsh-Bower, and Prilleltensky, 1996) and exonerates workers from responsibilities to fight inequitable structures (Weinberg, 2010). Charlotte made a distinction between her own agentic potential and the structures in which she operated. She stated, "I don't have power necessarily to change the whole system … [but], I do have control over myself." In this instance she viewed herself as distinct from the systems in which she worked, but did not understand her job as encompassing work to change structural aspects in the maternity home or that in each intervention she made, she contributed to the structures that affected practice.

Theorists have argued that there has been a withering of the political and moral underpinnings that have defined social work as a profession (Chu, Tsui, and Yan, 2009; Parton, 2000). Leonard (1990, p.9) argued that the impulse to social justice has been "subordinated to a technical practice from which these moral concerns seem to have been evacuated." He opined that the field has become disillusioned and overwhelmed by powerlessness. For social workers, according to Leonard (1990, p.12), this crisis of welfare is as much ideological as a crisis of resources, including personal ones. Most people desire to be liked and respected. Generally, to live comfortable lives, workers require the financial stability and remuneration that their employment provides. Workers must protect themselves from harm and the complexities of operating in an environment with limited resources, increasing need, massive expectations, serious consequences to poor decision-making, and considerable monitoring. Their practice, moreover, is taking place in an atmosphere that is suspicious, devaluing, and unsupportive of the work being done. Thus the possibility for discrepant and divergent thinking is reduced, as well as the potential for creative problem solving.

Multiple rationales were articulated by participants that explained accommodations, compromises, or 'playing it safe' around ethical decisions such as loss of credibility, fear of losing one's job, the 'contamination factor,' referred to above, not being in the decision-making position given the hierarchical nature of their positioning, exhaustion, fear of liability, loyalty to one's agency and/or co-workers, and concern about providing consistent responses to all clients.

At the same time, it is clear from the cases discussed here, that workers are not automatons without agency nor are they simply technocrats following orders and policies handed down from on high. Subjectivity is a shifting canvas. At times workers acquiesced, but at others, they used discretion and creativity, and took risks to work around constraints. Sometimes they drew on discourses that identified the macro factors influencing practice. The next chapter will explore those discourses and the ways that workers moved beyond the limitations to resist, finding alternatives that edged towards what they believed were more ethical choices.

Bibliography

Armitage, A. (2003). *Social Welfare in Canada*. (4th ed.). Toronto: Oxford University Press.

Aronson, J., and Sammon, S. (2000). Practice and social service cuts and restructuring. Working with the contradictions of "small victories." *Canadian Social Work Review*, 17(2), 167–87.

Aronson, J., and Smith, K. (2010). Managing restructured social services: Expanding the social? *British Journal of Social Work*, 40, 530–47.

Baines, C., Evans, P., and Neysmith, S. (1991). Caring: Its impact on the lives of women. In C. Baines, P. Evans, and S. Neysmith (Eds.), *Women's Caring. Feminist Perspectives on Social Welfare* (pp.11–35). Toronto: McClelland and Stewart.

Baines, D., Cunningham, I., and Fraser, H. (2011). Constrained by managerialism: Caring as participation in the voluntary social services. *Economic and Industrial Democracy*, 32, 329–52.

Baines, D., Davis, J.M., and Saini, M. (2009). Wages, working conditions, and restructuring in Ontario's social work profession. *Canadian Social Work Review*, 26(1), 59–72.

Baker, M. (1992). The adequacy of existing social programs for Canadian families: Trends in emerging needs. In T.M. Hunsley (Ed.), *Social Policy in the Global Economy* (pp.67–79). Kingston, Ontario: School of Social Policy Studies, Queens University.

Bakker, I. (1996). Introduction: The gendered foundations of restructuring in Canada. In I. Bakker (Ed.), *Rethinking Restructuring: Gender and Change in Canada* (pp.3–25). Toronto: University of Toronto Press.

Banks, S. (2011). Ethics in an age of austerity: Social work and the evolving new public management. *Journal of Social Intervention: Theory and Practice*, 20(2), 5–23. Available at: <http://www.journalsi.org/index.php/si/index> (Accessed January 4, 2016).

Brodie, M.J., and Bakker, I. (2007). *Canadian Social Policy Regime and Women: An Assessment of the Last Decade*. Ottawa: Status of Women.

CBC (2001, April 12). Jury rules baby's starvation death a homicide. Available at: <http://www.cbc.ca/news/canada/jury-rules-baby-s-starvation-death-a-homicide-1.264770> (Accessed January 4, 2016).

Chappell, R. (2014). *Social Welfare in Canada* (5th ed.). Toronto: Nelson Education.

Child and Family Services Act: 1990. Revised. (1996). Toronto: Queens Park Printer of Ontario.

Chu, W.C.K., Tsui, M.-S., and Yan, M.-C. (2009). Social work as a moral and political practice. *International Social Work*, 52(3), 287–98.

Clarke, J. (2004). *Changing Welfare, Changing States: New Directions in Social Policy*. London, England: SAGE

Cohen, M.B. (1998). Perceptions of power in client/worker relationships. *Families in Society*, 79(4), 433–42.

Cool, J. (July 29, 2010). *Wage Gap Between Men and Women*. Background paper. Publication number: 2010-30-E. Ottawa: Library of Parliament. Social Affairs Division. Available at: <http://www.parl.gc.ca/content/lop/researchpublications/2010-30-e.pdf> (Accessed January 4, 2016).

Davies, L. (1990). Limits of bureaucratic control: Social workers in child welfare. In L. Davies, and E. Shragge (Eds.), *Bureaucracy and Community. Essays on the Politics of Social Work Practice* (pp.81–101). Montreal: Black Rose Books.

DeRose, L., Corcuera, P., Gas, M., Fernandez, L.C.M., Salazar, A., and Tarud, C, (2014). Essay: Family instability and early childhood health in the developing world. In *Mapping Family Change and Child Well-being Outcomes. World Family Map*. Available at: <http://worldfamilymap.org/2014/articles/family-instability-and-early-childhood-health> (Accessed June 9, 2015).

Dunlop, J.M. (2009). Social policy devolution: A historical review of Canada, the United Kingdom, and the United States (1834–1999). *Social Work in Public Health*, 24, 191–209.

Edelman, M. (1988). *Constructing the Political Spectacle*. Chicago: University of Chicago Press.

Evans, P.M., and Wekerle, G.R. (1997). The shifting terrain of women's welfare: Theory, discourse, and activism. In P.M. Evans, and G.R. Wekerle (Eds.), *Women and the Canadian Welfare State. Challenges and Change* (pp.3–27). Toronto: University of Toronto Press.

Evans, T. (2010). *Professional Discretion in Welfare Services. Beyond Street-level Bureaucracy*. Burlington, VT: Ashgate.

Evans, T. (2011). Professionals, managers and discretion: Critiquing street-level bureaucracy. *British Journal of Social Work*, 41(2), 368–86. DOI: 10.1093/bjsw/bcq074.

Ferguson, K.M. (2012). Children in and of the street. In L.M. Healy, and R.J. Link (Eds.), *Handbook of International Social Work* (pp.160–65). Oxford: Oxford University Press.

Flynn, N. (2000). Managerialism and public services: Some international trends. In J. Clarke, S. Gewirtz, and E. McLaughlin (Eds.), *New Managerialism New Welfare?* (pp.6–27). London, England: SAGE.

Foucault, M. (1977). *Discipline and Punish. The Birth of the Prison* (A. Sheridan, Trans.) (2nd ed.). New York: Vintage Books. (Original work published in 1975)

Foucault, M. (1978). *The History of Sexuality. An Introduction. Vol.1*. (R. Hurley, Trans.). New York: Vintage Books. (Original work published in 1976)

Hair, H.J. (2014). Power relations in supervision: Preferred practices according to social workers. *Families in Society*, 95(2), 107–14.

Hoge, M.A., Migdole, S., Cannata, E., and Powell, D.J. (2014). Strengthening supervision in systems of care: Exemplary practices in empirically supported treatments. *Clinical Social Work Journal*, 42, 171–81.

Hugman, R. (2010). *Understanding International Social Work. A Critical Analysis*. New York: Palgrave Macmillan.

Imada, A. (1997). Changes to welfare legislation in Ontario: How much worse can it get? *Kinesis*, July/August, 5.

Jones, K.B. (1988). On authority: Or, why women are not entitled to speak. In I. Diamond, and L. Quinby (Eds.), *Feminism and Foucault. Reflections on Resistance* (pp.119–33). Boston: Northeastern University Press.

Johnson, J.T., and Bird, M.Y. (2012). Indigenous peoples and cultural survival. In L.M. Healy, and R.J. Link (Eds.), *Handbook of International Social Work* (pp.208–13). Oxford: Oxford University Press

Kondrat, M.E. (2002). Actor-centred social work: Re-visioning "person-in-environment" through a critical theory lens. *Social Work*, 47(4), 435–48.

Lawrence, M. (1992). Women's psychology and feminist social work practice. In M. Langan, and L. Day. (Eds.), *Women, Oppression, and Social Work. Issues in Anti-discriminatory Practice* (pp.32–47). New York: Routledge.

Leonard, P. (1990). Fatalism and the discourse on power: An introductory essay. In L. Davies, and E. Shragge (Eds.), *Bureaucracy and Community. Essays on the Politics of Social Work Practice* (pp.9–23). Montreal: Black Rose Books.

Lightman, E.S., and Riches, G. (2009). Canada: One step forward, two steps back? In P. Alcock, and G. Craig (Eds.), *International Social Policy Welfare Regimes in the Developed World* (pp.45–65). (2nd ed.). New York: Palgrave MacMillan.

Lipsky, M. (1980). *Street-level Bureaucracy. Dilemmas of the Individual in Public Service.* New York, NY: Russell Sage Foundation.

Luong, M. (May 2008). Life after teenage motherhood. *Perspectives on Labour and Income*, Statistics Canada, Vol. 9(5), Catalogue no. 75-001-X. Available at: <http://www.statcan.gc.ca/pub/75-001-x/2008105/article/10577-eng.htm> (Accessed January 4, 2016).

MacArthur, K. (1997, July 9).Women rely more on government transfers. *Globe and Mail*, pp. Metro A6.

Mandell, D. (2002). *"Deadbeat Dads." Subjectivity and Social Construction.* Toronto: University of Toronto Press.

Mapp, S. (2012a). Status of women. In L.M. Healy, and R.J. Link (Eds.), *Handbook of International Social Work* (pp.249–53). Oxford: Oxford University Press.

Mapp, S. (2012b). Violence against women. In L.M. Healy, and R.J. Link (Eds.), *Handbook of International Social Work* (pp.260–64). Oxford: Oxford University Press.

Margolin, L. (1997). *Under the Cover of Kindness. The Invention of Social Work.* Charlottesville: University Press of Virginia.

McAuliffe, D., and Sudbery, J. (2005). "Who do I tell?" Support and consultation in cases of ethical conflict. *Journal of Social Work*, (5)1, 21–43.

Midgely, J. (2000). Globalization, capitalism and social welfare. Social work and globalization. Special Issue. *Canadian Social Work*, 2(1), 13–28.

Nadkarni, V., and Dhaske G. (2012). Poverty and human needs. In L.M. Healy, and R.J. Link (Eds.), *Handbook of International Social Work* (pp.232–6). Oxford: Oxford University Press.

Newell, J.M., and MacNeil G.A. (2010). Professional burnout, vicarious trauma, secondary traumatic stress, and compassion fatigue: A review of theoretical terms, risk factors, and preventative measures for clinicians and researchers. *Best Practices in Mental Health*, 6(2), 57–68.

Noble, C., and Irwin, J. (2009). Social work supervision. An exploration of the current challenges of a rapidly changing social, economic, and political environment. *Journal of Social Work*, 9(3), 345–58.

Ontario Works Policy Directives. Ministry of Community and Social Services (2008). *Learning, Earning and Parenting Programme.* Available at: <http://www.mcss.gov.on.ca/documents/en/mcss/social/directives/ow/0802.pdf> (Accessed January 4, 2016).

Orlie, M.A. (1997). *Living Ethically. Acting Politically.* Ithaca: Cornell University Press.

Parton, N. (1996a). Social theory, social change and social work. An introduction. In N. Parton (Ed.), *Social Theory, Social Change and Social Work* (pp.4–18). New York: Routledge.

Parton, N. (2000). Some thoughts on the relationship between theory and practice in and for social work. *British Journal of Social Work*, 30, 449–63.

Parton, N., and O'Byrne, P. (2000). *Constructive Social Work. Towards a New Practice*. London: MacMillan.

Raychaba. B. (1993). *Pain Lots of Pain. Family Violence and Abuse in the Lives of Young People in Care*. Ottawa: National Youth In Care Network.

Razack, N. (2012). Racism and antiracist strategies. In L.M. Healy, and R.J. Link (Eds.), *Handbook of International Social Work* (pp.237–42). Oxford: Oxford University Press.

Regehr, C., Bernstein, M.M., and Kanani, K. (2001). Liability for child welfare social workers. Weighing the risks. *Canadian Social Work*, 3(2), 57–67.

Rice, J.J. and Prince, M.J. (2013). *Changing Politics of Canadian Social Policy* (2nd ed.). Toronto, ON: University of Toronto Press.

Rock, L.F. (2012). Child abuse and neglect. In L.M. Healy, and R.J. Link (Eds.), *Handbook of International Social Work* (pp.142–7). Oxford: Oxford University Press.

Rogowski, S. (2011). Managers, managerialism and social work with children and families: The deformation of a profession? *Practice: Social Work in Action*, 23(3), 157–67.

Rose, N. (1996). The death of the social? Re-figuring the territory of government. *Economy and Society*, 25(3), 327–56.

Rossiter, A. (1986). *In Private: An Inquiry into the Construction of Women's Experience of Early Motherhood* (Unpublished doctoral dissertation). University of Toronto, Toronto, Ontario, Canada.

Rossiter, A., Prilleltensky, I., and Walsh-Bowers, R. (2000). A postmodern perspective on professional ethics. In B. Fawcett, B. Featherstone, J. Fook, and A. Rossiter (Eds.), *Practice and Research in Social Work* (pp.83–103). New York: Routledge.

Rossiter, A., Walsh-Bowers, R., and Prilleltensky, I. (1996). Learning from broken rules: Individualism, bureaucracy, and ethics. *Ethics and Behavior*, 6(4), 307–20.

Thomas, R., and Davies, A. (2005a). Theorizing the micro-politics of resistance: New public management and managerial identities in the UK public services. *Organization Studies*, 26, 683–706. DOI: 10.1177/0170840605051821.

Wakefield, J.C. (1998). Foucauldian fallacies: An essay review of Leslie Margolin's *Under the Cover of Kindness*. *Social Service Review*, 72, 545–87.

Weinberg, M. (2005). The mother menagerie: Animal metaphors in the social work relationship with young single mothers. *Critical Social Work*, 6(1). Available at: <http://www1.uwindsor.ca/criticalsocialwork/the-mother-menagerie-animal-metaphores-in-the-social-work-relationship-with-young-single-mothers> (Accessed January 4, 2016).

Weinberg, M. (2010). The social construction of social work ethics: Politicizing and broadening the lens. *Journal of Progressive Human Services*, 21(1), 32–44.

Weinberg, M. (2014). The ideological dilemma of subordination of the self versus self care: Identity construction of the "ethical social worker." *Discourse & Society*, 25(1), 84–99.

Weinberg, M., and Campbell, C. (2014). From codes to contextual collaborations: Shifting the thinking about ethics in social work. *Journal of Progressive Human Services*, 25(1), 37–49.

Weinberg, M., and Taylor, S. (2014). "Rogue" social workers: The problem with rules for ethical behaviour. *Critical Social Work*, 15(1), 74–86.

Williams, L.O. (2012). Youth. In L.M. Healy, and R.J. Link (Eds.), *Handbook of International Social Work* (pp.265–72). Oxford: Oxford University Press.

Workfare Watch. [Issue #6]. (1997, December). Toronto: Community Social Planning Council.

Chapter 5
Mitigating Trespass

Introduction

The previous chapters have examined the inevitability of trespass. In this chapter, we will look at the possibilities for reducing trespass. In each moment of a helping relationship, a worker 'chooses', or not, to take up a subject position that is preferred and ego-syntonic. I put quotes around 'chooses' because I do not believe that these actions are necessarily consciously or overtly perceived as a choice, but at those moments, 'x' rather than 'y' occurs. Those take-ups represent the agency of the worker and construct the multiplicity of forms of help. They also represent the infinite possible subject positions of the helper. Butler (1995, p.46) remarks, "[T]o claim that the subject is constituted is not to claim that it is determined; on the contrary, the constituted character of the subject is the very precondition of its agency." In other words, because subjectivity is constructed, individuals have the possibility of altering the subject positions they take up.

Paradoxes in practice, by their very nature of being contradictory, open the way for multiple and consequently, alternate courses of action, some of which may be more liberatory than others (Davies, 2000). At the same time, with the paradoxes I have examined, what often constructs them as ethical dilemmas is that no route to resolution is entirely satisfactory from the standpoint of trespass. Only edging towards a reduction of trespass is feasible.

I have argued that institutional systems and structural inequalities profoundly influence the likelihood of workers controlling clients and of perceiving themselves to be controlled as well. However, Connell (as cited in Davies, 2000, p.68) suggests, "though one can never escape structure, structures are constituted through practice and practice can always be turned against structure." How workers interpret the institutional regimes – the policies, procedures, legislation, and funding expectations, as well as structural factors such as race, not only impact on what positioning they take up for themselves and their clients, but create the notion of 'help' in that instant in time and become the structures and discourses of that society.

In this chapter, I will examine workers' resistances to institutional regimes at the levels of the self, interpersonally, and politically. What are resistances? Foucault (1978, p.96) proposed that resistance is, "the odd term in relations of power; they are inscribed in the latter as an irreducible opposite." Resistances are practices that subvert and redirect power, representing the possibility of humans to transform society. There cannot be power without resistance, suggesting that domination is never total nor static (Giroux, 2001). Resistance provokes modifications and transformations both in the helping relationship (Knights and Vurdubakis, 1994) and in the management of one's own identity (Thomas and Davies, 2005a).

But resistance can work in the service of the status quo as well, since it is "never in a position of exteriority in relation to power" (Foucault, 1978, p.95). For example, in the case of Shari, Jannie resisted her supervisor's attempts to interpret policy more broadly. Because of Jannie's belief in the importance of a homogenous response, her resistance was designed to ensure compliance, thereby maintaining the power differential between Shari and staff.

Given my social justice goals, the emphasis in this chapter is on those aspects of resistance where a querying of the potential destructiveness of taken-for-granted notions occurred. Resistance includes thinking critically, reflecting on oneself and one's work, and acting 'outside the box.'

Resistance means exceeding "the commands of common sense" (Orlie, 1997, p.191). It offers glimpses in gaps or inequalities of dominant narratives and a commitment to undo their perpetuation. It proposes alternatives to inequities. Giroux (2001, p.111) argued

> the ultimate value of the notion of resistance has to be measured against the degree to which it not only prompts critical thinking and reflective action, but, more importantly, against the degree to which it contains the possibility of galvanizing collective political struggle around the issues of power and social determination.

For this chapter, two theoretical approaches have been used. Structural approaches which focus on collective acts and protest, and post-structural theories which target "challenging subjectivities and meanings" (Thomas and Davies, 2005b, p.715).

The dilemma of the elaboration that follows is that suggesting what approaches workers took to ameliorate trespass can then become themselves disciplinary practices through the implied assumptions that these actions are the correct and required actions. I am creating a discursive field about ethics that has its own limitations and exclusions. There can be no place of blamelessness. Any articulations of what is 'better' or more 'liberatory' does, in fact, ultimately produce its own forms of trespass. One feature that is significant is the context for practitioners. But any delineation on my part omits this key ingredient for individuals reading this text because they will have their own contexts to consider.

Nonetheless, I would argue that some information, albeit, partial and inadequate, is preferable to saying the problem is great, but you are on your own to solve it. This chapter is intended to be more illustrative than prescriptive. Social work is an applied science requiring concrete solutions, not just theoretical discussion. In part, the decision to submit ideas about the minimization of trespass comes from my need to offer hope and my belief that practitioners, with understanding, may do better in their attempts, despite the recognition that the issues are ultimately unsolvable. Consequently, in the face of this irresolvable challenge, this chapter is about my own judgment regarding what is less harmful; pointing in the direction of what I believe could create more ethical practice with clients.

I will begin with another of Patricia's stories. The risk of using one worker's narrative is that it suggests that Patricia was the most ethical in her work. In an attempt to correct that possible misimpression, in the discussion section I have used examples from other workers, since no worker is ever solely innocent or guilty of trespass. However, I believe this case illustrates an array of tactics of resistance and therefore, is useful for developing the ideas in this chapter.

Patricia's Story of Tanesha[1]

Client Behaviour – Dishonesty/Alcohol Use

Tanesha was a 17-year-old woman of colour, whom Patricia had been working with for over a year at the point our interviews began. Tanesha, "had been through the child welfare system herself as a child, and had been in and out of group homes and detention," "never finished high school" and had been "in prison."

When she was 16 she met her boyfriend, Lionel, who was quite a bit older. While "handsome and quite a smooth talker," he too had a "rap sheet" and drank "a lot." Their relationship was "very volatile."

Tanesha was referred to Patricia because "she had given birth to her son three-and-a-half months early." He "weighed a pound-and-a-half" and Tanesha "basically had no supports except for her boyfriend who really wasn't all that supportive." Tanesha was less involved with the baby than the medical and social service staff evaluated was necessary. Their concerns were that "she wasn't going to the hospital enough. She wasn't bonding with the baby."

While the baby was still in hospital, Tanesha told Patricia, "she couldn't go [to visit] because she didn't have any tokens" for public transportation. Accordingly, Patricia gave her "a week's worth" of bus tokens. One "freezing" day, Patricia agreed to accompany Tanesha to the hospital. According to Patricia, Tanesha said, "Let's take a taxi." When Patricia responded, "I don't have money to take taxi," Tanesha stated, "I've got ... money" and pulled out "this big wad of cash." Patricia retorted, "you know what, you little liar, you give me back all my tokens right now" and Tanesha answered, "okay ... I guess I shouldn't have pulled out" all the money. While they were both laughing, Patricia clarified, "I am not joking. You have enough money there to buy a roll of tokens ... Those are for ... people who really need them." So Tanesha returned the tokens.

Despite predictions of the medical establishment, the baby flourished and the plan was to release him from the hospital. Tanesha "had been drinking a lot." Her "father had been calling the hospital ... saying that ... [Tanesha] was a really disturbed kid and did a lot of drugs and alcohol and they shouldn't release the

---

1   For an elaboration of this case, see Weinberg, M. (2006). Pregnant with possibility: The paradoxes of "help" as anti-oppression and discipline with a young single mother. *Families in Society,* April–June, 87(2), 161–9.

baby to her." Both the father and the hospital contacted the CAS. Because of her drinking, Patricia also made a referral to the CAS. Shortly thereafter, while Tanesha "wasn't exactly thrilled!" with Patricia, she contacted her, saying she understood why Patricia had called the CAS and "she wanted a referral for treatment." So Patricia "made a referral to a programme." Tanesha followed through, although "she didn't see [the] worker consistently."

Notwithstanding Tanesha's attempts to change, the baby was eventually apprehended. After the apprehension, for a period of time, Tanesha did "really well." But when the baby was about 8 months, Tanesha began to "screw up" again. For example, the CAS made an appointment for her to take the baby to get his immunizations. Despite saying that she had gone, Tanesha had not taken the baby to the doctor, then lied, making up a whole story. Also "she was drinking a bit more." Patricia believed that her behaviour at that juncture was "kind of the beginning of the end for her."

CAS personnel "were deciding … whether to go for crown[2] wardship" and Tanesha's father re-contacted the Children's Aid, saying he "wanted custody of the baby." Lionel "had stopped going" to visits, but he "really blamed" Tanesha for the loss of the child. He too, decided to go for "lone custody of the baby."

The CAS awarded the baby to Tanesha's father and his girlfriend. When the CAS worker announced this to Tanesha, "she cried" like Patricia had "never (!) heard anybody cry." The next day, Tanesha fell apart and got very drunk. Lionel, worried, called Patricia, asking her to go to Tanesha's apartment. During the visit, Tanesha said "'I can't believe: my dad is getting my son.'" With prompting from Patricia, Tanesha disclosed that her father had sexually abused her. Despite her history of dishonesty, when Tanesha divulged this information, Patricia believed her and reported this disclosure to the CAS. But they did not judge it was the truth.

By the end of my interviews with Patricia, she evaluated that Tanesha was still drinking but she was attempting to limit it in an effort to get the baby back. Tanesha was trying to turn her life around, walking everywhere, losing some weight, not smoking, and going to an employment-counselling group.

Tanesha viewed her father's girlfriend as "a good person who would watch out for" the baby and that since he was male "nothing [would] happen to him." These statements implied a concern about the abuse she had suffered as a child but a hope that the girlfriend would protect her son from fate similar to her own. She wanted to "still see him."

Interpretation of Client Behaviour – History of Trauma/Fear of Bonding/Racism/ Unsupportive System

Patricia's understanding of Tanesha was that she had an extremely traumatic early history of abandonment, geographic dislocation, and rejection, with a mother who

---

2   Permanent wardship by the state, which has legal responsibility for the protection of children.

had a "substance abuse problem," and a father who sexually abused her. The other children in her family were perceived as "perfect kids" while Tanesha was seen as the "scoundrel."

Patricia speculated that drug use, as well as domestic violence between Lionel and Tanesha, might have precipitated Tanesha's premature labour.

Patricia evaluated that Tanesha was "quite an expert at lying ... it was one of her ... strengths." I asked her to explain her use of the word "strength" she responded that "it was how [Tanesha] survived ... her whole life, she was so skilled and ... believable and ... likeable." Patricia stated it "was really her coping strategy."

In making sense of Tanesha's avoidance of visits at the hospital, Patricia questioned whether a component was "not wanting to bond with the baby" in case he died "because he was so tiny." She also speculated that racism was "part of the reason ... she ... didn't want to go to the hospital ... because it was ... so blatant."

As in the case of Kelly and Marshall, Patricia felt that the "system" was part of the problem. For example, in describing why the nurses dumped Tanesha's breast milk, Patricia assessed that not only was it because she was "drinking a lot," and "smelling of alcohol," but it was a "compete judgment because she was young" and not going to the hospital "enough! for their ... liking."

Strategies of Help and Justifications

Patricia utilized many of the same strategies that she had employed in the case discussed in Chapter 4: supporting and emphasizing strengths, building trust, advocating, surveillance, confrontation, and setting limits. Similarly, her justifications were comparable to those in the previous narrative: mandated responsibility, professional obligation, the safety of the child, and ameliorating the effects of a punitive system. Therefore, I will only elaborate on these issues as they arise in the following discussion.

The remainder of this chapter will explore those conditions that may contribute to reducing trespass, starting with a discussion that problematizes the helping relationship.

Discussion

Problematization of the Helping Relationship

Privilege

Reduction of trespass requires inquiring what privileges the dominant have been able to accrue and preserve by their positioning. It is important to recognize that "*unearned advantage* and *conferred dominance*" (McIntosh, 1992, p.78, italics in the original) can foster the maintenance of the status quo at the expense of clients. Charlotte demonstrated that awareness when she spoke about workers having a "very white middle-class perspective on the job ... . We talk about ... privilege.

We come from a position of power, entitlement. I think that ... we have to be very conscious of our own location." Moreover, the subject position of 'professional' carries the risk of separating individuals from their personal values, potentially diminishing the independent and critical thinking needed to make ethical decisions (Kendall and Hugman, 2013).

Polakow (1995, p.268) added, "Countless middle-class people in the human services professions have built their careers as the direct beneficiaries of poverty." In Chapter 2, Frieda acknowledged this consciousness when she articulated that part of the rationale for the administrator's belief that Trina should return to the maternity home was the need for the monetary benefits for the residence when young mothers returned after the delivery of their babies.

Attentiveness to privilege must extend to being accountable for unjust gain. Utilizing a concept from Sandra Harding, Heldke (1998, p.90) avers that those who are "overprivileged" should attempt to undo those very systems that overprivilege them, becoming "responsible traitors." Accountability requires recognizing the needs and situation of the Other as potentially distinct and separate from the self, including the prospect that the Other does not share the benefits of one's own positioning. One such privilege is that of privacy, which shields the middle-class from surveillance. When Patricia said, "I can go home and close my door," she was acknowledging the contrast between the lack of scrutiny of her mothering practices and the extensive observation of her clients.

Being a responsible traitor must extend particularly towards those who suffer as a consequence of that overprivilege. Identification of the impact of institutionalized social exclusion and workers' privileged position as contributing to that exclusion are important ingredients. For example, Frieda described the expectation that the young mothers gather together a layette as one indicator that they are prepared for and able to mother. Not obtaining these purchases could be used as data that the child would be deprived, linking poverty with unfit mothering. De Montigny (1995, p.105) states, "social workers recognize the preponderance of 'poor' and 'minority' people among the reported cases of child abuse, yet their methods preclude recognizing the phenomenon they observe may be an artifact of their own institutionally grounded practices." Frieda recognized this conundrum and changed the maternity home parenting curriculum to reduce expectations on young mothers around the purchase of 'needed' articles for their newborns.

Another task in being a responsible traitor is engaging in actions that seek to unbalance and undermine that privilege (Heldke, 1998, p.97). In one instance, Tanesha decided she wanted to return to school and was required to meet with a guidance counselor to re-enroll. Patricia used her own dominant position to support Tanesha's budding awareness of issues of advantage when she asked Tanesha if she should accompany her to the appointment. According to Patricia, Tanesha replied: "oh yeah ... It doesn't hurt to have a big mouth, white woman with a business card." To which Patricia "started laughing and ... said that's good and [Tanesha] said, 'well, you're (!) the one who taught me that.'"

There has long been a debate about the potential of front-line workers to have discretion in fulfilling their responsibilities (Evans, 2010; Lipsky, 1980; Weinberg and Taylor, 2014), particularly in the neoliberal environment. Some theorists (Aronson and Sammon, 2000; Carey and Foster, 2011) found that workers were cut off and saw practice problems as individual dilemmas rather than as part of broader systems. And studies have suggested a variable picture of the relationship with managers in the neoliberal environment (Aronson and Smith, 2010; Evans, 2011). Nonetheless, in this research, workers spoke little of turning to others for input and support, suggesting a picture of isolation. However, in this study there were many instances of workers acting like responsible traitors.

Power and Authority

A problematization of power and authority in the helping relationship is another indispensable aspect of trespass reduction as Patricia demonstrated in this attitude towards her clients:

> I can give you [a client] some professional ... advice or the educational piece but you're really the expert of your child ... I think a lot of people who work in the field really see themselves as the expert of all children and you know, "I'm better than you because – I went to school or I work here – I'm not a pregnant teenager."

One aspect of professionals' power and authority is the mandate to determine what constitutes a problem. Questioning *authority* is central to finding alternative ways of practising. Asking who has defined it as such, and why it is perceived as a problem, sows the seeds for contesting and disrupting the interpretation of the norm by allowing for the examination of what stake that person may have had in defining the problem in a particular fashion and what benefits may have been garnered from that construction. In a workshop Kristine attended, she used a metaphor of a raccoon in a garage as an example of the possibility of questioning the framing of what constitutes a problem. The facilitator queried, "There's a raccoon in a garage. What are you going to do about it?" Kristine's first impression was, "who says it's the raccoon [that is] the problem."

Assessment, an integral component of the helping relationship, is, in part, a process of problem definition. Depth of field in photography is a useful metaphor. It is the zone of sharpness around the subject on which the lens is focused. Broadening depth of field by understanding the underlying dynamics of a client's behaviour, including political, structural and historical analyses, contribute to becoming a responsible traitor, since these analyses tend to provide explanations that expand workers' sensitivity beyond what they may have evaluated as inadequate or problematic functioning on the part of their clients, to see problems as systemic rather than solely intrapsychic.

To illustrate, Patricia was looking for explanations that allowed her to understand, from Tanesha's perspective, the barriers that prevented her from meeting the institutional expectations of making hospital visits. She stated, "I ...

made a ... point to ... explore with her why she wasn't going to the hospital." Patricia was aware not only of familial dysfunction, violence, and drug abuse for Tanesha; but also of racism, structural inadequacy, and injustice. All these factors played a part in her explanations of Tanesha's behaviour; and led her to view Tanesha as strong to have survived under these conditions. Patricia said, "the more I ... found out about her life and her childhood, I could see that ... her excellent ... skills at lying were just really what kept her going."

I will come back to this case illustration below. But now I would like to explore workers' responses to difference as another means to reduce trespass.

Response to Difference

Self and Others

At the heart of an interrelation between the self and the Other is a dilemma regarding difference: recognizing ourselves and our similarities in the Other, but also knowing we can never entirely know the Other. The response one takes to that dilemma entails risks. In this study, when workers expressed an attitude of 'there but for the grace of God go I,' there tended to be a coming closer to the young moms, due to having experienced some of these hardships for the workers themselves. In describing her early history, Kristine said, "I had people that could prevent me from going to the streets but ... it's not that far away. Like you can end up there very quickly."

At the same time, similar experience does not guarantee that kind of sensibility. One risk is denial of difference. A stance workers can construct from having had comparable life experiences is to assume that, since they were able to be successful, others should be as well.

Another risk in seeing difference as difference is to take oneself as the norm. This can lead to exoticizing, pitying, or abhorring the Other.

An additional risk is appropriating another's difference as one's own without due acknowledgement. This type of risk has been particularly problematic for First Nations' communities that rightly feel that their customs, knowledges, material possessions and even human remains have been taken by the dominant culture without permission or the appropriate training that should accompany particular rituals or customs.

We are limited in our knowledge of the Other by context and by representational systems such as discourse, which are always partial, and omit as well as define. Consequently, another peril is totalizing, or essentializing, taking one aspect of difference as the whole of that individual.

Certainty that we understand is also problematic because, according to Cornell (1992, p.57), "it turns against the generous impulse to open oneself up to the Other, and to truly listen, to risk the chance that we might be wrong."

But even valuing of difference can be tricky. As Minow suggests, "the stigma of difference may be recreated both by ignoring and by focusing on it" (as cited in Meyers, 1994, p.4). Kristine was well aware of that in her relationship with

Jessica. She fretted about raising the issue of race in her sessions. Kristine feared, "if I address it ... have I made an issue out of nothing?" However to appreciate and prize diversity is not easy without making it inappropriately the core of another's subjectivity.

All of these risks lead to misunderstanding and the potential to trespass.

These perils are amplified in hierarchical relations, such as in social work. Professionalism, with its implied authority and expertise, can also include a belief in one's right to articulate difference as pathological or criminal through processes of normalization, discipline and governmentality.

Whiteness and Difference

White social workers have particular challenges in working with difference, since the profession of social work is founded on whiteness as the norm. Racism and other relationships of difference are historically constructed processes through which domination and oppression are maintained (Yee, 2005). And our institutional structures have been established in ways that perpetuate white dominance and countenance racism; viewing racialized others as inferior or pathological (Razack and Jeffery, 2002). We have had illustrations of this phenomenon, particularly in Chapter 3 when we looked at who is judged; namely single, often racialized or minoritized, impoverished young mothers. Consequently, how do white professionals help those who do not meet social work benchmarks without contributing to the maintenance of racialized standards and contributing to the Othering of clients (Sakamoto, 2007)?

One gesture is to recognize the importance of the language. Jannie said:

> I ... think that the more you ... use the politically correct, the more sensitive lingo, the more ... tentative kind of approach; I think ... that really influences your practice. And the more you practice in that way you'll receive a different response from your clients.

Kristine queried whether it was bias on her part to use the term "mixed breed" when this had not been Jessica's preferred term. She also expressed anxiety about initiating discussion about Jessica's mixed race because she did not want to make Jessica feel she needed "to be white for" Kristine.

At the same time, Kristine stopped short of recognizing the privilege that came with her own fair skin. An examination of the privilege of Kristine's whiteness was avoided and consequently, she was able to maintain blamelessness from trespass. Kristine was not alone in failing to undertake this exploration. Frankenberg has proposed that whiteness is characterized as content-free and unnamed, effects of its dominance (1993). With the exception of Patricia, the other workers in this study did not confront with any regularity the implications of their whiteness in the maintenance of structures of oppression and privilege. Furthermore, in the cultural competence approach to difference, it has often been assumed that white workers can transcend their own culture, while clients do not (Yan and Wong, 2005).

Unsettling the understanding of the positionality of white workers requires disturbing the notion of 'virtue' that lies at the heart of social work identity (Jeffery, 2005, p.415). However, that creates another dilemma; namely, what happens to conceptions of competence and ethics if professionals cannot feel that they are good people (Jeffery, 2005).

It is important to see racism as relations of domination rather than personality traits (Razack and Jeffery, 2002). Otherwise, with the recognition of one's white guilt, how are white workers to reconstruct a sense of self without repudiating the historical and cultural context that is a component of one's identity (Alcoff, 1998)?

The deconstruction of binaries of all differences, and race cognizance in particular, are necessary steps in the minimization of trespass. Alcoff (1998, p.25) suggests that whites in particular must work on a "double-consciousness," which involves an acknowledgement of the legacy of the past on which current structures of inequality exist today, at the same time as one moves towards the future of social transformation in which racism is eliminated. In this way, there will be the possibility of "collective self-respect" (p.25) as the basis for white identity. Had Kristine understood that while she was not individually culpable for the existence of current racism and its impacts on Jessica, she could have recognized that those historical structures perpetuated the marginalized Jessica in the present and pledged herself to participate in the undoing of those structures. This would have been an example of the double-consciousness.

Teasing out the distinctions and not conflating one aspect of difference with all differences is an element in edging towards more ethical practice. In working with a Jessica who indicated self-hatred for her mixed-race heritage, Kristine tried to make a distinction between the dynamics in this client's own family and all black families. She proposed, "that's not what all black people are about. That's what your family's about."

Difference can be a "resource rather than a threat" (Sawicki, 1991, p.45) since it allows for strategic alliances of subjugated knowledges and people. By different groups such as Aboriginals, people of colour and whites banding together, a coalition that would be more powerful than one group fighting alone could be constituted to fight racism, for example.

Underpinning workers' response to difference is their management of reason and affect. The next section will investigate the complex web of emotions, judgement and empathy in practice, particularly in ethical deliberations.

Moral Link between Reason, Affect and Empathy

Empathy
What is empathy? Meyers refers to empathy as "imaginatively reconstructing another person's feelings" (1994, p.33). Alternatively, "it is the capacity to maintain a sense of self that permits the therapist, while being deeply affectively connected, to make the complex clinical judgements that must be made" (Kaplan, 1991, p.47). The affective component is an "interpenetration of feelings between

two people" (Jordan, Surrey, and Kaplan, 1991, p.46), the clues of which are physiological responses and affects. Foucault argued that feelings are the part of the self that are "most relevant to our morality" (1984, p.352) since they open opportunities for self-transformation (Zembylas, 2003a) and for resistance. Frieda demonstrated a capacity for empathy in her awareness of how wards must feel when they are being "put under a microscope." But it is not a symbiotic, regressive merger. While it is directed at the Other, it is not a matter of identification as if one were the same, but a bond with the other person.

Emotions are not just inherent personal qualities but are also shaped by institutions, culture, history, politics, and the discourses that arise in a particular period (Zembylas, 2003a). They might not occur at all had not particular discursive constructions been dominant in social work of that era or had they not created paradoxical circumstances that required resolution in practice. Thus, emotions should be understood as "both personal and social" (Zembylas, 2003b, p.112).

The constitution of the self, occurring as it does at the nodal point of conflicting or inconsistent discourses, can be emotionally fraught (Zembylas, 2003b). For example, Tanesha's mendacity about the bus tokens was a way of Tanesha saying to Patricia, 'gotcha!' you've been taken in by my play at 'poor me.' This was a test for the subject positions taken up by both Patricia and Tanesha. Someone who is a competent mental health professional is expected to be able to see beneath the surfaces of behaviour and to understand the 'true' person. While Tanesha had been caught at only playing at the 'good and needy client,' Patricia also had been caught at not being skilled enough to spot deception. Additionally, Tanesha had potentially upset the normative one-up, one-down power relationship of client and helper by undermining Patricia's authority to make determinations of who required monetary assistance.

Despite being duped, with the accompanying possibility of allowing herself to be positioned as an 'inferior worker,' Patricia refused that positioning, by reminding herself that "it wasn't directed at [her] personally." She saw the exchange as a form of "testing [Patricia] to see how much [Tanesha] could... push; to see if [Patricia] was going to get angry with her." So the subject position taken up by Patricia was one of the 'understanding' worker, rather than the 'misled,' demonstrating empathy.

Affect and Reason

Theorists (Jordan, Surrey, and Kaplan, 1991, p. 27) have proposed that empathy has both affective and cognitive components. It requires maintaining some analytical distance about what is being said, and using reasoning skills to make judgements. However, at times, discourses about objectivity clash with those regarding empathic emotional engagement, creating discrete and possibly contradictory options for the take-up of particular subject positions.

Vetlesen suggests that in empathy, "the emotional bond is not morally neutral" (1994, p.179, italics in the original) and it is this emotional bond that potentially may be violated or suspended when one adopts an attitude of objectivity. In the case of Shari, Jannie wished to view all the individual clients in a homogenous way, to ensure fairness and consistency. She was subscribing to a philosophy of "impartial reason" (Meyers, 1994). The difficulty with this position is that it does not take difference and disadvantage into account. Furthermore it "fails to accord due respect to individuals who regard their difference as central to their identity and to individuals who suffer from disabilities few others share" (Meyers, 1994, p.6). Additionally, it did not provide Shari with a voice in her exclusion. The maxim 'do unto others as you would have them do unto you' presupposes similarity and excludes the Other's point of view. It also allows those who judge to be centre and to use themselves as the moral baseline, resulting in seeing difference as inferiority or pathology (Meyers, 1994). In order to maintain equity and to respond to difference ethically, clients may require differential responses, so impartial reason is inadequate.

Broad Empathy

Instead of impartial reason, the use of broad empathy is more likely to edge towards minimizing trespass. *Broad* empathy extends beyond specific incidents to question more generally "what is it like to be you?" (Meyers, 1994, p.35) imaginatively querying the shape of someone's entire existence, including how that life is different from the professional's. This query moves an individual beyond an identification of the Other as like the self. Kristine demonstrated an ability to use broad empathy when she commented about Jessica,

> it's really hard for the women to talk about ... being resentful, of being the one who gets pregnant, has to maintain the pregnancy and change her whole life and raise a baby on her own and fight for support ... .

To approach ethical reflection, an important question that can be asked is "do you want to be the sort of person who would do such-and-such" (Meyers, 1994, p.17). Meyers elaborates, "moral judgment synthesizes empathic understanding of others with understanding of one's personal moral ideal and one's knowledge of one's options" (p.17). Consequently, it requires an individual to search for an understanding of what would constitute ethical conduct by examining one's own values, no matter what the circumstances of the Other. It calls on individuals to be the best they can be, given the current conditions.

Critical Reflection

"Feelings entail judgements about the situation eliciting them" (Vetlesen, 1994, p.215). What is significant about this claim is that it opens the individual up for reflection and the possibility of changing how one feels. Emotions are not passively beyond one's control, outside of the realm of the ethical, but a central constitutive part of the minimization of trespass.

Critical thinking requires examining one's assumptions, biases and values; scrutinizing situations from multiple perspectives; and reframing one's understanding within socio-political contexts (Chu, Tsui, and Yan, 2009). And such thinking requires self-reflexivity; asking questions about why one responded as one has, and the investment in particular self-images (Heron, 2005).

Reflexivity has been defined in multiple alternate ways in social work literature (D'Cruz, Gillingham, and Melendez, 2007). I am referring to a critical awareness by practitioners of the processes of knowledge generation and the implications of power in that creation. Kondrat suggests that for critical reflexivity, a worker must pose three types of questions regarding: 1) the world and particularly the structures that reinforce inequality; 2) an individual's world, including values and assumptions; and 3) the disjunctures and correspondences between these two worlds (1999, p.465–6).

For example, Kristine liked "to be challenged" and was receptive to looking at her own part in the helping relationship. In explaining why raising topics such as race were difficult, she questioned, "maybe I do have an issue with them," demonstrating self-reflexivity and the concern about amplifying Jessica's marginalization. In referring to Jessica as a "mixed-" rather than a "half-breed," she wondered, "have I given a message of bias?" The recognition about the impact of one's conduct on others and the feelings this evokes in the Other are variables in the potential to reduce trespass (Meyers, 1994.)

Nonetheless, some social work scholars (Heron, 2005; Margolin, 1997; Rossiter, 2001) have argued that practitioners can utilize concepts of reflection as a means of appearing egalitarian whilst obscuring the use of power and thus maintaining their 'innocence.' What was missing from Kristine's analysis about the mixed-race issue was a more contextualized understanding of the subject position of helper and the problematization of the power in that relationship. She did not ask what investment she might have in appearing as an anti-racist or what self-image she was attempting to construct (Heron, 2005).

One method of developing self-reflectivity that has the potential to address this critique is referred to as critical reflection (Fook and Gardner, 2013, Fook, 2007, Napier, 2010). It is a procedure developed in social work that emanated from the work of Schon (1983) who identified that practitioners' actual practice is often different from their espoused theories, and that one must look at the underlying assumptions and emotions that support those assumptions. The approach involves evaluating the presuppositions on which a worker's beliefs are built (Napier, 2010). It requires uncovering how, in particular situations, one makes meaning through the language utilized, unearthing the suppositions at play, and analyzing the underlying power dynamics. It includes both an analytical deconstruction of a critical incident for a practitioner and a reconstruction to revise one's practice based on the reflections generated.

Critical reflection on the categories that ground biases, especially power dynamics, is a necessary element in self-reflexivity. Humility about fallibility and the biases of one's own perspective are essential. Tolerance of ambiguity is important. Innocence is not a possibility.

Working on Counter-transference

Another beneficial procedure is the exploration and control of counter-transference. Counter-transference is a Freudian concept that refers to a worker's unconscious reactions to a client that arise from the practitioner's own unresolved neurotic conflicts, activated by the material in the therapeutic relationship (Cooper-White, 2001).

Benjamin has hypothesized that we all experience the Other as both a part of the self and discrete (1995). "The inner representation of the other can either represent an ideal for the self (a preferred self) or a disowned part of the self" (Weinberg, 2007). That disavowed aspect can be viewed as a "monster, the Other within" (Benjamin, 1998, p.86). The anxiety and distress of that recognition can be projected onto the client and retaliated against. I would speculate that a component of Jannie's discomfort with Shari in Chapter 2 was that Shari evoked unresolved feelings about Jannie's emotionally immature mother, leading to, at times, harsh responses toward Shari. This could have been a counter-transference reaction.

Workers must reach out to the Other in oneself, those aspects which have been denied. Neither denying difference, nor rejecting it are solutions. "Relations of reciprocal symmetry can only come into existence if the Other remains unassimilated" (Cornell, 1992, p.16) and individuals must recognize the Other in themselves. The monster, the Other within, must be acknowledged.

Focusing on such reactions requires putting emphasis on the significance of one's emotions as they impact on practice (D'Cruz, Gillingham, and Melendez, 2007). This is especially important in ethical considerations, as we discussed in Chapter 3. Had Jannie acknowledged and worked on her emotional reaction to her own mother, perhaps she might have been more compassionate to Shari.

More recent theoreticians have viewed emotional material as not solely problematic and have expanded what is understood by counter-transference. For these thinkers, it includes unconscious aspects of a worker's personality that help that individual be therapeutic, as well as objective emotional reactions to problematic behaviour or personality characteristics of clients (Bochner, 2000). For example, in Chapter 2, because Charlotte had been told "lies" about herself, had experienced sexual assault, and did not receive much support from parents, she felt she had engaged in behaviours that might be viewed by others as 'pathological.' But because she understood those actions as being the best she was able to do at the time and her only way to survive, she might have had more tolerance and empathy for her clients' behaviour that could have been judged as 'acting-out' by someone who had not had those formative early experiences.

Besides counter-transference reactions, feminist theorists have added that there are two other levels in the therapeutic relationship to which one must attend (Brown, 1994b): the real world encounter and the symbolic components of difference, aspects addressed above.

Supervision and Consultation

Supervision and consultation are vehicles for regulating the effects of counter-transference (Gibbons, Murphy, and Joseph, 2011; McTighe, 2011). However, there are complexities to the employment of supervision for this purpose (Agass, 2002; Tosone, 1997), since counter-transference can be reactivated in the supervisory session both for the worker, but also the supervisor. When this enactment occurs, with a particularly skilled supervisor who understands her own and the worker's counter-transference and where there is space within the supervisory relationship, this type of exploration can be fruitful. Unfortunately, there is little of this sort of supervision available in an era of managerialism. Consultation also holds potential for the examination of counter-transference reactions with the advantage that power dynamics are likely less acute.

Supervision is also heralded as a key mechanism for promoting ethical practice more generally (Barsky, 2010). Supervisors are expected to be aware of ethical standards, and in some jurisdictions, are held responsible for the misconduct of their supervisees. This system does offer some promise for workers to be their most effective and ethical selves, with the caveats raised above.

I will now discuss a few other therapeutic elements that can lessen ethical trespass.

Other Relational Skills

Further components that incline towards trespass reduction in the helping relationship are honesty, nurturance, persistence, and care. To illustrate, Tanesha had "difficulty connecting" and trusting other people. When she was asked by a psychiatrist why she had related so well to Patricia, Tanesha, according to Patricia, replied, "'I think it was that day when she … told me I was a little liar and she wanted her tokens back.'" Notwithstanding denying Tanesha bus tokens, Patricia's realistic assessment of Tanesha, without the moralistic sting, allowed her to solidly connect with Patricia. I would speculate that, for Tanesha, there was comfort and release in being known, especially those parts of her that normatively had been evaluated negatively. There was productive power in the nurturance provided (Brown, 1994b).

In addition to her honest but caring and positive framing of Tanesha, Patricia's nurturance included significant persistence (Jermier, Knights, and Nord, 1994, p.12), and the extension of the boundaries beyond the normative in-office, nine-to-five involvement. For example, Patricia went to Tanesha's apartment after the decision of CAS for crown wardship. By this action, Patricia demonstrated a caring that went beyond the masculinist model of objective and distant boundaries of the traditional therapeutic relationship and supported an understanding that some boundaries in the social work relationship should be permeable and negotiated (O'Leary, Tsui, and Ruch, 2013).

As an aside, while this example portrays potential alternatives that can edge towards more ethical behaviour, it simultaneously demonstrates the possibility of a trespass on my part. I fear that I will inadvertently reinforce the need for workers to be ever-present and altruistic towards their clients, regardless of their own personal needs and obligations (Weinberg, 2014). In the process, I may be viewed as supporting the essentialist, cultural feminist notions of women as all-giving. It is necessary for professionals to have boundaries and I am not suggesting by this example that workers must always go the extra distance, since there may be occasions when this is damaging to the practitioner, unhelpful, or even destructive for clients.

Now, I will outline a series of specific strategies of responsible traitors.

Strategies of the Responsible Traitor

Not Doing/Limiting One's Use of Power

Passive resistance, by not doing or limiting one's exercise of power, are strategies. For example, Foucault (1977) described the disciplinary power of documentation by classifying individuals and developing norms and diagnoses. Records are shaped to support the decisions taken by workers (Davies, 2014). Smith (1990, p.24) identified that "for any set of actual events, there is always more than one version that can be treated as what happened." Professional training acts as a device to frame what particulars from the ongoing work are relevant to present as reportable data. The detachment from the local and particular, as well as the objective and professionalized language contribute to their truth claims (Smith, 1987; Smith, 1990).

But a record "stands in" for the actual flesh and blood young woman, leaching out feelings, objectifying the client (Smith, 1999), and limiting identified subject positions.

To illustrate, when Tanesha's baby was apprehended, she said to Patricia, "don't cry because you know, we have to be strong." Patricia stated, "if that was me, I'd be holding onto the bumper of the car, throwing up and screaming like a lunatic." Tanesha's response, according to Patricia, was "I can't do that ... because you know what, that would go in my file." The record has moral implications for clients and workers, particularly when the assessments cast a negative light on their motivations or behaviour.

These processes can reinforce inequities and contribute to hierarchical power relations (Davies, 2014; Askeland and Payne, 1999). At times, the caseworkers attempted to minimize these risks by omitting or limiting what was written into the formal records. Therefore, in resisting, workers used their discretion about what was said, in order to protect clients from potential negative readings by others. Patricia explained in her written reports there was "no interpretation" because "things can be misinterpreted ... things can be dragged up and used against young women in court a lot."

Not using the language of power was also used. Employing psychiatric terminology gives credence to the expertise of the worker while separating her socially from her clients (De Montigny, 1995). It is a "lexicon of deficit" rather than strength, framing clients as ill and needing to be healed by professionals (Saleeby, 2001, p. 183). The highly political nature of diagnosis continues to pathologize the Other (Saleeby, 2001) while ignoring the resources that these individuals bring to solving problems. I asked Frieda why she rarely used psychiatric jargon to describe her clients, despite her clear knowledge of the terms. She responded that she did not "like to put people in boxes and label them" because of others making "judgments" and because of the "connotations" associated with those labels. Charlotte was conscious of the impact on the clients themselves for available subject positions: "It's people making diagnoses and statements that just affect the way you [a client] look about [sic] yourself."

Another tactic was to restrict workers' own access to information. Kristine's general policy was to avoid receiving background information on clients from the CAS records, because she "didn't want to be tainted." There are times when not reading case material can open an individual caseworker, or client to danger; so, as with many situations in social work, there is no simple ethical route to take. Despite the expectation that as part of distributing food vouchers, workers were expected to verify how the vouchers were used, Frieda rarely confirmed the purposes for which money was used. I wish to add a caveat here.

A further strategy was not enacting rigid or problematic policies. Decisions to refrain from contacting the CAS could be seen as a dereliction of statutory responsibility. But sometimes workers did refuse. One worker explained that "everybody else is quick to judge," and she had seen "so much dysfunction as a result of CAS ... coming in to help." She felt there was "a different set of standards" for impoverished clients, and that it was "a threat" that was held "over their heads constantly."

Doing and Not Telling/Subversive Activities

The obverse to passive resistance was "doing and not telling." Studies have shown that these acts run the gamut from individualized deviance to more politicized radical acts to fight restructuring (Aronson and Sammon, 2000; Carey and Foster, 2011; Evans, 2011; Smith, 2007; Weinberg and Taylor, 2014). In one instance, in her Catholic-sponsored agency, Jannie described that, while the director of her program "was supportive," she "did not want to know" about staff providing education about birth control. Consequently, Jannie "shut the door" to the classroom so her insurrection would not be as apparent, a form of impression management (Clegg, 1994). Kristine, too, acquiesced to a request for condoms in her Catholic agency, confessing, "I guess that's my little bit of rebellion."

In workers' subversive moves, there were complex internal rationales used in drawing from their discursive fields to justify taking positions that they believed were contrary to the dominant discourses. Often it was in the weighing of harms and "attention to 'particular others in actual contexts'" (Walker, 1992, p.166) that workers chose to act against the dominant institutional frameworks. In Kristine's decision to provide the condoms, she said, "There's no other way she can get them." Of course clients have other ways to acquire condoms. But Kristine's rationale included an awareness of this client's subordinate positioning and context. She argued, "How is she going to get to the public health department to pick up a supply of condoms? You know, drive her two children on the bus with her ... for a two minute stop-over? No, no."

The worker who did not contact the CAS, utilized a discourse of harm when she said, "I don't want to see them [clients] hurt any more than they've already been hurt and ... I'm not going to be the person that does the hurting."

It seemed that when workers were more comfortable with non-compliance and defiance, they were more likely to take up non-privileged readings around difference, which led to being responsible traitors. Those individuals who view ethics from the standpoint of principles were less likely to take these stances than those who are skeptical about principle-based morality (Fine and Teram, 2009). Also, there is a typology regarding individuals' responses to rules more generally (Evans, 2012). There are those who believe in the value of rules in and of themselves (*nomocracy*) and those who see rules as a means to an end (*telocracy*). Those who queried the purposes and the outcomes of rules tended towards telocracy and more often resisted. In my interviews, Frieda, in her subject position of "devil's advocate" and Patricia, in that of "anarchist," saw themselves as resistors and were the workers who most often questioned the dominant narratives about their work and their clients. Jannie, on the other hand, more closely illustrated nomocracy. However, later research suggests a more complex picture. Even individuals who believe in the importance of rules, for stability and fairness, at times struggle with accepting the rules when they feel that the best interests of their clients are not being served (Weinberg and Taylor, 2014).

However, even when workers adopted subversive subject positions, these strategies were frequently accompanied with feelings of ambivalence, discomfort, or fear, in part because workers understood that they were behaving in ways that could have significant consequences, including for credibility and job security. Furthermore, it is understandable that in diverging from the taken-for-granted notions of dominant discourses, one would question one's own position. In not appraising clients' uses of food vouchers, Frieda shared, "I don't know if it's right or not." Charlotte, on rereading the transcripts when her behaviour had been transgressive, retracted what she had said originally. Participants often framed their own resistances as personal inadequacy or as dangerous behaviours. For example, the worker who did not contact the CAS wondered if her resistance was "a weakness" on her part. She also expressed that perhaps she would "get in a lot of trouble."

There are questions about the efficacy of covert actions, since they may mask structural problems; perpetuating current operations and bypassing needed dialogue about organizational change (Fine and Teram, 2012; Weinberg, 2014). However, there are times when the need to respond directly to individual clients outweighs decisions to invest the time and energy to confront injustice in systems more broadly (Fine and Teram, 2012; Weinberg, 2014).

To be a responsible traitor, the respectability of disobedience must be extended to clients, allowing for encouragement of their resistance and a tolerance of opposition towards workers themselves. At times, Patricia was on the receiving end of Tanesha's anger. Patricia viewed it as 'normal.' Patricia believed that the anger needed to be expressed, rather than repressed, and that it constituted a form of energy that could be redirected into active confrontation and opposition to oppression, increasing the potential for a sense of mastery and for more reciprocal human relationships for Tanesha (Barrett, Berg, Eaton, and Pomeroy, 1974, p.14). Patricia's goal was to turn a victim into an effective fighter.

Dissident Speech

Another strategy is the use of dissident speech. Dominant discourses become a type of shorthand, fossilizing norms (Meyers, 1994, p.53) and structuring the imagination of both the marginalized and the dominant, consequently shaping ethical choices. Wetherell (1998, p. 393) has suggested that power is "the capacity to 'articulate' and to make those articulations not only 'stick' but become hegemonic and pervasive." Dissident speech is the act of constructing positive discursive reframes to nonconscious material that has hitherto contributed to the maintenance of culturally accepted prejudices (Meyers, 1994). Thus, dissident speech (Meyers, 1994. p.93) can be used to create new norms and healing subject positions that repair story lines that have pointed towards culturally normative and oppressive positionings (H. Nelson, 2001).

Clinical assessment is one means to accomplish potentially more constructive subject positions and be used as dissident speech. Assessment is a form of "mind-reading" in the accounts provided for the actions of the Other (Mattingly, 2008). Workers can rely on familiar discourses about the Other, utilizing stereotypical tropes to understand those who are different. Meyers (1994, p.44) suggests that "prejudice is encoded in culturally entrenched figurations of 'different' social groups" and results in prejudice that is accepted as a norm. For example, in explaining why a 'troublesome' client such as Tanesha went infrequently to the hospital to visit her infant or lied, Patricia could have used familiar discourses of 'neglectful' or 'pathological mother' that abound for poor, single, racialized women. Instead of Patricia adopting these dominant discourses, she relied on those of 'racism' and 'fear of the infant dying.'

This is the flexibility of discourse to be used for resistance. In assessing Tanesha's evasion of hospital visits, there were many possible explanations. One can never know the 'truth' of what motivated Tanesha to behave in the way that she did. Many truths may have been operating at the same time: pathological lying, exhaustion, lack of bonding, laziness, avoidance of the racism, as other examples. By 'choosing' to perceive Tanesha in the way she did, this manoeuvre provided the option of a more positive construction of a subject position to be taken up by Tanesha rather than to simply perceive herself as 'bad' in the eyes of others. It also allowed for Patricia herself to understand Tanesha in the same constructive way, becoming a means to facilitate empathy on the part of a worker in a dominant position, because it disrupted a familiar way of understanding the Other.

Assessment, a potential form of dissident speech, is also consequential for the actions taken by workers since it frames the definition of the 'problem' to be remedied by helpers. To assess 'pathological mother' could lead to apprehension of the child, whereas 'racism' might result in activism.

One form of dissident speech is referred to alternatively as counterstories (H. Nelson, 2001), or counterfigurations (Meyers, 1994, p.12). Counterstories always maintain certain elements of the master narratives (in part because they dispute them) (Bamberg, 2004). So how can one distinguish figurations that support emancipation from those that are repressive (Meyers, 1994)? The "critical test of the viability of a counterfiguration is its impact on empathy" (Meyers, 1994, p. 14). Emancipatory figurations allow marginalized groups liberating subject positions so they do not become "complicit in their own subordination" (Meyers, 1994, p.14). They offer the possibility of improvising new storylines for oneself that are more morally exemplary too (Bamberg, 2004).

Hilde Nelson (2001) identified two steps in the construction of counterstories. The first is identification of those aspects of the master narratives that are damaging (p.50). For Patricia, a component of the helping relationship was "dispelling the myths of motherhood." Patricia spoke about the dominant discourse that "every women is going to be immediately bonding with their infant ... and breast feeding is going to be so easy and ... you're going to fall in love with your baby the minute you see it." This statement refers to the psychological discourse discussed in Chapter 4 that there is a natural mothering instinct and those who do not feel an immediate attachment are in some way abnormal. Patricia disputed this discourse, "That's a lot of pressure and ... [a] lot of us don't feel that ... the minute we see our baby."

The second component, according to H. Nelson (2001, p.50), is retelling a story "to make visible the morally relevant details that the master narrative suppress." Patricia continued that it was "okay" to look at the baby and say, "'oh my God,' what is this little screaming red thing in the bassinet beside my bed?" She continued, "I don't expect every person to be like the most amazing mother right off the bat. I know how hard it is." Key was her sentiment, "it's ... normal to feel like that."

A third component, I believe, is the development of new storylines that are creative, redemptive, and encourage a repressed group to see themselves as ethically worthy. One such counterfiguration was exemplified by Patricia. With another client, she tried to reassure her about the legitimacy of receiving financial assistance while her baby was young. Patricia argued, "You're doing a job and ... if I went on maternity leave for a year, I'd be getting government money. You're getting paid to be a mom and it's a really important job." In this instance, Patricia articulated the feminist chestnut of mothering as unpaid domestic labour, rather than accepting the reactionary conservative discourse of Chapter 1 in which those mothers who take financial assistance are viewed as economically dependent and morally reprehensible.

While one can 'choose' to reject damaging subject positions, that stance is dependent on one's ability to trust one's own judgments (H. Nelson, 2001) and belief in one's capacity to take an alternate subject position (Davies, 1990a). Patricia had been frustrated with Tanesha's stance when people spoke to her with overt racism because, according to Patricia, Tanesha said, "'people talk to me like that all the time. It's not a big deal.'" Of course it is possible that there were other motivations to Tanesha's claim that it was no big deal. One possibility is that the naming of racism was too painful. Another is that perhaps Tanesha did not sufficiently trust a white woman with the power to take away her baby to express her responses to the bigotry directed toward her. However, it is also possible that the damaging subject position impaired Tanesha's sense of her capacity to act (H. Nelson, 2001).

Davies (1990a) identified that access to others who will support alternative positionings fosters agency. Through Patricia's openness about the dynamics of racism and classism, there was the prospect of a "growing awareness that the order of things is not inevitable or fated and can be changed" (Moneyhun, 1996, p.245). By sharing an anti-oppressive framework, Tanesha was encouraged to articulate how bigotry had been operating in her own life. When in anger over the surveillance of her mothering by the CAS, Tanesha asked Patricia, "how come you can go home and stick your kid in front of the TV and have a glass of wine and nobody says anything?" Patricia responded with possible explanations but also provided the entrée to alternative positionings that supported a shift in Tanesha. Patricia asked Tanesha what she thought, to which Tanesha speculated she was scrutinized "because I'm black and I'm poor and I don't have an education." And Patricia replied, "wow, I've never heard you say that before ... all I've ever heard you say is 'whatever, doesn't matter' ... and ... she said, 'well, you know what? It does f_cking! matter.'" Tanesha was expressing the "bigger picture on how she [had] been treated"; namely, that intolerance and oppressive structures had impinged on her life as a young single, unmarried, black mother. According to Patricia, this was a "major breakthrough."

Sharing Formal Knowledge

Lorde (1984. p.110) argued that the "masters tools will never dismantle the master's house." However, the workers did use the master's tools to take apart and rebuild dominant discursive frameworks. By filling clients in on the rules of the game (Clegg, 1994), clients were able to cross a cultural divide and were provided the keys to the house. One aspect of teaching the rules was helping clients understand the risks of their involvement with the helping professions.

An instance occurred when Patricia explained the dangers of an assessment of Tanesha that was on file with the CAS. Patricia believed that the version on record had negative implications for Tanesha because of terms such as "developmentally delayed," and "unable to make eye contact."

Ambiguities in texts are particularly important since they require readers to interpret what is meant and can creep into one's consciousness "and take over ...

Not necessarily to agree with it ... but to adopt its organizing framework" (Smith, 1997, p.234). One such ambiguity is the expression "unable to make eye contact." This type of phrase allows for different interpretations that rely on alternate discursive frameworks. One psychological discourse suggests that those who avoid eye contact are unable to engage in and/or maintain relationships. However, another discourse recognizes that there are cross-cultural discrepancies where eye contact would be inappropriate (such as Inuit people speaking to someone in authority).

Part of the power of the text is its permanence and lack of temporality. While people change and grow, individual parts of the record stay as is. While additions can be made which can 'dilute' the significance of earlier entries, those entries set the parameters of what must be disputed in order to change earlier impressions. "Records from the past brought forward allow social workers to meet clients as already discursively organized" (De Montigny, 1995, p.72).

Furthermore, the information in a file is *about* the client, not *from* the client (Pence, 1996, p.75). Patricia tried to bring the client back into the discussion. She asked Tanesha "do you feel ... you're developmentally delayed?" When Tanesha said, "I don't think so," Patricia concurred. She responded to the traps she saw in the text by teaching Tanesha about the power of this documentary evidence and its implications for Tanesha. According to Patricia, eventually Tanesha reached a point that she said, "I'm really worried ... this is in my file and if I ever have another child, it's going to come up again." Consequently, Patricia arranged for another assessment to be done, which "came out quite positive." The new assessment was also placed on file so that there could be an alternate reading of Tanesha's capabilities.

Another method of giving the master's keys to clients is sharing middle-class strategies so that they can enter the house, should they so choose. With one client, Frieda described "warning [her] against the system." She laid out a script, providing the client with "ammunition" to protect herself, suggesting:

> go to a lawyer and find out the specific criteria that CAS is going to [need to] be able to apprehend your child ... and come prepared to your intake interview ... know this knowledge ... don't [say] ... "I'm so scared that you're going to take my baby." ... come in and say ... "this is what I need, and I have some concerns about Children's Aid, but I'm aware that this is where I stand".... .

This is Foucault's nexus of knowledge and power discussed in Chapter 1. An agency must have concrete grounds for apprehension and Frieda wanted the client to know what criteria would be used to judge her mothering. Knowledge of legal strategies and assertiveness about one's rights are the tools the middle-class use to wage battles.

Frieda was also presenting a potential subject position for the client that was not weak and submissive but strong in the expectations of what was needed and anticipated from the agency. This was a form of active resistance, supporting a client to be a fighter on her own behalf.

Advocacy and Activism

Advocacy and activism are forms of 'renovation' of the master's house because they are designed to alter actual structures. Advocacy is supporting a cause and actively engaging in the influence of public policy or resource allocations. Activism is human action to bring about socio-political change. It takes courage to overtly confront injustice and carries risks for practitioners (Fine and Teram, 2012). Strategies fall on a continuum from local to more broad-based activities.

Charlotte induced management to alter the design of her agency to include more opportunities for respite from the children for the young mothers. In the newly designed agency, she described her fantasy of how things might have been different for the client whose baby had earlier been apprehended, in part due to a lack of respite. She hypothesized, "if it had happened today ... maybe one of the workers ... would've said, 'go to bed for a couple of hours, and we'll feed the baby.'"

Many of Patricia's attempts centred on advocating with others outside her agency for what these clients needed: inveigling others to get diapers or a spot in shelter, and reducing expectations around clients' involvement with the social service system. In the case of Kelly and Marshall, Patricia worked the system, knowing how to move an issue through the hospital bureaucracy. She took her dissatisfactions through the institutional structures, from the hospital social worker to the head of obstetrics. She also used her connections to get her grievances placed on the agenda of a meeting. Various strategies were employed to prevent her from disrupting the status quo. She was "uninvited (!) ... at the last minute!" from "a big meeting to discuss this whole thing." She was also informed that she would need to "follow up [with] a letter." With persistence, Patricia did respond with a letter, in which she expressed a wish to build bridges, stating that she knew the committee was "forging ahead and building a relationship ... and that at a management level they were trying to put structures in place" to better respond to the needs of patients. By emphasizing the best in the individuals who were in a position to effect change in the organization, Patricia finessed the situation by opening up the possibility for the hospital management to move towards subject positions of succor to their patients, rather than as unresponsive subjects.

She was successful both in being heard at a subsequent meeting and, ultimately, being invited to join the committee. Being forthright and asking "point blank" if she had been "ditched" from the earlier agenda opened the way for honesty, not just about content, but also about the process of decision-making which recognized the politics of avoidance that operated in the hospital. Her efforts were an illustration of contextual practice (Fook, 2002) in which practitioners work with whole contexts, attempting to form alliances with like-minded individuals, whilst knowing that those coalitions will shift depending on issues and the changing subjectivity of participants.

One of the difficulties with moving towards more resistant stances in agencies is the isolation of most workers. The pluralism in organizational settings results in ambiguity about what constitutes an ethical stance, but also opens the door for liberatory action since more than one response might be viewed as ethical (Fine and Teram, 2012). Strategies of dividing and conquering leave individuals perceiving the problems as individualized and personal rather than systemic and structural. Solidarity does not mean everyone sharing the same perspective, but being able to find common ground on which to act. This is difference as a resource. There is less likelihood of being outflanked when people function as a group, since a collectivity is more powerful than a sole individual (Clegg, 1994). An individual's integrity and authority can be tarnished, but it is more difficult to incriminate whole factions. Additionally, there is the proverbial strength in numbers to fight back if accusations occur.

Since all differences cannot be bridged, worker-client alliances can be a resource in political struggles since they both "multiply the sources of resistance" and aid in discovering "the distortions in our understandings of each other and the world" (Sawicki, 1991, p.28). Client self-advocacy and activism amplify service users' agency and reduce the paternalism of social work. Patricia asked if she could use her clients' names since she anticipated that there might be a request to follow-up with individual nurses who had been involved in particular racist incidents. She also kept these young women actively involved by informing them afterwards about the outcome of committee meetings.

One client wanted to write her own letter of complaint and resistance, and Patricia encouraged this. Similarly, she provided the name of the CAS supervisor so Kelly could complain directly about her treatment by the intake worker, rather than Patricia doing this for her. Her rationale was "she's a young strong woman and she's more than capable of advocating for herself far better than I could."

Patricia organized for Tanesha to be part of an interview team to hire a student social worker at her clinic. There was a progression from, at first, Tanesha being "very quiet," to, by the third interview, "own[ing] the place." By Tanesha participating in the hiring process, there was a reversal of standard positioning and it contributed to Tanesha having the sense that the clinic was for clients – "theirs."

Through these strategies, Patricia enacted her understanding of clients' strength to fight for themselves, and their right to be informed. In doing this, she contributed to the possibility of agentic subject positions for service users and of political resistance.

Conclusion

While trespass cannot be eliminated, it is feasible to reduce its effects. This chapter looked at a variety of possibilities for both workers and clients. Resistance to dominant discourses that encouraged more liberatory readings was an important element. How one responded to Others' difference was essential. The use of broad empathy, critically reflecting on affective reactions and cognitive judgements, while searching for the best in oneself as a practitioner were also key components. When workers problematized the helping relationship, their power and privilege, the prospect of trespass minimization was enhanced. The chapter concluded with a wide range of tactics employed by workers to enrich care and reduce disciplinary practices of clients.

Bibliography

Agass, D. (2002). Countertransference, supervision and the reflection process. *Journal of Social Work Practice*, 16(2), 125–33.

Alcoff, L.M. (1998). What should white people do? *Hypatia*, 13(3), 6–26.

Aronson, J., and Sammon, S. (2000). Practice and social service cuts and restructuring. Working with the contradictions of "small victories." *Canadian Social Work Review*, 17(2), 167–87.

Aronson, J., and Smith, K. (2010). Managing restructured social services: Expanding the social? *British Journal of Social Work*, 40, 530–47.

Askeland, G.A., and Payne, M. (1999). Authors and audiences: Towards a sociology of case recording. *European Journal of Social Work*, 2(1), 55–65.

Bamberg, M. (2004). Considering counter narratives. In M. Bamberg, and M. Andrews (Eds.), *Considering Counter-narratives: Narrating, Resisting and Making Sense*. Philadelphia: John Benjamins North America.

Barrett, C.J., Berg, P.I, Eaton, E.M., and Pomeroy, E.L. (1974). Implications of women's liberation and the future of psychotherapy. *Psychotherapy: Theory, Research and Practice*, 11, 11–15.

Barsky, A.E. (2010). *Ethics and Values in Social Work. An Integrated Approach for a Comprehensive Curriculum*. Toronto: Oxford University Press.

Benjamin, J. (1995). *Like Subjects, Love Objects. Essays on Recognition and Sexual Difference*. New Haven: Yale University Press.

Benjamin, J. (1998). *Shadow of the Other. Intersubjectivity and Gender in Psychoanalysis*. New York: Routledge.

Bochner, D. (2000). *The Therapeutic Use of Self in Family Therapy*. Northvale, New Jersey: Jason Aronson Inc.

Brown, L.S. (1994b). *Subversive Dialogues. Theory in Feminist Practice*. New York: BasicBooks of HarperCollins.

Butler, J. (1995). Contingent foundations: Feminism and the question of "post-modernism." In S. Benhabib, J. Butler, D. Cornell, and N. Fraser (Eds.), *Feminist Contentions: A Philosophical Exchange* (pp.35–57). New York: Routledge.

Carey, M., and Foster, V. (2011). Introducing "deviant" social work: Contextualizing the limits of radical social work whilst understanding (fragmented) resistance within the social work labour process. *British Journal of Social Work*, 41, 576–93.

Chu, W.C.K., Tsui, M.-S., and Yan, M.-C. (2009). Social work as a moral and political practice. *International Social Work*, 52(3), 287–98.

Clegg, S. (1994). Power relations and the constitution of the resistant subject. In. J.M. Jermier, D. Knights, and W.R. Nord. (Eds.), *Resistance and Power in Organizations* (pp.274–325). New York: Routledge.

Cooper-White, P. (2001). The use of the self in psychotherapy: A comparative study of pastoral counselors and clinical social workers. *The American Journal of Pastoral Counseling*, 4(4), 5–35.

Davies, B. (1990a). Agency as a form of discursive practice: A classroom scene observed. *British Journal of Sociology of Education*, 11(3), 341–61.

Davies, B. (2000). *A Body of Writing. 1909–1999*. New York: Alta Mira Press.

Davies, H. (2014). Working inclusively with the socially excluded. *Ethics & Social Welfare*, 8(4), 417–22.

Davies, L. (1990). Limits of bureaucratic control: Social workers in child welfare. In L. Davies, and E. Shragge (Eds.), *Bureaucracy and Community. Essays on the Politics of Social Work Practice* (pp.81–101). Montreal: Black Rose Books.

D'Cruz, H., Gillingham, P., and Melendez, S. (2007). Reflexivity, its meanings and relevance for social work: A critical review of the literature. *British Journal of Social Work*, 37, 73–90.

De Montigny, G. (1995). *Social Working*. Toronto: University of Toronto Press.

Evans, T. (2010). *Professional Discretion in Welfare Services. Beyond Street-level Bureaucracy*. Burlington, VT: Ashgate.

Evans, T. (2011). Professionals, managers and discretion: Critiquing street-level bureaucracy. *British Journal of Social Work*, 41(2), 368–86. DOI: 10.1093/bjsw/bcq074.

Evans, T. (2012). Organisational rules and discretion in adult social work. *British Journal of Social Work*, 43(4), 739–58.

Fine, M., and Teram, E. (2009). Believers and skeptics: Where social workers situate themselves regarding the codes of ethics. *Ethics & Behavior*, 19(1), 60–78.

Fine, M., and Teram, E. (2012). Overt and covert ways of responding to moral injustices in social work practice: Heroes and mild-mannered social work bipeds. *British Journal of Social Work*, 1–18.

Fook, J. (2002). *Social Work. Critical Theory and Practice*. London: SAGE.

Fook, J. (2007). Reflective practice and critical reflection. In J. Lishman (Ed.), *Handbook for Practice Learning in Health and Social Care* (pp.363–75). Philadelphia: Jessica Kingsley

Fook, J., and Gardner, F. (2013). *Critical Reflection in Context. Applications in Health and Social Care*. New York: Routledge.

Foucault, M. (1977). *Discipline and Punish. The Birth of the Prison* (A. Sheridan, Trans.) (2nd ed.). New York: Vintage Books. (Original work published in 1975)

Foucault, M. (1978). *The History of Sexuality. An Introduction. Vol.1.* (R. Hurley, Trans.). New York: Vintage Books. (Original work published in 1976)

Foucault, M. (1984). On the genealogy of ethics: An overview of work in progress. In P. Rabinow (Ed.). *The Foucault Reader* (pp.340–72). New York: Pantheon Books.

Frankenberg, R. (1993). *White Women, Race Matters. The Social Construction of Whiteness*. Minneapolis: University of Minnesota Press.

Gibbons, S., Murphy, D., and Joseph, S. (2011). Countertransference and positive growth in social workers. *Journal of Social Work Practice*, 25(1), 17–30.

Giroux, H.A. (2001). *Theory and Resistance in Education. Towards a Pedagogy for the Opposition* (Rev. ed.). Westport, Connecticut: Bergin & Garvey.

Heldke, L. (1998). On becoming a responsible traitor. A primer. In B.-A. Bar On, and A. Ferguson (Eds.), *Daring to do Good. Essays in Feminist Ethico-politics* (pp.87–99). New York: Routledge.

Heron, B. (2005). Self-reflection in critical social work practice: subjectivity and the possibilities of resistance. *Reflective Practice*, 6(3), 341–51.

Jeffery, D. (2005). What good is anti-racist social work if you can't master it?: exploring the paradox in anti-racist social work education. *Race, Ethnicity and Education*, 8(4), 409–25. DOI: 10.1080/13613320500324011.

Jermier, J.M., Knights, D., and Nord, W.R. (1994). Introduction. Resistance and power in organizations: agency, subjectivity and the labour process. In J.M. Jermier, D. Knights, and W.R. Nord (Eds.), *Resistance and Power in Organizations* (pp.1–25). New York: Routledge.

Jordan, J.V., Surrey, J.L., and Kaplan, A.G. (1991). Women and empathy: Implications for psychological development and psychotherapy. In J.V. Jordan, A.G. Kaplan, J.B. Miller, I.P. Stiver, and J.L. Surrey (Eds.), *Women's Growth in Connection. Writings from the Stone Center* (pp.27–50). New York: Guilford Press.

Kaplan, A.G. (1991). Empathic communication in the psychotherapy relationship. In J.V. Jordan, A.G. Kaplan, J.B. Miller, I.P. Stiver, and J.L. Surrey (Eds.), *Women's Growth in Connection. Writings from the Stone Center* (pp.44–50). New York: Guilford Press.

Kendall, S, and Hugman, R. (2013). Social work and the ethics of involuntary treatment for Anorexia Nervosa: A postmodern approach. *Ethics and Social Welfare*, 7(4), 310–25.

Knights, D., and Vurdubakis, T. (1994). Foucault, power, resistance and all that. In J.M. Jermier, D. Knights, and W.R. Nord. (Eds.), *Resistance and Power in Organizations* (pp.167–98). New York: Routledge.

Kondrat, M.E. (1999). Who is the "self" in self-aware: Professional self-awareness from a critical theory perspective. *Social Service Review*, 73(4), 451–77.

Lipsky, M. (1980). *Street-level Bureaucracy. Dilemmas of the Individual in Public Service.* New York, NY: Russell Sage Foundation.

Lorde, A. (1984). *Sister Outsider. Essays and Speeches by Audre Lorde.* Freedom, California: Crossing Press.

Margolin, L. (1997). *Under the Cover of Kindness. The Invention of Social Work.* Charlottesville: University Press of Virginia.

Mattingly, C. (2008). Reading minds and telling tales in a cultural borderline. *Ethos*, 36(1), 136–54.

McIntosh, P. (1992). White privilege and male privilege: A personal account of coming to see correspondences through work in women's studies. In M.L. Anderson, and P.C. Collins (Eds), *Race, Class and Gender: An Anthology* (pp.70–81). Belmont, California: Wadsworth.

McTighe, J.P. (2011). Teaching the use of self through the process of clinical supervision. *Clinical Social Work Journal*, 39, 301–7.

Meyers, D.T. (1994). *Subjection and Subjectivity: Psychoanalytic Feminism and Moral Philosophy*. New York: Routledge.

Moneyhun, C. (1996). Not just plain English. Teaching critical reading with *I, Rigoberta Menchu*. In A. Carey-Webb, and S. Benz (Eds.), *Teaching and Testimony, Rigoberta Menchu and the North American Classroom* (pp.237–46). Albany, NY: State University of New York Press.

Napier, L. (2010). Practising critical reflection. In A. O'Hara, Z. Weber, and K. Levine (Eds.). *Skills for Human Service Practice* (pp.1–11). Don Mills: Oxford University Press.

Nelson, H.L. (2001). Identity and free agency. In P. DesAutels, and J. Waugh (Eds.), *Feminists Doing Ethics* (pp.45–62). New York: Rowman & Littlefield Publishers, Inc.

O'Leary, P., Tsui, M.-S., and Ruch, G. (2013). The boundaries of the social work relationship revisited: Towards a connected, inclusive and dynamic conceptualisation. *British Journal of Social Work*, 43, 135–53.

Orlie, M.A. *(1997)*. *Living Ethically. Acting Politically*. Ithaca: Cornell University Press.

Pence, E. (1996). *Safety for Battered Women in a Textually Mediated Legal System*. (Unpublished doctoral dissertation). University of Toronto, Toronto, Canada.

Polakow, V. (1995). Naming and blaming: Beyond a pedagogy of the poor. In B.B. Swadener, and S. Lubeck (Eds.), *Children and Families "at Promise." Deconstructing the Discourse of Risk* (pp.263–70). Albany: State University of New York Press.

Razack, N., and Jeffrey, D. (2002). Critical race discourse and tenets for social work. *Canadian Social Work Review*, 19(2), 257–71.

Rossiter, A. (2001). Innocence lost and suspicion found: Do we educate for or against social work? *Critical Social Work*, 2(1). Available at: <http://www1.uwindsor.ca/criticalsocialwork/innocence-lost-and-suspicion-found-do-we-educate-for-or-against-social-work> (Accessed January 5, 2016).

Sakamoto, I. (2007). An anti-oppressive approach to cultural competence. *Canadian Social Work Review*, 24(1), 105–14.

Saleeby, D. (2001). The diagnostic strengths manual? *Social Work*, 46(2), 183–7.

Sawicki, J. (1991). *Disciplining Foucault. Feminism, Power, and the Body*. New York: Routledge.

Smith, D.E. (1987).*The Everyday World as Problematic. A Feminist Sociology*. Toronto: University of Toronto Press.

Smith, D.E. (1990). *Texts, Facts and Femininity. Exploring the Relations of Ruling*. London: Routledge.

Smith, D.E. (1997). Discourse as social relations: Sociological theory and the dialogic of sociology. [Earlier version of Chapter 7 in *Writing the social*]. (Unpublished manuscript). Toronto.

Smith, D.E. (1999). *Writing the Social. Critique, Theory, and Investigations*. Toronto: University of Toronto Press.

Smith, K. (2007). Social work, restructuring and everyday resistance. In D. Baines (Ed.), *Doing Anti-oppressive Practice. Building Transformative Politicized Social Work* (pp.145–59). Halifax: Fernwood Publishing.

Thomas, R., and Davies, A. (2005a). Theorizing the micro-politics of resistance: New public management and managerial identities in the UK public services. *Organization Studies*, 26, 683–706. DOI: 10.1177/0170840605051821.

Thomas, R., and Davies, A. (2005b). What have feminists done for us? Feminist theory and organizational resistance. *Organization*, 12(5), 711–40.

Tosone, C. (1997). Countertransference and clinical social work supervision. *The Clinical Supervisor*, 16(2), 17–32.

Vetlesen, A.J. (1994). *Perception, Empathy and Judgment: An Inquiry in the Preconditions of Moral Performance*. University Park: Pennsylvania State University Press.

Walker, M.U. (1992). Moral understandings: Alternative "epistemology" for a feminist ethics. In E.B. Cole, and S. Coultrap-McQuin (Eds.), *Explorations in Feminist Ethics. Theory and Practice* (pp.165–75). Bloomington, Indiana: Indiana University Press.

Weinberg, M. (2006). Pregnant with possibility: The paradoxes of "help" as anti-oppression and discipline with a young single mother. *Families in Society*, April–June, 87(2), 161–9.

Weinberg, M. (2007). Ethical "use of self." The complexity of multiple selves in clinical practice. In D. Mandell (Ed.) *Revisiting the Use of Self: Questioning Professional Identities* (pp.213–33). Toronto: Canadian Scholars Press.

Weinberg, M. (2014). The ideological dilemma of subordination of the self versus self care: Identity construction of the 'ethical social worker.' *Discourse & Society*, 25(1), 84–99.

Weinberg, M., and Taylor, S. (2014). "Rogue" social workers: The problem with rules for ethical behaviour. *Critical Social Work*, 15(1), 74–86.

Wetherell, M. (1998). Positioning and interpretive repertoires: Conversation analysis and post-structuralism in dialogue. *Discourse and Society*, 9(3), 387–412.

Yan, M.C., and Wong, Y.-L.R. (2005). Rethinking self-awareness in cultural competence: Toward a dialogic self in cross-cultural social work. *Families in Society*, 86(2), 181–8.

Yee. J.Y. (2005). Critical anti-racism praxis: The concept of whiteness implicated. In S. Hick, J. Fook, and R. Pozzuto (Eds.). *Social Work. A Critical Turn* (pp.87–103). Toronto: Thomson Educational Publishing.

Zembylas, M. (2003a). Emotions and teacher identity: A poststructural perspective. *Teachers and Teaching: Theory and Practice*, 9(3), 213–38.

Zembylas, M. (2003b). Interrogating "teacher identity": Emotion, resistance, and self-formation. *Educational Theory*, 53(1), 107–27.

Chapter 6
Conclusion

Ethical Trespass and its Inevitability

This book has argued that, regardless of intention, social workers are caught in a web of tensions, complexities, and contradictions, a morass of irresolvable strands, resulting in inevitable and unavoidable trespass.

Multiple paradoxes are endemic to the social work field and result in no completely adequate solutions. One of the most significant is that social workers function as agents of discipline and care in society (paradox 1), a contradictory and ambiguous space from which ethical tensions will arise and no resolution will be entirely satisfactory. How do practitioners support emancipatory directions and empowerment for clients when workers' positionality includes being the agents of moral regulation?

Also, practitioners have, as their clients, more than one individual for whom they are responsible, resulting in a helping relationship which is never strictly between one worker and one client (paradox 2). Working with an array of players whose stakes in the outcome may diverge, every situation calls for judgments made on the basis of incomplete information. But the fact of there always being a third, according to Levinas (1991), obliges humans to attempt to create a system that is intelligible, ordered and fair.

Someone must make the judgments necessary to construct such a system. Context is critical but can never be fully known or understood. Furthermore, while judgement is necessary given the positioning of social workers in our society, non-judgementalism is required to engage service users and form positive relationships that undergird successful practice. Nonetheless, judgements are an unavoidable and indispensable responsibility in a just society. Someone must be charged with providing protection for those who are at risk for injury, neglect, or harm. Social workers are one of the groups with this mandate. This is paradox 3, judgement versus non-judgementalism. Wise (1990, p.248) argues,

> social work *is* about social control and especially the protection of children and other vulnerable people, and this is a morally proper function in feminist terms because feminism is concerned with adopting a moral-political stance to questions of power and powerlessness.

There are children who are abandoned, ignored, and abused. There are young mothers, too, whose own resources, both emotional and material, are insufficient to meet the challenges of successful and healthy living, and who, consequently, require support and aid.

Thus, judgment is intrinsic to the positioning of social workers. There is no client outside of normalizing judgment and no social worker outside of the subject who judges. Social workers rely on moral evaluations to determine acceptable behaviour, and responsibility (Chu, Tsui, and Yan, 2009). Yet judgment is complex and problematic. It is a necessary component in attempts to create a just society and to facilitate change, yet it carries with it disciplinary and dominating aspects. How does a social worker know when her judgments are inaccurate or even unnecessary? How does she avoid judgment that shames or marginalizes? How does she foster change and growth without imposing her vision and consequently ignoring or devaluing the individuality of the client?

Today, in the Euro-Western world, on what terms have we attempted to create a just society? Attention should be placed on, "how practitioners form their moral judgments and their capacity, given the current socio-political context" (Asquith and Cheers, 2001, p.24). We need to examine the forms of power in social processes that organize the frameworks for the distribution and construction of what is taken as 'good' or 'adequate' mothering. Who are the people in our society that become the objects of power and who of surveillance? Who is named as 'high risk'?

In the process of those determinations, paradox 4 occurs. While empowerment, human rights, and free choice are values in the profession, social workers are setting the norms of what constitutes health, adequacy, and moral fitness on a whole range of behaviours for many subjects, including young single mothers. Consequently, workers are caught between wanting to support those values and their social responsibility to evaluate those behaviours that contribute to 'acceptable' standards in a society. How are workers to evaluate a range of issues from parenting capacity or health, as examples, if clients do not give them information on which to make those judgements?

This leads to paradox 5, which directly impacts service users; the paradox of clients needing to reveal themselves to be seen as cooperative subjects, while those revelations may put them at risk for disciplinary practices. Those judgments carry dangers, at the same time that they are necessary for practice to be effective both for the worker and the service users themselves.

However, the picture that is painted by these judgements often keeps the focus at the individual level without sufficient exploration of context and structure. Western society is rife with structural imbalances that disadvantage marginalities of all kinds: people of colour, ethnic minorities, the poor, women, the young, the old, religious minorities, and those with disabilities. The structures in which the young mothers in this study had to function were inexcusable in their inadequacy and punishment. These women (poor, young, unmarried mothers, often of ethnic or racial minorities) were frequently marked as inadequate or at fault for what befell them. I agree with Margolin (1997, p. 105, italics in the original) when he states, "[b]y focusing on the characteristics of clients, on *their* pathology, *their* delinquency, *their* failures, attention was diverted from the conditions external to them that constrained and limited their choices." And at times the workers in this study did perceive change as exclusively the responsibility of the individual client.

I believe individualizing client accountability will contribute to trespass. By continuing to make individual clients exclusively answerable for changing themselves and their circumstances, the structural inequities and institutional power relations do not surface as part of the depth of field, thereby maintaining current systems of capitalism and patriarchy. The broader societal framework of neoliberalism supports a politics of scarcity which places both clients and workers under enormous strain, and in which punishment and inadequacy of resources is the norm, regardless of the personal motivations and efforts of individual practitioners. The "headlessness" (Orlie, 1997, p.51) of modern rule that I discussed in Chapter 1, does not ensure its benevolence. Arendt (1958, p.40) states the converse, that "the rule by nobody is not necessarily no-rule; it may indeed, under certain circumstances, even turn out to be one of its cruelest and most tyrannical versions."

As a society, we have made choices. Polakow (1995, p.265) was referring to the United States when she argued that "poverty in a wealthy industrial society such as ours can hardly be seen as a product of national scarcity and dwindling resources; rather, it is a product of acquisition, of the politics and priorities of distribution." The same could be said of many countries in the Euro-Western world. As long as young women are scapegoated for more general ills, and the politics of scarcity reigns, we will continue to create categories of haves and have-nots, regardless of the creative and determined efforts of workers on the front-lines to reduce those disparities.

In part, the politics of scarcity is supported by another paradox we have discussed; namely paradox 6, equality versus equity. The need for fairness and equality is an outgrowth of liberal ideology. But equality does not take into account the barriers that many service users encounter. Not everyone starts at the same starting gate. For example, a social worker could support a parent's plan to spend more money on a child with special needs than on his sister in order to meet his particular requirements to thrive. This is the principle of *equity* rather than *equality*. But the sibling without special needs could feel this is unfair to her interests, a lack of equality. This paradox relates to that of paradox 2 – having more than one client whose needs and interests may be discrepant.

There are multiple players with different stakes and needs in the outcomes, including the personal and vested interests of the workers and agencies that employ them. I have addressed my concerns about the social reproduction of power in the profession of social work and the benefits that accrue to the field by the maintenance of certain definitions of the problem with this population. However, to locate ethics within the actions of individual practitioners, as if they were free to make decisions irrespective of the broader environment in which they work, is to neglect the significant ways that structures shape those constructions and erect difficult standards for those embodied practitioners mired in institutional regimes, working with finite resources and conflicting requirements and expectations.

The workers in this study often assumed that their struggles were idiosyncratic and outside the norm. Power dynamics have been under-emphasized in traditional theoretical orientations in social work (Finn and Jacobson, 2003). Thus, "a power relation studied in isolation from its cultural and institutional context is easily perceived as an anomaly, and not as part of a larger system of domination like sexism, racism, and so on," argues Allen (1996, p.286).

In order to be effective, any critical analysis must take into account structural inequities that workers both perpetuate and fight against, such as those that contribute to the construction of the category of 'client.' An examination of ethical practice should also be broadened to include the significant constraints under which practitioners operate and explore how workers respond to those restrictions. Such explorations should recognize the precarious location of workers as both agents and critics of the state, as administrators of social order, and representatives of social justice.

Practice is messy, contradictory, and indeterminate. The more individuals involved in an ethical conundrum, the more relative an ethical stance one must acknowledge and withstand (Hugman, 2005a). Historically, I believe that the traditional treatment of ethics in the social services has failed to provide schemas that adequately take into account factors that both reflect and constitute the challenges of ethical issues on either micro or macro levels. Prilleltensky, Walsh-Bowers, and Rossiter (1999, p.316) stated that the current dominant model based on codes of ethics, is restrictive, "rule driven and mechanistic, has a narrow definition of what constitutes an ethical issue, is minimally relevant to daily practice, and regards harm as the aberrant behaviour of few professionals."

The emergence of ethical dilemmas and trespasses for the workers in this study were rarely resolved solely by formulaic rules of ethics or decision-making models. Other authors support this finding (e.g. Gough and Spencer, 2014; Keinemans and Kanne, 2013; Richardson, 2014). Kristine was the lone worker who mentioned codes of ethics as influencing how she had behaved and that was only in reference to one case. Orlie (1997, p.195) explains that "code-oriented moralities tend to normalize principle because rather than continually questioning proper conduct, they express a desire to find the true ground of our being." Since this is not possible, codes are both inadequate and result in the perpetuation of trespass.

In part, trespass "originates when we conceive and live the limited as if it were limitless" (Orlie, 1997, p.187). Orlie's explanation for this narrowing of perspective is that, as finite beings, we cannot comprehend the infinite (p.187). Consequently, we may foster dogmatism rather than humility (p.27), and support models of ethics that are overly rule-bound, and linear without due regard for context and the inescapability of the insufficiency of our attempts. The emphasis in ethics on the face-to-face interaction, up until the present, has required the practitioner to apply rules in a mechanical fashion, despite the complexities involved in making ethical decisions (Prilleltensky, Rossiter, and Walsh-Bowers, 1996).

"Ethics is not about eliminating moral uncertainty" (Kendall and Hugman, 2013, p.315). Nor is it about having the right answer, but about making the best choice (Gray and Gibbons, 2007) from an array that will always in some way fail to totally capture all the current and future variables and potential harms. Rather than a focus on a set of principles and formulas for decision-making, a problematization of those very formulae (Hugman, 2005a) and the helping relationship as a whole are required. Acknowledging the "oppressive potential of professional discourses" is essential (Kendall and Hugman, 2013, p.322). It is also vital to place an examination of the privilege, power and authority in one's positioning, as well as one's subjectivity as an agent of discipline and moral regulation at the forefront of one's consideration of what it means to be ethical. We are always in the process of becoming, which makes such an examination both an ethical responsibility and ethical imperative (Clarke, 2009). Ethics should involve recognition of moral uncertainty and support for the agentic morality of the professional (Kendall and Hugman, 2013).

More robust tools than the traditional arsenal of codes and decision-making models for ethical practice must be offered to practitioners to aid in that analysis. This book has offered some alternate analytical devices, summarized now.

Tools for Ethical Practice

Discursive Fields

The attention to the concept of discursive fields is a useful means for scrutinizing ethical decision-making. What each worker understood as problems varied significantly and could be understood by reference to examining her discursive fields. These diverse understandings for accomplishing the 'helping relationship' led to very divergent anxieties, articulations of dilemmas, and senses of trespass that each worker experienced. There were no dilemmas outside of the discursive logic of specific workers. What they took to be problematic or violative emerged from their discursive fields, as did their choices for how to resolve dilemmas.

To illustrate, a central belief for Jannie was the importance of correcting deficiencies she perceived her clients as having as a result of poor upbringings, components of the dominant reactionary discourse on these young women. This led to utilizing impartial reason and providing consistency as main strategies from her discursive field. Alternatively, a primary discourse Patricia adopted was a strengths discourse when she viewed even the most troubled clients as having potential and wanting the best for their children. Her explanations of their struggles included a revisionist discourse of an inadequate government. That led to advocacy and activism to rectify the structural imbalances, main tactics in her repertoire. Thus, the practice of these two workers was appreciably different. And the dilemmas that arose for each also came from their dissimilar discursive fields. In the interviews, it was not a dilemma for Patricia to provide divergent services to different clients, whereas for Jannie, being expected to make exceptions became a central dilemma in my interviews with her.

Preferred and Actualized Selves

Within an individual worker's discursive field, opposing discourses existed. What determined which route would be taken was both subtle and cumulative, leading to very dissimilar effects for different workers. It is productive to speak about 'preferred' and 'actualized' subject positions because these terms provide an analytical device to explore the notion of what might arise as an ethical dilemma for an individual from the context of divergent subject positions within that individual. They offer a language for explaining an intrapsychic phenomenon from a post-structural perspective. These notions help make sense of the shifting and contradictory stances that an individual worker might adopt in providing 'help.'

They also aid in explaining the emotional reactions that accompany the take-up of certain subject positions. In this study, some subject positions were a better internal 'fit' for the worker, but whether a particular favoured position was enacted was influenced by the client's behaviour, the view of the category 'client,' as well as myriad other micro and macro relations, including work contingencies.

Davies (2000) explains that desire is more than a physiological response; it is a psychic quality as well. It is through desires that we know ourselves. "Although those desires are demonstrably discursively produced and thus collective in nature, they are 'taken on' by each individual as their inner core" (Davies, 2000, p.75). These are the 'preferred subject positions' that participants saw and wished for others to see as the 'true core' of that individual's identity. When a worker was able to actualize a favoured subject position there was little, if any, sense of conflict.

However, when the factors pushed a worker to adopt subject positions that were not preferred, they experienced this as an ethical dilemma. It was workers' desires to be interpreted in certain ways that spoke the contradictions and dilemmas into existence. When workers enacted a subject position that was ego-dystonic, justifications and/or reservations might have been articulated or felt. At those moments, they might have sensed an ethical trespass. Those occasions where what they felt they had to do conflicted with what they wanted to do, signaled discomfort with dominant discourses or practices, and indicated a recognition (perhaps not fully conscious) that a required way of acting might have inherent harms in its implementation. The discomfort demonstrated thoughtfulness about social conduct. It gestured towards an attempt to question the limitations of conformity to social rules even while executing those rules. At times, the social workers fought against and resisted the discrepancy between preferred positions and those they perceived of as required or normative, with the potential of reducing trespass.

Affect was a critical component to the take-up of a particular subject position. But historically, the requirement that a worker be an objective judge, a blank slate on which a client projects her unconscious material has often been viewed as the recommended route for practitioners. Dominant discourses on rationality and objectivity, in fact, operate as discourses of control (Niesche and Haase, 2012) and strategies of governmentality. But given the struggles around subjectivity, these stances are both impossible practically and limited ethically. Being an ethical human being is an identity project that requires the recognition and management of not just one's thoughts but also one's emotions. Emotions are not constructed outside of human relations. Our emotions are constituted through the discourses of the society in which we live and consequently are both individual and communal, and hence always politicized. They are performative and provide "spaces for self-formation and resistance" (Zembylas, 2003b).

Awareness of 'rogue' or conflicting emotions are often signals of disquiet about dominant discourses that highlight the need for dissident speech or action. Together, reason and emotion help to explain the processes whereby workers take up particular subject positions. Foucault referred to ethics as a life-long process of negotiation with oneself (Foucault, 1990; Foucault, 1994; Niesche and Hass, 2012). That work should include self-reflexivity, critical reflection, and work on one's counter-transference reactions, which entail both thought and affect. Consequently, the melding of thinking with emotion and passion are tools that are necessary in the amelioration of trespass (Banks, 2009).

Ethical Trespass

Another central analytical tool that is valuable in a study of ethics is the notion of trespass. I believe that the causes of trespass are complex and primary to the human condition. One aspect of trespass relates to the paradox of individuals being both like others in their humanity and therefore obliged to the Other, but also singular as human beings and consequently, never totally able to 'know' the Other. Another facet of trespass is that no matter how much good is enacted, any act will have ramifications and repercussions that can lead to other harms. There is an element of unpredictability that is intrinsic and unavoidable in human action. Arendt (1958, p.233) states,

> He (sic) who acts never quite knows what he is doing, that he always becomes "guilty" of consequences he never intended or foresaw, that no matter how disastrous and unexpected the consequences of his deed he can never undo it, that the process he starts is never consummated unequivocally in one single deed or event, and that its very meaning never discloses itself to the actor ... .

Any set of practices is always incommensurate with the adequacy of its intentions for justice. Those practices become a form of violence in attempts to create a just society.

Trespass occurs in the normalization of some standards over others, leading to taken-for-granted ways of being, which limit other ways of being that deny the uniqueness of the individual. Social workers are particularly implicated in trespass because they are authorized to determine the normal, healthy, and acceptable which privilege some subject positions over others. Therefore, their judgments, no matter how sound, are always limited, not totally accurate or just, and, regardless of intention, lead to other forms of harms, including the injury of limiting or ignoring the distinctiveness of a client.

Given the inevitability of trespass, it is easy to look for someone to blame for the ineffectiveness in efforts to create a just society. A system of culpability has been created, as was described in Chapter 4, in which clients get sent from one service to another with no one wanting to take responsibility. Both clients and workers are scapegoated for structural inequities and the blaming game occurs (Parton, 1996b; Weinberg, 2010). Orlie's (1997, p.27) explanation is that "in the absence of a natural order of things, the perpetual contest among our makings and unmakings initiates an apparently insatiable will to control our circumstances and fosters increasing resentment as a result of our failures to do so." Thus individuals look to others to take responsibility for the suffering in the world.

Social workers, who are seen as 'contaminated' by their proximity to those who are marginalized, become easy prey for this type of thinking. Being a female-dominated profession with limited prestige, status, or clout, also sets social work up as a target for frustration about irresolvable societal ills.

Trespass Reduction

For Young Single Mothers Specifically

Despite the targeting of social workers for blame around societal problems, there is little to be gained by focusing on fault, particularly given the inescapability of some level of failure in resolving social ills. The question becomes how to move towards more ethical practice. Are there ways to maximize help and minimize trespass?

For the group studied, young single mothers, the concept of 'choice' should be re-examined. Choice in the discourses of the workers in this research was predicated on an individualistic model where it was identified with independence and the ability to stand on one's own (Ruddick, 1993). Tenets of empowerment and self-determination omit an analysis of structural oppression that render implementation difficult, if not impossible, for those Others marked by differences such as skin tone, accent or limited financial resources. Furthermore, for 'minority' women, where kin and community may be central, "[w]hen the dominant culture opposes self-regard to responsibility for others and identifies choice with the independent self, young women may appear to be passive even as they make what are, to them, self-respecting and self-defining choices" (Ruddick, 1993, p.131).

I think the dominant discourse of 'choice' is unrealistic and ultimately uncaring, putting the onus on young single mothers to resolve, on their own, significant, pervasive problems and inadequacies that are endemic to Western society generally. These narrow notions of choice, when mapped on individuals, remove state and social responsibility. Additionally, they privilege individualism discourses over communitarian discourses as 'good' approaches to living.

The inexcusable constraints on these young women are so extensive that it is a wonder any of them are successful at maintaining and mothering their children. There should be no expectation of mothers being willing or able to put attention towards more psychologically-based issues until basic survival needs are adequately met. 'Empowerment' is an empty gesture until structural barriers are reduced to make choice a viable possibility in these young women's lives. Instead, I think a model that reinforces mutuality and interdependence would be better suited for the requirements of young, single, impoverished mothers.

We have to stop expecting these young women to 'cope,' on their own, and instead ask what needs to be put into place to help them function adequately *with help and ongoing supports*. I think we should move to a politics of these young women as "at promise" rather than "at risk" (Swadener and Lubeck, 1995). Policy considerations should include work on changing the social conditions for these young women. Without improved housing options, child care resources, and respite as important examples, we will continue to promote the principle of 'less eligibility,' a stance that I believe should be repugnant in a humane and civil society. Fundamentally, what is required is recognizing young single mothers' importance to the future of our country as a "*resource*" (Krane, 1997, p.72, italics in the original) and as an asset to our communities rather than as a liability.

What would be the consequences if, instead of the emphasis being on individuals to make change, we looked more broadly at the environment in which practice occurred, and examined possibilities for partnerships, collaborations, and community? The young women who were the clients in this study often seemed to wish to maintain ties with people that the social service system discouraged. I believe that the general trend in the field omits seeing boyfriends, the fathers of the babies and extended family as part of the 'case' that requires intervention, to say nothing of utilizing them as potential resources for young single mothers. While often these individuals have been a source of abuse for these young women, thus contributing to practitioners perceiving them as a danger, the isolation and lack of supports for young single mothers is also a major contributing factor to the ongoing stressors and oppression of this client group. Exploring the possibility of enlarging client networks to include the men in their lives and their extended families could transform the individualistic nature of definition of the problem and potentially result in added supports and decreased isolation for these women. Of course, this option is recommended only when it will not exacerbate the risks to and dangers for these young women.

For Social Workers

What general directions should be proposed for trespass mitigation for the workers? Wise (1990, p.248) states,

> Once we accept that vulnerable people need protection, we can then begin to pose other feminist questions, like what feminism can tell us about what should

be "acceptable standards," who should decide what these are, and how they should be imposed.

Inherent in this quote is the idea that some forms of practice are preferable to others, which, as I outlined in Chapter 5, has its own potential for forms of disciplinarity. At the same time, I do not believe the field of social work is morally bankrupt and I wish to contribute to attempts by embodied social workers dealing with a messy quotidian reality by offering possible insights into more ethical practice. I do not want to evacuate a notion of standards for the field. I think it is more fruitful to open up discussion about ideals that takes into account the paradoxes and institutional forms of regulation to which social workers are subject, while still holding on to both the reality of ethical trespass but the possibility of its reduction.

Orlie (1997, p.146) queries,

> How, if at all, can we be responsible for our effects upon others when those effects themselves are the effect of what we have been made to be? How, if at all, can individuals be free who are subjects of normalizing power?

Her answer is that "we must better understand how we become subjects" (1997, p.148). She is concerned with *process*. Social workers and clients become subjects through the infinite instances in which theories are interpreted, principles of practice are enacted, policies are implemented, and individuals are 'helped.'

It is in these moments that the possibility of trespass is reduced or enlarged. "[W]e live responsibly and freely when we put what we are in question by refusing merely and passively to reinscribe social rule," opines Orlie (1997, p.169). Therefore, could workers analyze how relations of power may be operating and pose questions, such as: what is missing in this analysis, why is X taken for granted, who benefits from this definition, or what would happen if we turned our thinking around on this? Problematization of standards helps to guard "against principles becoming merely normalizing norms" (Orlie, 1997, p.195). By challenging current social rule and imagining other possibilities, while recognizing the exercise of power throughout those deliberations, we can mitigate trespass.

One set of norms that might be productively problematized is the framework of liberal individualism and how it has impacted both clients and workers. Such a problematization might be supported by reflecting on an expanded view of the construction of issues not usually considered under the terms of this theoretical discourse. I believe, as part of the scope of the study of ethics, the analysis should extend beyond individual issues between a worker and her client, to take into account structural disadvantage.

Racism, for example, is "so embedded in social structures, it appears both normal and natural" (Razack and Jeffery, 2002, p.260). Orlie (1997, p.141) states, "we need to be able to think about invisible powers, as well as to discern our active role in their extension and elaboration." Class, racial, and ethnic biases of the institutions that are in place recreate structures that perpetuate discrimination and inequity, and social workers contribute to their construction and maintenance.

Recognizing whiteness as racialized and dominant, in ongoing social relations in which social workers have the power to construct what is normal and what is aberrant, could be highlighted (Razack and Jeffery, 2002).

Individual workers may feel guilty, resentful or even victimized, given what they perceive to be their own location in social structures and prevalent structural inequalities. This, for instance, is often the case for white workers in dealing with issues of racism. These feelings can lead to either fleeing what one is or ignoring trespasses inflicted on others (Orlie, 1997). Cycles of resentment can be interrupted by forgiving ourselves and others. At the same time, Orlie (1997, p.184) clarifies that it is not a formulation between "an 'I' and a 'you' fully present and self-made." That is because we are not sovereign but subjects of social processes that are not totally of our own making.

If social workers could recognize their involvement in relations of power (such as the maintenance of the domination of white people) and their authority in processes of normalization and dividing practices, while acknowledging the limits and dangers of trespass as part of that exercise of power, they would move a step closer to trespass reduction. Respect, consideration, and kindness in judgments might follow from recognition of the unavoidability of trespass. Leavening a stance of justice with one of mercy would support these aims. Strengths of clients, as a default position for workers, and redefining symptoms as often understandable responses to impossible situations, could move practitioners towards more ethical practice.

As we have seen, the Kantian doctrine of impartial reason privileges sameness over difference without recognizing the deeply systemic nature of certain forms of inequality, reinforcing the middle-class over the poor, male over female, and those who are white over those of 'colour.' A response to difference could be fostered, not as inferiority, but as distinctiveness and uniqueness that enrich society through multiple ways of being. Particularly in processes such as assessment and diagnosis, broadening one's depth of field and asking 'what is it like to be you,' are important practices to help correct for the tunnel vision of one's own meaning making and to enhance understanding and compassion. This is the key question posed for utilizing broad empathy. It is an especially important consideration for workers who represent dominant groups, such as able-bodied, white, or straight workers, since they may more likely adopt the taken-for-granted 'truth' of prevailing discourses.

Care should be taken to avoid highlighting intra-psychic issues at the expense of understanding broader structural restrictions. Ethical practice is always political (Chu, Tsui, and Yan, 2009; Infinito, 2003). Integrating a macro and advocacy stance in social work, even in one-to-one practice (Morrow and Hawxhurst, 1998), such as that provided by Patricia when she was able to raise her concerns on the homelessness committee at the hospital, might also reduce the emphasis on individual responsibility, increase the importance of community accountability, and begin to address systemic inequality. By enlarging explanations of the constitution of the client to include categories such as poverty, race, and ethnicity, workers could begin to be sensitized to the lack of contextual framing in understanding the client's world, and could move in the direction of political action for change.

Utilizing dissident speech: deconstructing and undermining dominant discourses, and reconstructing more constructive counter-stories that work to elevate subjugated discourses can also support those who have been disenfranchised.

The irony of paradox is that in the ambiguity, possibilities for resistance and moving towards ethical practice exist (Clarke, 2009). While constrained by broader structures of neoliberalism and managerialism, embracing that ambiguity of paradox (Roose, Roets, and Bouverne-De Bie, 2012), and viewing it as opening opportunities for social transformation are useful approaches to professional practice. A plethora of strategies identified in Chapter 5, such as sharing the tools to the master's house, are available to practitioners and arise in part from those paradoxes. Then one's potential to be an agent of emancipation is enhanced.

Yet we will always fail to totally reach the goal of ethical practice because we will never know the Other completely (Cornell, 1992) and there are many Others with alternate needs and wishes. Ultimately, since all practices will contain their own forms of discipline and correction, trespass will always be with us. Perhaps the most one can hope for is to open up the discussion by approaching the conundrums of practice with a stance of self-effacement and reservation about one's efficacy.

The current state of affairs where, in order to look competent, professionals must act autonomously, is destructive to both the personnel in social service agencies and to their clients. How might agencies create a safe space for workers to discuss concerns about the paradoxes and dilemmas they encounter? What structures could be created that would allow for active encouragement to explore the complex and irresolvable dilemmas confronting practitioners?

When opportunities are provided for supervision, reflection, and consultation about the constraints and the paradoxes of practice, the strain, anxiety, and pressure on front-line workers could be lessened and the potential to move towards more ethical practice could be enhanced. In an era of austerity where supervision has become primarily administrative, one logical forum for this type of work has been diminished. But supervision, consultation, education and ongoing professional training are important potential sources for enhancing the types of thinking and practices advocated in this book.

I support the notion of a "collaborative conscience" (Orlie, 1997, p.168) because I think the field would be strengthened by the solidarity of a community that recognizes the inescapability of trespass and allows for humility, doubt, and clemency. Arendt (1978, p.175) states, "but if the wind of thinking ... has shaken you from sleep and made you fully awake and alive, then you will see that you have nothing in your grasp but perplexities, and the best we can do with them is share them with each other ... ."

Why Not Concede Defeat and Give Up?

Given the inevitability of ethical trespass and doing damage in the relationship with the Other, why try to help? Why not just give up? What should prevent one from simply living in a narcissistic bubble, unconcerned about striving towards goodness and ethical behaviour?

Levinas undertook to answer these concerns in his critique of Euro-Western philosophy. He believed the fundamental philosophical question was "how being justifies itself" (Levinas, 1989, p.86). In answer to ones' right to be, Levinas spoke about the uniqueness of each individual human being and the irreplaceability of one by another. This inimitability has significant consequences: to illuminate the trace of God in humanity and to gesture to each individual's responsibility to change the world through a relationship with the Other, even as we recognize that that Other is fundamentally unknowable (Critchley, 2002; Levinas, 1993).

This is a grave responsibility, preceding intention, desire or our very birth, according to Levinas (1991). We cannot evade or be replaced by someone else. It is this call to responsibility that justifies our existence and is the essence of ethics (Critchley, 2002) In other words, our uniqueness makes us each responsible to the Other; no one else can take our place. And our right to exist rests on that responsibility to each other. It is a means to move closer to the infinite or God (or however one defines the ineffable in life).

Another consequence of our individuality and, consequently, accountability to the Other, is that in that responsibility, individuals are made as beings. Through difference and relationship, we are each altered. Subjectivity is always relational and shifting. The Other is crucial to one's own constitution of the self.

The responsibility of social workers is to attempt to cross the chasm, knowing that each will fail to ever fully understand or help the Other. At the same time, both the responsibility and potential of coming closer to the infinite prevent a nihilism that would have one concede defeat. Like moving towards the horizon, which will never be reached, there is the beauty and promise in the travel. More importantly, only through these attempts, will a more ethical society be created.

This monograph has attempted to demonstrate that social workers are not powerless victims and, while they are constituted by social processes and discourses, they constitute them as well. It is necessary to see ethics in every act that a practitioner undertakes (Banks, 2009). The power of workers can be constructive in the potential to enhance self-reflexivity, to strengthen and support clients, and for the betterment of society. Judgement, too, can be a tool for anti-oppressive practice, if there is ongoing recognition of the nuances and complexities of judgement and non-judgementalism as both necessary and contradictory components in practice.

For change to occur in our world, social workers must move beyond talk about ethics to action and political solidarity. "Ethical conduct," according to Orlie (1997), "requires more than thinking about the limits of the self, it also demands ethical political work on those limits" (Orlie, 1997, p.183). Through advocacy and activism, in partnership with those entrusted in practitioners' care, social change can occur. But it will not materialize from an immediate intention or desire to make it happen. It will be constructed out of little pieces, brick by hard-earned brick, as social workers struggle to be ethical in their dealings with the Other.

Arendt articulates (1958, p.178) "[t]he fact that man (sic) is capable of action means that the unexpected can be expected from him, that he is able to perform what is infinitely improbable." Rabbi Tarfon adds, "We are not called upon to complete the work, yet we are not free to desist from it" (Pirkei Avot, chapter 3, verse 2). Despite the perils, paradoxes and inevitability of some level of failure, I believe social workers should move towards that horizon, knowing that while they will never reach it, the attempts will bring us closer to a just, caring and ethical society.

Bibliography

Allen, A. (1996). Foucault on power: A theory for feminists. In S.J. Hekman (Ed.), *Feminist Interpretations of Michel Foucault* (pp.265–81). University Park, Pennsylvania: Pennsylvania State University Press.

Arendt, H. (1958). *The Human Condition*. Chicago: University of Chicago.

Arendt, H. (1978). *The Life of the Mind*. New York: Harcourt Brace Jovanovich.

Asquith, M., and Cheers, B. (2001). Morals, ethics and practice – in search of social justice. *Australian Social Work*, 54(2), 15–26.

Banks, S. (2009). From professional ethics to ethics in professional life: Implications for learning teaching and study. *Ethics and Social Welfare*, 3(1), 55–63.

Chu, W.C.K., Tsui, M.-S., and Yan, M.-C. (2009). Social work as a moral and political practice. *International Social Work*, 52(3), 287–98.

Clarke, M. (2009). The ethico-politics of teacher identity. *Educational Philosophy and Theory*, 41(2), 185–200.

Cornell, D. (1992). *The Philosophy of the Limit*. New York: Routledge.

Critchley, S. (2002). Introduction. In S. Critchley, and R. Bernasconi. *The Cambridge Companion to Levinas*. Cambridge: Cambridge University Press (pp.1–32). Available at: <http://www.myilibrary.com?ID=42090> (Accessed May 15, 2015).

Davies, B. (2000). *A Body of Writing. 1990–1999*. New York: Alta Mira Press.

Finn, J.L., and Jacobson, M. (2003). Just practice. Steps toward a new a new social work paradigm. *Journal of Social Work Education*, 39(1), 57–78.

Foucault, M. (1990). The use of pleasure. Volume 2 of *The History of Sexuality*. New York: Vintage Books.

Foucault, M. (1994). The ethics of the concern of the self as a practice of freedom. In P. Rabinow, and N. Rose (Eds.) *The Essential Foucault* (pp.25–42). New York: The New Press.

Gough, J., and Spencer, E. (2014). Ethics in action: An exploratory survey of social worker's ethical decision-making and value conflicts. *Journal of Social Work Values and Ethics*, 11(2), 23–40.

Gray, M., and Gibbons, J. (2007). There are no answers, only choices: Teaching ethical decision-making in social work. *Australian Social Work*, 60(2), 222–38.

Hugman, R. (2005a). Exploring the paradox of teaching ethics for social work practice. *Social Work Education*, 24(5), 535–45.

Infinito, J. (2003). Ethical self-formation: A look at the later Foucault. *Educational Theory*, 53(2), 155–71.

Keinemans, S., and Kanne, M. (2013). The practice of moral action: A balancing act for social workers. *Ethics and Social Welfare*, 7(4), 379–98.

Kendall, S, and Hugman, R. (2013). Social work and the ethics of involuntary treatment for Anorexia Nervosa: A postmodern approach. *Ethics and Social Welfare*, 7(4), 310–25.

Krane, J.E. (1997). Least disruptive and intrusive course of action ... for whom? Insights from feminist analysis of practice in cases of child sexual abuse. In J. Pulkingham, and G. Ternowetsky (Eds.), *Child and Family Policies. Struggles, Strategies and Options* (pp.58–74). Halifax: Fernwood Publishing.

Levinas, E. (1989). Ethics as first philosophy. In S. Hand (Ed.), *The Levinas Reader* (pp.75–87). Oxford: Blackwell.

Levinas, E. (1991). *Otherwise than Being or Beyond Essence* (A. Lingis, Trans.). Boston: Kluwer.

Levinas, E. (1993). *Outside the Subject.* Stanford: Stanford University Press.

Margolin, L. (1997). *Under the Cover of Kindness. The Invention of Social Work.* Charlottesville: University Press of Virginia.

Morrow, S.L., and Hawxhurst, D.M. (1998). Feminist therapy: Integrating political analysis in counseling and psychotherapy. *Women and Therapy*, 21(2), 37–50.

Orlie, M.A. (1997). *Living Ethically. Acting Politically.* Ithaca: Cornell University Press.

Parton, N. (1996b). Social work, risk and "the blaming system." In N. Parton (Ed.), *Social Theory, Social Change and Social Work* (pp.98–114). New York: Routledge.

Parton, N. (2000). Some thoughts on the relationship between theory and practice in and for social work. *British Journal of Social Work*, 30, 449–63.

Pirkei Avot. [Sayings of the fathers]. (1994). Chapter 3, verse 2 [citing R. Tarfon]. [A new translation with notes by Eliyahu Touger]. New York: Moznaim Publishing Corp.

Polakow, V. (1995). Naming and blaming: Beyond a pedagogy of the poor. In B.B. Swadener, and S. Lubeck (Eds.), *Children and Families "at Promise." Deconstructing the Discourse of Risk* (pp.263–70). Albany: State University of New York Press.

Prilleltensky, I., Rossiter, A., and Walsh-Bowers, R. (1996). Preventing harm and promoting ethical discourse in the helping professions: Conceptual, research, analytical, and action frameworks. *Ethics and Behaviour*, 6(4), 287–306.

Prilleltensky, I., Walsh-Bowers, R., and Rossiter, A. (1999). Clinicians' lived experience of ethics: Values and challenges in helping children. *Journal of Educational and Psychological Consultation*, 10(4), 315–42.

Razack, N., and Jeffrey, D. (2002). Critical race discourse and tenets for social work. *Canadian Social Work Review*, 19(2), 257–71.

Richardson, J. (2014). In pursuit of philosophy and best practice- the challenges of an ethical dilemma. *Ethics and Social Welfare*, 8(4), 399–407.

Roose, R., Roets, G., and Bouverne-De Bie, M. (2012). Irony and social work: In search of the happy Sisyphus. *British Journal of Social Work*, 42(8), 1–16.

Ruddick, S. (1993). Procreative choice for adolescent women. In A. Lawson, and D.L. Rhode (Eds.), *The Politics of Pregnancy, Adolescent Sexuality and Public Policy* (pp. 126–43). New Haven: Yale University Press.

Swadener, B.B., and Lubeck, S. (Eds.). (1995). *Children and Families "at Promise." Deconstructing the Discourse of Risk*. Albany: State University of New York Press.

Weinberg, M. (2010). The social construction of social work ethics: Politicizing and broadening the lens. *Journal of Progressive Human Services*, 21(1), 32–44.

Wise, S. (1990). Becoming a feminist social worker. In L. Stanley (Ed.), *Feminist Praxis. Research, Theory and Epistemology in Feminist Sociology* (pp.236–49). London: Routledge.

Zembylas, M. (2003b). Interrogating "teacher identity": Emotion, resistance, and self-formation. *Educational Theory*, 53(1), 107–27.

Appendix A
Interview Schedule

Overall Outline

- the nature of the helping relationship
- the problem
- the forms of practice
- the identity of the helper
- the client – how is the client created in this encounter
- the interaction between the helper and the client
- the goals of helping

Prompts

1) The worker's own positionality
   - their own background, race, class, etc.
   - their educational background
   - why they went into the field
   - their agency
   - what their current job entails

2) Their understanding about the helping relationship
   - whom they believe to be their client (i.e. the mother, the child, the boyfriend, the whole family, a broader systemic approach)
   - what they believe to be their responsibility
   - what they believe to be their roles
   - their involvement and attitude towards professionalization
   - their response to legislation such as CAS mandate
   - their response to funding constraints such as Learning Earning And Parenting Programme
   - their response to resources and their allocation
   - their goals for the helping relationship

3) Their beliefs about the young women
   - sexuality
   - birth control
   - mothering practices
   - rules and regulations

- "causes" of single teen mothering

4) The tensions
  - what they see as paradoxes in the work that arise between principles and actualities
  - what makes these contradictions for them
  - what their understanding of how these tensions came to be problematic
  - how they resolve or live with these paradoxes
  - what tactics or resistances they use
  - what they articulate as the underlying principles that inform their work
  - what is considered and isn't considered
  - structural constraints
  - enablers
  - how contradictions are handled

Cases and range of options in the helping relationship

Index